THE LIFE AND RHYMES OF BENJAMIN ZEPHANIAH

A pioneer of performance poetry, Benjamin Zephaniah's talents as a lyricist and story-teller emerged at a young age, helping him to survive the racism he faced growing up in 1960s Birmingham. He now speaks candidly of his time living outside the law, and how he broke away from the path his schoolteachers told him was inevitable. With the flame of creativity burning inside him, Benjamin came to London in the 1980s and emerged as a uniquely dynamic performer. Nelson Mandela formed a close friendship with him after hearing his musical tribute to him recorded with the Wailers — the first artist to do so after the death of Bob Marley. Benjamin's memories provide a vivid portrait of an extraordinary life that celebrates the power of poetry and the importance of pushing boundaries.

Benjamin Zephaniah is best known for his dynamic performance poetry, but he is also an award-winning playwright, novelist, political activist, and musician. He has travelled the world speaking about his art and his humanitarianism, and is an outspoken campaigner for human and animal rights. He has written several novels for teenagers and has appeared on long-running radio and TV shows such as *Desert Island Discs* and *Question Time*. Benjamin continues to record and perform with his reggae band, whose most recent release is *Revolutionary Minds*.

BENJAMIN ZEPHANIAH

THE LIFE AND RHYMES OF BENJAMIN ZEPHANIAH
The Autobiography

Complete and Unabridged

CHARNWOOD
Leicester

First published in Great Britain in 2018 by
Simon & Schuster UK Ltd
London

First Charnwood Edition
published 2019
by arrangement with
Simon & Schuster UK Ltd
London

A catalogue record for this book is available
from the British Library.

ISBN 978–1–4448–4190–9

Published by
F. A. Thorpe (Publishing)
Anstey, Leicestershire

Set by Words & Graphics Ltd.
Anstey, Leicestershire
Printed and bound in Great Britain by
T. J. International Ltd., Padstow, Cornwall

This book is printed on acid-free paper

Dedicated to me.
And why not?
There was a time when I thought
I wouldn't live to see thirty.
I doubled that, and now I'm sixty.
Well done, Rastaman, you're a survivor.
A black survivor.

CONTENTS

Introduction

I hate autobiographies. They're so fake. The ones I hate the most are those written by individuals who have spent their lives deceiving people and then, when they see their careers (or their lives) coming to an end, they decide it's time to be honest. But they never really are. They feel the need to put 'their side of the story', as if they were in a court of law, or they suddenly want to tell you about secret affairs they were having with people who were really ugly, but really powerful. And don't get me started on the people who write autobiographies a couple of years after they're born: the eighteen-year-old pop star who feels life has been such a struggle that it can only help others if he lets the world know how he made it. Or the models who want to tell us exactly how much they've spent on cosmetic surgery. And don't get me started on the politician who once said you should vote for him because you can trust him, then you voted for him and he broke that trust, and now he wants to tell you how much pressure he was under. In my humble opinion, someone who has spent years in a corrupt government, or playing politics with people's lives, is never going to completely open up about what they've done, or what they've seen. They will still want to protect certain people and show themselves in the best light. So don't get me started . . . and why am I writing this anyway?

I didn't want to write an autobiography, but I had a beautiful agent called Rosemary Canter, who just loved books. She originally worked in publishing, and then went on to be an agent, so she knew the business well. She looked like Lady Penelope from *Thunderbirds*, was a little posh, with pointy shoes and pointy glasses, and she always looked like she'd just stepped out of the hairdresser's. She had a touch of sophistication about her, but I often felt I could take her to the dub club and see another side of her. Anyway, she kept going on at me about writing my autobiography. We used to lunch together once a year, and we'd have several other meetings throughout the year, and every time I saw her she would tell me to start writing that autobiography.

I used to tell her I was too young, and there was no sex scandal or kiss and tell. I tried to convince her that the few people who knew about me knew enough about me, but she kept insisting. Even when I was delivering other books to her, she would remind me there was another book outstanding. Then, one day, I met Andy Richardson. Andy was a journalist from Shrewsbury who had written a few pieces about me, usually when I was performing at Theatre Severn in Shropshire. He seemed to know a lot about me, and he gave me the distinct feeling that if I didn't write my own life story then he would write it for me.

After meeting Andy I told Rosemary that I felt the time was right, but I didn't want a contract

— so she shouldn't go looking for a publishing deal — and I didn't want deadlines or to feel under pressure in any way, and I certainly didn't want to do it for money. So Andy and I met up and I began to talk. I spoke fast, but he took notes faster, stopping every now and again to ask a question, but for the most part it was just me rambling on.

I've spent all my life trying to be as honest as I can. I have tried to be completely open about my political views and my personal life, even when it got me in trouble with my family. I have also been honest about the bad, wrong or naughty things I've done. I've always talked about my life of crime and my mistakes, but I did this in poetry or in various interviews. Until I started working with Andy, I'd never put them all together in one place.

When I'd done talking, he handed over what he'd written and told me to get on with it. It was a great kick-start. I then began reviewing my life, exploring my memories and pouring my heart out. I was writing, and my subject was me. Rosemary saw an early rough draft of this book, but that was all, sadly, as she passed away before I finished it. I owe a great deal to Andy for helping me to get started; his help was invaluable, and I thank him for his encouragement, but it really wouldn't have happened without Rosemary. It would sound a bit corny to say I'd like to dedicate the book to her, so I'm not. I don't have to, because I know that not one of these pages has been written without me thinking of her.

1

Early Days in Old Birmingham

'Mum, can I have some more hot water?'

It's Sunday, and I'm sitting in a tin bath in our back yard. My twin sister Velda is wrapped in a towel, looking at me while I'm shivering. At least I now have the bath to myself, even though the water's going cold. There's a two-at-a-time rule in our house that means we have to share baths, as there's already five of us. Mum and Dad don't share though. Just us kids.

There's a chill in the air. Time for conkers and kicking through leaves in the park, and soon Mum will let us have our baths indoors.

'Benjamin, this is the last kettle of hot water I'm gonna bring you. You better make sure you wash yourself through and through. Don't you think I got better things to do?'

I look around and count all the other tin baths hanging on the wall of the yard we share with our neighbours, hearing Mum speaking to me in rhyme. She does this all the time; it's part of her nature, her sing-song way of interpreting the world that makes me feel close to her.

She steps outside with the steaming kettle as I wedge myself against the back of the bath, anticipating the lovely feel of the fresh hot water on my body, making me all shiny. When I get out of the bath I'm going to play with the Lego I've hidden upstairs that I took from Michael O'Reilly. I love the bright colours — blue, yellow, red — and I love snapping them together in different shapes.

Most of everything else around me is grey. Grey tin baths, grey pavements, grey sky. Especially grey sky. Birmingham is full of smoke and fog from all the factories and foundries. They make cars down the road from where we live, here on Farm Street in an area called Hockley, and someone told me that nearby they make all kinds of metal stuff that's useful for building things.

Michael is a white kid and he lives next door. His mum is fierce. She doesn't talk in rhyme like my mum. She bustles about very quickly and is always scrubbing things and saying to Michael, 'Holy Mary, d'you think I'm made of money?'

Her voice sounds different to those of the other white neighbours. It's because she's Irish. I know that from my mum. No one has any money round here but Michael gets sixpence a week pocket money. I don't get pocket money. I'm too scared to ask my dad for it but I'm waiting for the right moment to ask Mum. Michael doesn't know I've got ten pieces of his Lego. I've been taking one piece from him each time we play together. If I keep doing that, I'll end up with a whole set and then I can have something that's all mine.

I have to share everything: my bed, with one of my siblings — Velda, Millie, Joyce or Tippa — as there isn't room for us to each have a bed; and my crayons and whatever toys come my way. We even have to share our toilet. We don't have one in the house; the toilet is down the bottom of the yard, beyond where the tin baths are kept. I hate going down there, especially if it's dark. I've been scared of going there since I saw the man with the metal leg using it. I watched him go in and he was in there ages. Then he came out and was walking funny and he saw me; he looked right at me and didn't smile. I went in there afterwards and it stank so bad! I quickly did what I had to do and used the horrible shiny toilet paper called Izal, then went running back into the house and told Mum.

'Mum, a scary man with a metal leg went in our toilet and now it's all smelly.'

She bent down to listen to me and told me it was maybe because he'd had something called polio. That's why he had to wear a brace on his leg. It wasn't his fault. Lots of people had things like that, she said, which meant they weren't able to move around as well as others. They were handicapped. I repeated the word a few times, listening to the sound of it in my mouth. Mum knows things like this because she's a nurse. She works nights in Marston Green Hospital. She has to get the double-decker cream-coloured bus into the centre and then take a Midland Red to Marston Green. I wish I could take a bus to faraway places. Even better, I wish I had a car. Hardly anyone on Farm Street has one, but I look at pictures of them and I'm going to get lots of cars as I soon as I grow up.

Dad works during the day at the GPO, which

is something to do with telephones, although we don't have one. There's only one lady in our street who has one and she charges people tuppence to use it, but only if there's an emergency. She won't let people go round there to just chat.

Dad's very proud of being at the GPO and he says it's a 'job with prospects', but he doesn't seem very happy. He doesn't laugh and never plays with us. It's only Mum who cuddles us and listens to us, but she looks sleepy a lot of the time and she's always saying she's exhausted. She doesn't play football with me — and neither does Dad — but I know she loves me. She was so very proud to have us twins, even though it was quite a drama bringing us into the world.

Mum tells me that I fought my way out of her like a semi-pro boxer. I was in such a hurry to get on with life that morning of 15 March 1958,[1] that I came into the world by the reception of the hospital, on a stretcher. This caused my dad much agitation, and he paced up and down the corridor, shouting and crying, extremely anxious. By the time my sister Velda arrived fifteen minutes later, they were able to get Mum into a ward. She says the best rest she ever had since coming to England was the nine days she spent in hospital after having us.

She lay in her bed admiring her twins by day, receiving her visiting friends — most of them

---

[1] My birth date is the subject of much speculation. All my official documents say it is 15 April 1958 but my mum swears it was 15 March.

nurses — and at night, when me and my sister would sleep like perfect little babies, my dad would come in. She didn't get such a long rest when my other siblings were born, though — her life got busier and busier — and now there are so many of us in the house that she never gets time to herself. And she also has to do all the cooking and cleaning and shopping.

'Come now, Benjamin, out of that bath. Don't mek me go over there, jus come over here; mek me do your hair.'

She brings me a towel and I stand in the yard as she dries me down. 'School tomorrow and you can't be slow. I know you like to laze about, you know.' She hums a song while she pats me with the towel and blows kisses and raspberries on my arms, making me giggle.

Adults always want everything done in a hurry. On my way to school I like to look at all the people and the tightly packed houses of my street. Sometimes I see the wild dogs that roam around by the wasteland where the bomb 'pecks' are. This is because there was a war before I was born and all the houses were destroyed in a Blitz. So now the only creatures that live there are the packs of dogs and wild cats that hunt mice and rats. I saw a big dog fight one day. It was exciting and scary. You could tell which dog was the leader because the fight didn't end until the toughest one was wounded.

If I see the dogs coming too close then I run, and I can run really fast. I'm like 'greased lightning', so old Frank, the man down the road, says. I ran all the way home one day to avoid the dogs, but Velda got bitten and she screamed and cried the house down. I felt a bit guilty for not staying with her and trying to fight it off, but she always says she wants to do things for herself, so I left her to it and it felt like instinct to run.

It also feels like instinct to explore my surroundings and make up words about it that I repeat to myself, which means I take longer doing things than adults like. I remember on the very first day we moved into our house, Dad surprised me. He said, 'Time this boy did some errands. Take this five shilling and go get some light bulbs from that corner shop.'

He wrote it down on a piece of paper so I could hand it over to the man behind the counter. I set off determined to do a good job. All I had to do was go to the shop, hand over the note, take the bulbs and return home. But my concept of time was different to my dad's. On the way to the shop I saw some boys playing football, so I stopped and asked if I could play with them. They said yes, and I did. After that I saw some kids swinging on a rope from a tree. So I stopped and asked if I could have a go and they said yes. So I did. I saw boys playing conkers, so I joined in, and girls skipping, so I stopped and skipped and made up a little rhyme about it: 'Hop one-two, then lose my shoe.' And that was just on the way to the shop. On the way back I stopped off for some other playful adventures before getting home, where it was beginning to get dark and the rest of the family was waiting for me.

I was really proud that I did so much without

losing the money and managing to return with the bulbs intact, but I received a good telling-off from the whole family. My mum said, 'Benjamin, why you make us worry so?' And my dad said: 'The boy have his head in the blasted clouds.' I maintain to this day that I did what I was told to do; no one mentioned time.

★　★　★

I don't want to go to school tomorrow. It's only at the end of Farm Street and it's called St Mathias, but it's boring and strict and I don't understand why the teachers are so horrible to me. As Mum tucks me into bed with Tippa, I think about the strange way they talk to me sometimes, those teachers. It's different from how they speak to all the other kids — the white kids. It's not fair they made me the captain of the cricket team the first day I joined the school. I'd never played the game before and I didn't know the rules or anything. They expected me to be good at it because I am 'West Indian', but I stood there not knowing what to do and then they were cross with me. I kept saying I was born in Birmingham like them, but they didn't take any notice.

Soon afterwards all the children in our class were told to bring in their favourite golliwog. The next day all the kids flocked around us, eager to show us their drawings, badges, jam jars, or their actual golliwog toys. Velda and me stood there grinning politely, too embarrassed to move or speak. I felt upset and I thought about it a lot.

11

Did they think we were 'golliwogs' because we weren't white like them? A golliwog was a silly toy, not a real person. I wasn't sure what was going on but I was too shy to ask the teachers what they were doing. I know they think we're very different from them because we're the only black family in the street — although they call us 'coloured' — but is this what it's going to be like for the rest of our lives?

I look forward to the gypsies coming back next year. The white people talk about them in an even worse way than they talk about us, but I've played with them and been over the bomb pecks with them and their adults never make me feel uncomfortable and unwanted like the white teachers do. They sing songs, play musical instruments, make fires and mend things from the old rubbish they find. And their eyes light up when they see me. The gypsy children are rough and tough but they're really friendly. They shout out, 'Let's do things' or 'Come with us, friend, let's have some adventures.'

We sometimes run over to the bomb pecks and look for farthings — tiny bronze coins with a little bird on. We've found quite a few of these, so it's a shame they're no longer used. Occasionally we find a penny or two and then we'll dash to the shop where the shopkeeper keeps a tray of penny sweets for us.

Some of the local kids are formed into little gangs and you don't want to bump into a group from another area — like round the corner or the next block of streets away. Sometimes, if one gang meets another, there'll be a little scrap.

Some punches get thrown but we always run off at the sight of an adult. It's definitely the gypsy kids that are known for being the best fighters.

A girl called Carol, who lives a few doors down from us, tried to stop me playing with them one day, saying they were all thieves and tricksters. When she asked me why I liked to play with them so much I told her: 'Their girls have scars, and I like girls with scars. Fighting girls. Not crybabies like you lot.'

I like them because they don't keep asking where I'm from or talking about my skin colour. I asked one of the neighbours why nobody likes the gypsies and she said, 'They're not like us; they come from another culture, and they do things differently.'

Culture. It was the first time I'd heard that word. I didn't think the lady who said it meant it in a nice way but I liked the sound of it. I admired the gypsies and their culture. I liked the way they did things. And I liked their girls with scars.

2

Wake Up and Smell the Racism

You see, back in those days, Hockley was a traditional white working-class area, even though it was only a couple of miles away from Aston, where there were lots of black families. Up until we moved to Hockley, my parents had been renting wherever they could find a landlord willing to let a house to a black family, which wasn't easy in the early 1960s. But now we had our first council house. Like everyone else on the street, we just about made ends meet, with both my parents working all hours. Money was tight, but all the families around me were at the same level. You didn't have rich people living side by side with poor people. You didn't have kids with fancy clothes and toys living next door to kids with nothing. So no one compared themselves to their neighbours on the basis of wealth because we were all living the same way.

But of course there was one immediately obvious way in which Valerie and Oswald Springer and their family were different. From the day we moved to Farm Street everyone knew there was a 'coloured' family in the neighbourhood. And from about the age of five or six, once I was going to school, I was coming up against people who didn't want us there.

14

As the months passed and I tuned my ear to the language of the people around me, I started to realise that some people were hostile; they used words to express their dislike of us that they didn't use about white people. I was only small but I sensed in my heart that nobody around us was going to defend us. There was no point going to my teachers. Although they didn't use horrible words, they were frosty and strict and religious, and ran the place along Victorian lines. Anyone who was regarded as different in some way had to fend for themselves. I did this by making friends with the other outcasts — the gypsies and the Irish kids.

One day, someone had been horrible to me and I was sitting by myself in the playground when this kid with a really strong Irish accent came up and said, 'I'll be your friend.'

'Why?' I asked. 'You're still white.'

'Yeah, but I'm a Catholic and I'm Irish. They pick on me too. We can be mates.'

So we became friends. We found a game we both loved — we started nicking apples together, mostly from gardens. This soon became easy. One day he dared me to take an apple from a grocer. I dashed across the road and a car caught the very edge of me. I wasn't hurt but I was shocked. I said, 'I don't think I wanna do that kind of scrumping anymore.' But by this time we were really close, me and the Catholic boy.

I was thinking that people in authority were uptight and not to be trusted to help you if you were in trouble. So in a bid to coax me in the direction of conforming, like the boys and girls that weren't black or Irish or from a travelling family, I was enrolled in the Boys' Brigade. The local branch met at St Mathias at the weekend and some other boys from the school had joined up. They told me there'd be orange squash and adventures but it didn't seem much fun compared to the adventures I'd had with the gypsies and my Irish friend. Mum bought me a new uniform, which looked like something a sailor would wear, and I had to do an initiation: running from one tree to another, counting from one to ten, and swearing to save all the boys and girls in the world from folk that were not like us.

The orange squash was OK, but there wasn't much adventure, apart from marching in the street on Sunday mornings and banging drums, which I didn't enjoy very much. We were rivals with the Boy Scouts, but we were forever being told that the Scouts were odd, doing weird rituals, and patting each other on the back all the time. But we didn't pat each other on the back. We were the Boys' Brigade, and we were soon to become the Man's Brigade. So we did drill, our clothes were regularly inspected, which seemed a pointless waste of time, and we had to stand to attention a lot.

It was all too regimented for me. I lasted three and a half weeks. I knew it was time to go when I stood in line with a group of boys and a rather intimidating moustache attached to a uniform went down the line and asked the boys what they wanted to do when they grew up. They all seemed to want to join the army, be firemen or policemen, but when it came to me I said I wanted to be a poet.

'A poet!' shouted the moustache. 'A poet! When was the last time you saw a poet skin a rabbit? Think of something better, and when you do you'll be one of us.'

I knew then and there that was never going to happen. I was never going to be part of the authority culture.

* * *

It was around this time that I suffered my first physical racist attack. I'd been called names at school but at least no one tried to hurt me. I had been playing football in the street with some friends one day, and I was walking home down Farm Street. It was hot and sunny. Birds were singing, dogs were barking and I was happy. I skipped with joy and made up rhymes about the sun and the moon and the dogs, reciting them quietly to myself. Then I heard someone behind me shout, 'You black bastard!'

I didn't even have time to look around before the full-sized house brick hit the back of my head. The boy actually had the brick in his hand, and he hit me with it as he rode past me on his bicycle, so the force was terrifying. It was as if the brick went through my brain, bringing with it 2,000 watts of electricity. He looked back at me as he rode off and shouted, 'Go home, wog!' and for the first time in my life I had to ask myself where home was.

I ran to Mum with my head pouring with blood, not crying but confused. As she cleaned me up, I asked, 'Mum, where is home?'

'This is home, Benjamin,' she replied. 'This house is your home.'

Then I had to ask the big question, the one I really wanted to know the answer to: 'What is a bastard?'

I had heard the word black before, even the word wog, but not the word bastard. I needed to know what a bastard was, and no matter how much my mum asked me about the attack and how much pain I was feeling, all I kept asking was, 'What is a bastard, Mum?' But all she could say was, 'Is a bad word, son.'

After my first physical racist attack, the attack of the golliwogs, and other strange happenings, I was becoming more and more aware that some people didn't like other people because of the way those other people were born. Not because of anything they'd said; not because of anything they'd done; not because they didn't share their sweets or pass the ball when playing football — but because of the way they were born. I thought about it for a while and a big question arose in my little head. If you wanted to be treated well, and you wanted to be liked by everyone, was there anything you could do *before* you were born to make sure that you were born 'right'? Or was there anything your parents could do?

Around this time I'd found another friend; someone to play with when the gypsies weren't in town. His name was Tommy. Tommy had lots of board games and he would let me go to his house after school and play with them. He had a

18

sister, who was okay, but she didn't have any scars, and sometimes I would see his mother, who, if she was going to explain anything to me, would start the explanation with, 'In this country we . . . ' Or, if she was talking about the past, she would say, 'In the olden days, before the country started going downhill . . . ' I used to find it all very confusing. By saying 'in this country' was she telling me that she came from another country? And if the country was going downhill, did this mean we were all going to fall off the edge of the country because it would be too much of a steep slope? Yet more big questions for me to ponder, as I tried to understand the workings of civilisation.

One day, as I was walking to Tommy's house from school, his sister, who had gone ahead of us, came running back to us. She looked panicked.

'You can't bring him home because Dad's at home,' she said to her brother. Tommy looked at me, unsure what to say next. I thought the problem was one of space. I thought the house was too small for us, so I said, 'That's okay. I've always wanted to meet your dad. I'll just say hello and then I'll go.'

Tommy's expression quickly went from unsure to worried. His sister ran off back home, shouting, 'Don't say I didn't warn you.' And then Tommy said, 'Sorry, you can't come home. My dad doesn't like black people. He thinks they should all be slaves.'

I wasn't educated enough to be angry. 'What's a slave?' I asked Tommy.

'I don't know,' he replied. 'But whatever it is, he thinks you should be one.'

As soon as I got home I asked my mother what a slave was and she said: 'A long time ago our people sinned, and God punished us for those sins, and slavery was part of that punishment. But don't worry, just be good, and if you are good you can receive redemption and go to heaven.' She smiled and finished by saying, 'There's no slavery in heaven.'

Trying to work out civilisation was hard enough, but now I had to work out the merits of heaven, which I immediately thought was a strange concept, but then I thought most of the concepts and stories that came out of the Bible were strange. I remember thinking at that very moment that as a place to hang out for eternity heaven sounded okay — a place where there was peace and clouds and women playing harps and, best of all, no slavery. But I didn't like the idea of having to wait until I died to get there, and to get there I had to be so good, so perfect, so well behaved that I couldn't play with the bad gypsies. So I said to my mother: 'Mum, I don't want to wait until I die to be free from slavery, and there must be some good white people alive, or why would God make us live? We could have all stayed dead or unborn.'

My mother looked at me as if I was mad, and I looked at her as if we were living in different dimensions. We might have sprung from the same heritage, but our experiences were already diverging.

3

Journey to the Motherland

The story of my poetry can be traced back to my mother. It was she who gave me words, she who gave me rhythm, and it was she who gave me my appetite for verse. At times she spoke in rhyme, not necessarily to encourage me to become a poet, but because it was the way she spoke. For instance, when me and my brothers and sisters were young, Mum would say things like: 'Let's go to the show; we have to go now, you know, cause if we don't go now we cannot go tomorrow.' She would stretch out syllables to make sure certain words rhymed, which is something all dub poets do. That's me mummy.

Rhyme was in everything she did and said, and so rhyme was part of our day-to-day lives. She was always singing and there were plenty of nursery rhymes or skipping songs for the girls. She never wrote any of this down, but she could rhyme a line for just about every situation. She would never call herself a poet; for her it was a great way to aid her memory and entertain us.

Lineve Faleta Honeyghan was born in the parish of St Elizabeth, in the southwest of Jamaica, on 29 June 1934. Her little area was known as Bluntas District, thirty minutes' walk from Treasure Beach. I've been there many times and I've always been struck by the appearance of people from that area. Most of them are very light-skinned and there is a reason for this. The history of the area shows that at times African slaves were allowed to mix with some of the Irish and Scottish folk who were sent there for being naughty in Britain, so many of the names and the physical features of the people reflect that. When I was young I remember my mother boasting of her Scottish ancestry and feeling ashamed of any African connection she might have.

There's a story that members of my family tell, which all of my Jamaican relatives believe to be true. It's the story of a ship that sailed from Britain with a mainly Scottish crew of forty men who got into trouble at sea. They fetched up on the coast of Panama and the captain asked if they could land but they were refused permission, so they turned around and managed to get to Jamaica. At Treasure Beach they were given permission to land. They soon recovered from their ordeal but it was so nice that instead of moving on they decided to stay, and being all men it wasn't long before they began to chase and marry local girls. We were always told that we partly descended from these explorers, and not the 'criminal' kind.

My mother's grandfather was William Moxam — not your average Jamaican guy but a Scottish white guy whom my mother still remembers. He had a shocking temper and used to smack her and beat her all the time. He would come down on her with fury for any little 'wrong' thing she did. Even though she was only a little girl, William would not spare her.

My mother was born in the same house as William and his African-Jamaican wife, Caroline. Their daughter, my grandmother, Adelyn Moxam, married a dark-skinned man called Honeyghan, and they had a baby, my mother. My mother's sister went on to marry another mixed-race man, so all of her cousins are very light-skinned, but my mother was darker than all of my auntie's kids because her father had been black, so she was a shade darker.

Jamaicans used to comment on the colour of people's skin all the time. Sometimes it's hard for non-Jamaicans to understand, and to some it sounds racist, but that's not the case. It's a bit like saying, 'Pass me the black ball, not the green one.' It's just how they recognise and describe people; they simply mention such things in passing. People were called black, red, yellow, collie (Indian) or Chinee (Chinese), but most of the people in my mother's family were light-skinned, or 'red'.

The Jamaican side of my family was neither rich nor poor. By no stretch of the imagination were they wealthy — they had very little money but they had lots of animals, including cows, goats, chickens — and my mother even had her own horse. A lot of that was down to William Moxam. He had a strong work ethic and he strove to buy land and ensure that even if the family was short of cash they would still have food. They would grow yams, sweet potatoes, tomatoes, corn, cashew nuts and more. So they always had food and clothing, most of which was homemade by them or by neighbours, and most of the food — animal and vegetable — was grown in their yard.

My mum remembers with some pride (to my horror), how she actually drank milk straight from the cows' udders, especially from her favourite cow, Rose, who was particularly quiet and demure. At night she would tie up Rose's calf so he couldn't get to her to take the milk. Then, in the morning, Rose's udders would be full and ready for my mother to drink from. She claims that the cow didn't mind, and would shake her tail approvingly. I think differently, but I wasn't around then to object.

The most important person in my mother's life was her uncle, Richard Moxam, known to everyone as Moody. Her mother washed her and put her to bed, but Moody played with her, he gave her money and advice, and he would listen to her if she had something to say. He, like many Jamaican men of that time, went to Cuba to find work, and it was he who gave my mum her names: Lineve Faleta. It was said that he was a bit of a ladies' man, and my mum thinks she was named after one of his Cuban girlfriends. To family and friends my mum was known as Faleta.

So Faleta was born at the family home in Bluntas. That was a perfectly normal thing to happen. There were midwives in the area, but they weren't trained as professionals; they were just women with experience (which usually meant they'd had a few kids of their own) who

24

would pass on their knowledge to other women by word of mouth, and sometimes trial and error. If there was any trouble during a delivery they would call the hospital and a bed would be made available if they could get there on time.

My mother came from a big family; she had two sisters and five brothers. She was the eldest girl and the second eldest child, but the older boy died young, so my mother ended up being the eldest. By Jamaican standards she had a good education, starting school at seven and leaving at sixteen. By all accounts she enjoyed it, using her time constructively to learn as much as she could. She loved school so much that she attended even on days when she didn't have to. On Fridays lots of pupils didn't turn up, attendance was very lax, but she never missed a lesson.

After my mum finished her school studies she went to Munro College for a further two years. Now, don't start thinking of European-type private education, as it was nothing like that. It was as far away from fee-paying college in England as you could get. It had very few facilities, very few up-to-date books, and the staff looked like they weren't being paid, but she still had to pay and, as ever, Uncle Moody funded her. The family lived by the seaside, so to reach Munro College she had to take a long bus ride up a steep hill, which she hated, so she stayed at the college and only went home at weekends.

She graduated when she was eighteen, and spent the next couple of years enjoying herself, going to parties and dances, but living at home.

She had a carefree life with few problems and she always had a bit of money in her pocket. Although her father was around he had very little to do with her. He never gave her a dime — he didn't have much money anyway — but he was a distant figure. Uncle Moody was the complete opposite. He travelled, he owned land and hired people, and he gave her all she needed. He loved giving presents, and my mum loved receiving them. He was particularly generous on birthdays or during celebrations like Christmas and Easter. My mum, and the rest of the community, recalls how she once had six new dresses — an almost unheard-of abundance. She was the talk of the town, and for the following few months wherever she went they could see her coming along the street in one of her lovely new dresses.

Inevitably her first child came along during that fun-filled post-college period. She met a young man and they courted Jamaican-style — under the moonlight with the palm trees swaying; a little bit of dancing and a little bit of rum. Both were enjoying themselves after leaving college, and then my mother fell pregnant and Tina came along.

★ ★ ★

One day in the mid-1950s, Mum and her sister stopped to look at one of the many posters that were put up around Jamaica around that time as part of a campaign headed by a Conservative politician. The poster said: 'The Motherland calls. Jobs and a great future await you in the land where the streets are paved with gold'. It is now well known that there was an extensive campaign in Jamaica and other Caribbean islands to get people to apply for the jobs that English workers wouldn't do after the Second World War. The British were desperate for people from overseas.

My auntie said there was no way she was going to England; she had heard it was cold and dark, but my mother wanted to give it a try. Once again, Uncle Moody stepped in. He was convinced it would be a good move for her, and she was very eager to go, but her daughter Tina was only two, so it would mean making a tough decision.

The culture around having and raising children was a lot less formal in the Caribbean compared to Europe. In Jamaica big families were the norm, and they tended to live together and look after each other. Living under one roof you could find mothers, grandmothers, aunties, brothers and sisters, and all would offer support. Even members of the local community who weren't blood relatives would provide plenty of free childcare, so she knew Tina would be well-cared-for.

People were also fairly happy; it was only when they started coming to the UK and comparing themselves to people around the world that they began to consider themselves poor. But my mum never thought like that. She had money in her pocket, lots of dresses and lots of shoes.

The decision to migrate to England was made easier by the fact that another uncle, Neville, was already there, and she would listen to the radio and hear advertisements calling for people to go to England and work. Neville would write regularly saying how good it was, so Uncle Moody paid her fare, and her mother said she would look after the baby. So that was that, the decision was made: my mum would go to the UK and stay with Neville in Sheffield.

4

Come on Over, Valerie

The weeks leading up to her departure were exciting because there was a lot to do. She had to go to Kingston, the big city, to get the papers and her passport, which in itself was a big adventure for her and the family members who went with her. There was great anticipation, but the mood changed on the day she left because, when it came to it, she found it difficult saying goodbye to her family and daughter and making the break. She remembered hearing people crying as the minibus came round to pick people up. Those being left behind were in tears because they didn't know whether they would ever see their loved ones again.

My mother and the others, mainly women, were taken to Kingston, to a hotel, where she paid £70, and the next day they boarded a huge cruise liner called the SS *Peniah*. The journey started in Jamaica, and then the ship went to St Kitts to pick up more people bound for the Motherland. When it was full of Caribbean people, it headed towards Europe. It stopped off on the coast of Spain, and my mother got off to buy souvenirs, which she found a peculiar experience. For the first time in her life she encountered people who didn't speak any

English. Suddenly she was very important; people wanted to shine her shoes, for a price, and offer her gifts, at a price.

On the boat there were hundreds of migrants carrying the many possessions they had brought from Jamaica and the other islands. They slept in bunks in large dormitory-like berths, and they were called into a dining area for breakfast and then called back again at dinnertime. The passengers were speculating about what it would be like when they arrived; they talked about the weather and the conditions they might encounter. They talked about the people: Were they clean? Could they cook? Would they be nice? They spent seventeen days at sea in total. The conditions were good, and they all had a reasonably pleasant time, but most of all they had great expectations.

Now, here's a mystery. Mum says she came over on this ship called the SS *Peniah*, but I looked really hard — so hard I think I have the right to call it research — and I could find no ship from that time with that name. I spoke to the historian Arthur Torrington and other experts of the *Windrush* generation, who migrated from the Caribbean, and none of them have found a ship with that name, but my mum swears that's the ship she came on. I can only conclude that either she has simply got the name wrong (maybe the *Peniah* was a nickname and the ship had a different official name), or she was an illegal immigrant. In which case it would have to be said that she did a great job, and I'm very proud of her.

When the ship (whatever it was called) landed at Southampton in the first week of June 1957, people from companies that had advertised for workers were waiting. One such group met my mother and took her to a train station so she could make the journey to Sheffield. One of her earliest memories was of English houses. As the train headed north all she could see were factories with smoke billowing out of their chimneys, thousands of them.

She clapped her hands in joy; with so many factories, work would never be scarce. Then a friendly native told her the truth. All those factories were in fact houses. It was a big letdown. In Jamaica only factories had chimneys, but in England every house had them, and every house lit coal fires to keep warm. She had made the mistake many people from the Caribbean made when they first arrived in England. Back in Jamaica most houses were painted in vivid colours and were usually only one storey, so Mum was confused by the small English homes, all drab and made from brick, and all so very tightly packed together.

She arrived in Sheffield and found her way to the small house that was to be her new home. It was in stark contrast to the comfortable conditions she'd enjoyed in Jamaica. She had to sleep in the same bed as the other people she was staying with — three of them — until she eventually got a room of her own. The landlady found it difficult to say Faleta, so she suggested that she change her name to Valerie. She stuck to it, and when people asked her what her name was she would reply, quite proudly, 'Valerie.' Faleta was a beautiful name that conjured up images of the Caribbean sun and dancing on the beach, but Valerie suited Sheffield; it sounded much more English.

Her Uncle Neville had wanted her to get straight into nursing but her first job was working for Batchelors Peas in a canning factory. She was swept away by the adventure of her new life but she missed her mother, Uncle Moody and other members of her family — and most of all she missed her baby, Tina. Like a lot of people from the Caribbean back then, she told herself she'd only stay in the UK for five years, make some money, then return home; but five years turned into ten, ten into fifteen, fifteen into twenty. The twenty turned into fifty.

She tried to make a go of things in Sheffield, but after a few months she realised that as much as she loved peas she didn't want to spend her life processing them, so when one of the people who'd travelled with her from Jamaica suggested that she look over the horizon to Birmingham, she did, and after nine months she left Batchelors Peas and made the move to the Midlands.

She'd been told to be prepared because England would be freezing cold, but when she arrived in June it was quite warm. She'd also been told she would have to drink tea all the time, otherwise she would freeze from the inside out. There were lots of little stories about other people's experiences, and lots of advice was offered, but everyone's experiences were different. Much depended on the time of year they arrived, the city they arrived in and the houses they lived in.

She kept in touch with her family back home by writing plenty of letters in which she would describe her living conditions: the carpets (or lino), the wallpaper, the pictures on the walls, even the smells she encountered. The moment she received a letter from someone back home, she would respond straight away. If, for any reason, she took too long to reply, another letter would soon drop on the doormat, prompting her to write.

Her big dream was to one day bring her mother over to England, but it was a struggle raising the money, so when she wrote home telling the family she hadn't yet earned enough they told her not to worry, they were happy just to receive her letters. Despite some difficult conditions, Valerie, as she was now known, had begun to make a life in England; she made it her home and she was growing to love it.

One of the things she found most exciting was the absence of authority. For the first time in her life she didn't have anybody to answer to. There were no parents monitoring her every move, and if she wanted to spend her wages on soaps, perfumes, dresses or shoes, then she could.

The home in which she found lodging was being shared with a nurse, who very kindly asked her matron whether there were any more jobs. There were jobs, so matron gave my mum a form to fill in, and pretty soon she'd passed the interview. She flew through her training, taking the transition from factory worker to nursing in her stride. And that was it: she was now an SRN, a State Registered Nurse.

★ ★ ★

Now, my mother will tell you that she has never ever experienced racism, not since the day she arrived in England from Jamaica. She insists nobody has ever said anything racist to her or been unpleasant to her because of the colour of her skin. She doesn't deny there is racism; she just says it's never happened to her. This is something we disagree on. As a child I remember people calling her names as she walked past them, but she would insist they were saying something else and not talking about her. I remember being in shops where the shop assistant would serve everyone else before her, even when my mum was next in line, and she would say, 'She's serving them first because they're in a hurry.' Even when people were racist directly to her face she would make excuses for them, saying they were confused or upset. She was always trying to see the good in people, even when the people weren't good.

She had only one close friend in Birmingham — another woman who'd been on the ship with her. Mum was always looking for somewhere better to live, so her friend got her a better room in a larger house in Aston. It was while living there that she met and started to date Oswald Springer. He was from Barbados and had started to work as a packer in what was then called the GPO, the General Post Office. Now that was a good job, a job with a future. My mother's future was beginning to look good too. She worked hard and she studied hard and, after taking more exams and getting a few promotions, she was soon working in a mental hospital, in the Chelmsley Wood area of Birmingham. She began to earn good money; enough to start sending some home.

5

Marriage, Music and Rhyme

Her relationship with Oswald got serious; so serious that they got married. I don't know much about my dad; he didn't tell me much and, to be honest, he didn't even talk to me that much. Most of what I know about him I've learned from Mum, but I knew that his mother died when he was still young, so his dad remarried, and he had two brothers and one sister.

The GPO was the only company he ever worked for. He started as a packer, which strangely meant that he swept the floor a lot, and he worked his way up to management. He was very proud of his progression through the ranks, but even more proud of his dedication to one company. He really believed that by getting letters and parcels dispatched in and out of the country, he helped to make Britain great. The pinnacle of his career, much later on, was overseeing the upgrade of the telephone system in Barbados, so that Barbados had what was then the most advanced telephone system in the Caribbean.

Marriages between people from different Caribbean islands were not actually that common. People from Barbados called Jamaicans loud, uncontrollable criminals, and Jamaicans called people from Barbados small-minded, small-island people who ate monkeys' fingers. Marrying in England would have been easier than marrying in the Caribbean, but when Mum wrote home to tell the family who she was marrying they were all surprised. Some said they thought England had run out of Jamaican men, and she must have got very desperate; others said they were worried he might eat her.

In late summer 1957 she was working at Marston Green Hospital and all was going well, but one day she felt unwell. She went to a doctor in the hospital and told him she was having stomach problems and, without checking her, he said: 'Now, you just got married. Could you be pregnant?' She said it was a possibility but she didn't think so. She was sent next door to the maternity unit and was examined straight away. She was pregnant, and the newly married husband and wife were happy, but when she went for a check-up a few months later, she was X-rayed and was told she was carrying twins.

Mum had been forewarned of the possibility of having twins in the future after having her first baby back in Jamaica. The nurse had given her an examination and told her she could see 'twin eggs' on her womb. I don't know that much about reproductive biology but I'm sure it doesn't work like that. Mum swears the nurse was right, though, and after the arrival of me and Velda, it's hard to convince her otherwise.

Having children in England was a very different experience to having them in the Caribbean. When Velda and I were three months old, Mum had to return to work. There were no grandmothers, aunties, sisters or friends to look after us. No network of neighbours who would lend a hand. That's why she started working nights — she had that option as a nurse — while Dad took over when he got home from his day at the GPO.

After Velda and me came Millie, in May 1959, Joyce, in September 1960, and Tippa in January 1962. And then, in 1963, Mum had yet another set of twins, Mark and Paul. By this time the house was full, with nine mouths to feed. Eventually it became impossible for both parents to work and maintain their ships-in-the-night marriage. There were so many children, with so many demands, that Mum had to stay at home. We were noisy, playful, naughty children who were always up to something. Our house sounded like a school playground. Someone was always hurt or kicking a ball around; someone else was demanding food, and another was trapped in the cupboard.

We didn't have much to distract us. There were no smart phones or fancy electronic devices; we didn't even have a television. Only well-off people had television, but we did have a radio and Mum and Dad listened to the BBC Home Service.

Then there was the music. My parents had an old-fashioned Blue Spot radiogram in the front room — the room reserved for entertaining, with its three-piece suite and cushions and colourful wall hangings showing a map of Jamaica and a hummingbird and a picture of Jesus with a slogan saying something like: 'Christ is the head of this house'. A typical scene would go like this:

Most likely it would be a Saturday afternoon and the drinks trolley had been wheeled out to entertain Dad's friends and my uncles (Mum's brothers), who had not long arrived from Jamaica. The men would be pouring rum and wearing suits and ties, and the women were in the kitchen mixing punch and looking crisp in their colourful dresses. There would be much chat and gossip and laughter. Everyone would be excited and looking forward to hearing the latest sounds from back home as if they were a gift from God.

And then Uncle Everett would bring out some new records from his bag and there would be much excitement — such as when the needle landed on Prince Buster's 'Al Capone' for the first time. The men liked the theme of Buster's lyrical characters: gangsters from the 1920s, whose 'guns don't argue', or catchy songs about horse races. Prince Buster had already established himself as a star in Jamaica with 'Madness', rhyming with gladness, 'Blackhead Chinaman' and 'Wash Wash'. Next up maybe we'd hear Mum's rather scratched copy of 'Oh Carolina', and soon everyone would be swaying to the sound and having a good time.

The records were all played lots of times — there'd be Alton Ellis, Desmond Dekker and Millie Small, who'd recently had a chart hit with 'My Boy Lollipop', but Prince Buster most often won the day with his cheeky-sounding voice and lyrics that spoke of Caribbean life and places I didn't yet know, like Orange Street, in Kingston, where the majority of the records were produced.

I'd be in among the adults, tangling myself up in all the long legs and loving the sound of the bass and the beat. I knew not to touch the radiogram anymore, though. Once I tried to be the DJ, and I was doing quite well until I pretended it was a jukebox and dropped coins onto the turntable. Although it didn't affect the functioning of this wonderful contraption, Dad went crazy and told me never to go near it again. I obeyed him for at least a week.

But the main reason I loved the music is that this was where my rhyming began in earnest. When the record finished playing I carried on. I'd pick up the theme of the song and put my own spin on it, talking about what was happening in the kitchen or about one of my brothers or sisters being told off. I would do a running commentary, similar to my playground game at school where I'd make up rhymes for the girls I liked when we played kiss chase. So while all the other boys were getting out of breath running around, I'd make up a sweet little rhyme about the girl and she would pay me by giving me a kiss. No running required.

For me, rhyming was normal. Poetry, storytelling and music were a part of everyday life, not as I imagine it would be in a middle-class white family, where a parent might sit a child down to read poetry and then praise him if he did it well. We just did it. It was how we communicated with one another.

★ ★ ★

I don't know how she fitted it in with nursing, but around this time Mum found a part-time job at the local cinema. Every now and then, if a film was suitable, she'd take us to see it. Mostly it was really boring stuff like *The Sound of Music* but there'd also be westerns. The first western I remember enjoying was *True Grit*, starring John Wayne. For once he had a woman as his sidekick. Usually he would be slapping a woman one minute then kissing her the next. I didn't care about him; we liked the gunslinging.

One night there was bandit action closer to home. We came back from the cinema and found we'd been robbed. In those days, low-level burglars were looking to rob gas and electric meters. Ours were in the cellar. A few weeks later, we were all in bed and they came again. And my dad caught them! He put them in the living room, then said to me, 'You watch them', while he went to fetch the police. Can you imagine me, a little kid, sitting there with two big burglars?

As soon as he left, one of them jumped straight through the window, glass and all. The other one stayed, though, and Dad came back with the police and they nicked him. The next day the cops returned and said to my dad, 'We're going to drive around. Would you be able to spot the other one?' Less than an hour later Dad came back and said they'd got him. In those days burglars looked like burglars, and because he'd gone through the glass he had all these cuts on his face, which he'd covered with plasters. It was like something from the *Beano*.

As I grew up, I started to become aware that something was wrong in our house. It began early one morning. It was a school day but I was woken up much earlier than normal by noises downstairs. I went to see what was happening and there was my mum in the kitchen crying and rubbing her head. I'd never seen my mother cry before; in fact, I'd never seen an adult cry. I thought it was something only kids did. I asked her what had happened and she pointed to my father and said slowly, 'He hit me.' Then she pointed to the floor, where there was a frying pan, and said, 'He hit me with that.'

I looked at my mum crying, then looked at my dad in utter shock. *My dad had made my mum cry . . .* in my young head this was a declaration of shock and a question all happening at the same time. I was trying to process it and I couldn't.

This moment has stayed with me all my life. It's not very often you'll see a frying pan on a floor; it's a strange place for a frying pan to be, unless you're camping or something like that, and even then the frying pan is usually on something. But if I do ever see a frying pan on a floor I get a flashback straight to that morning. It happens from my child's eye view: I see my mum crying and my dad looking angry, then that frying pan on the floor, looking out of place. And then I hear my mother saying, 'He hit me with that.'

6

New Beginnings, Old Problems

It's 1968 and we've all moved to a new council house. Mum is expecting everyone will be happier here, as we've now got an inside bathroom and toilet. We're in Fentham Road, back in Aston, and Mum and Dad are saying it's like moving back to Jamaica. The smell of Caribbean and Asian food fills the air, the houses are colourful, and we hear bluebeat and ska as we walk past them. The best thing is I'm going to a new school, with colourful pupils and colourful teachers, called Deykin Avenue.

Now I'm a bit older I have to be organised and responsible. As the eldest I'm the leader of the pack. We have to get up early, eat breakfast then walk to Witton Road to get the number 5 or 7 bus. We all have to carry our biscuit money and bus fare, and if anyone messes with us I beat them because I'm the big brother and this is the big world where feral kids and highwaymen can nick your biscuit money, or so I'm told.

I love Deykin Avenue School. I make up poems in the playground and perform them for friends. I even read poems in school assembly and get a kiss on the cheek from one or two of the teachers. That's how different this school is from the horrible St Mathias. Kiss chase is even more popular here, so I can earn kisses in accordance with my creative output. I'm collecting girlfriends. I've got seven of them. One day, a couple of weeks ago, I was playing football and a boy told me to look around and all these girls were lined up in the playground, and all looking cross. I'd made Valentine's Day cards for them and they'd been talking.

'You can't have this many girlfriends, Benjamin,' one shouted at me. 'It's not fair.'

'Yeah,' said another. 'You've got to pick one of us.'

'I like you all,' I said. 'I'm not going to choose. You're all nice. But right now I've got to play football.'

As well as having lots of girlfriends, I've also had to protect my brothers and sisters a few times, so I've already gained a reputation as a good fighter. In fact, I'm now declared 'cock of the school', which means I'm someone to be feared, and for a while I enjoy the notoriety.

But nothing stays the same, and one day a new boy comes on the scene. His name is Mervin Francis and he has a bit of a reputation. Rumours circulate about his strength and the speed of his fists, and there's talk that he could take me on, and possibly take me down.

One day, I'm tired of hearing rumours. I push out my chest and go and find him playing marbles in a corner of the playground.

'Alright, Mervin Francis, if you think you're bad. Come den.'

The whole class and some of the older years have gathered around, all chanting, 'Fight, fight,

fight', and some of them are betting on who will win, but he won't fight! I push him and dig the toe of my shoe in his side and say, 'Whassup, you scared?' But still he won't react. I call him names and kick his marbles away, but still no reaction, and the crowd gets bored and the kids disperse.

I'm now declared undisputed cock of the school, the guns, the champion of champions, and now is my moment of triumph. The truth is I'm actually glad he didn't react, because I'm not sure I could have beaten him. I go on to admire Mervin Francis for not fighting. He tells me straight that he can see no reason to fight, and he isn't going to fight simply to see who's best.

But it's me who has the glory now, and if there's ever any problem with my siblings or friends, then other kids run to me and I sort it out. As long as it's a problem in the under-elevens category, 'cos that isn't serious stuff; the serious stuff is happening at home.

School is cool, but family life is beginning to fall apart. My father has started losing his temper more, and Mum is becoming unhappier. After that first incident with the frying pan in Farm Street, there hasn't been any more physical violence but there is always tension in the air. Then things suddenly change; it's as if my father has decided we are now old enough to see the violence for ourselves.

I'm always amazed at how something small and insignificant ends up in domestic carnage. Sometimes he comes home from work and beats Mum because his dinner isn't ready, or because she's spent too much time shopping, or too much money shopping. The other night she was ironing his shirt when he demanded a cup of tea. She said she would do it after she finished the shirt, but he demanded she do it straight away. When she told him she needed a minute, he hit her.

This is the only marriage I've seen up close and it's not like the stories I hear about adults being in love. I'm scared when I think about the future and what's going to happen. I've also started to realise that some of the wars I see on our black and white TV are real wars, and the suffering is happening to real people. There are children around the world who are going really hungry — not just the hungry I feel when dinner is a bit late. The news talks a lot about black people in the United States fighting for something they call civil rights and people are dying because of it. I keep hearing the names Martin Luther King and Angela Davis. There's war in Vietnam, and there's war at 35 Fentham Road.

The other day I went to this kid and asked him, 'What do you do when your dad hits your mum?'

He said, 'My dad doesn't hit my mum.'

So I said, 'I know, you've got one of those hippie families. What about when your mum hits your dad?'

Then he said, 'My mum doesn't hit my dad. They don't fight. You should go to the police. He's a Bad Dad. Some Bad Dads do that.'

Now I'm confused. Now I know that not all families are like mine. There are lots of families where the dads don't hit the mums, but I don't want to go to the police.

★   ★   ★

Around this time the UK was becoming more colourful and people were trying out new fashions and ideas. Pop music was exploding out of radios and things didn't seem quite as stuffy and grey as they had been. I remember our old neighbour Maria O'Reilly paying us a visit, saying, 'Cat Stevens is in the Top Ten', and being really happy about it. She explained the pop charts to me.

I was watching things on TV like *The Avengers*. I loved Emma Peel! When I saw her wearing her catsuit I started thinking, *Is that what they call sexy?* Later on I was excited by *The Man from U.N.C.L.E.*, and at some point I got a *The Man from U.N.C.L.E.* set for my birthday. You got the briefcase and the pass into the secret bunker.

The only time I would watch TV with Dad was when Muhammad Ali, who had previously been known as Cassius Clay, was in a big boxing match. That was an event! But he never really spent time with me. We never sat down and watched a film together or had those father/son good times in the park. He was chatty, but there were never proper conversations.

My uncles would come round and all the men would sit in the front room and drink rum. Jamaicans wouldn't normally socialise with 'Bajuns' (Barbadians) back home, so these gatherings were unusual in Caribbean cultural mixing. Sometimes they'd give me some booze — enough to get me a bit wobbly — and they'd call me 'Cock'. They'd get me to do something that was a bit difficult, such as hand me a full glass and say, 'Walk 'cross the room wit dis, Cock.' They'd watch me wobble and falter and then they'd laugh and there would be much hooting and thigh-slapping. This was probably the happiest and most animated I saw my dad.

He worked a lot and started to grow his own veg — sprouts and cabbages — which we ate, and this made him quite proud. I can't remember him passing on wisdom or talking to me about life, though. I remember my uncles doing that, sometimes taking me aside and saying, 'Hey boy, you gotta watch out for that one', and that sort of thing.

There was violence against my mother, and then there were the beatings that we all got — the kind of punishment many Caribbean kids used to get often for being naughty, rude or for making an adult vex. This is one of those culturally sensitive areas, as almost every Caribbean elder I've met of my parents' generation thinks there's nothing wrong with giving children a beating every now and then. In fact, it's not simply called a beating, it's 'a damn good beating', and they really believe it's good for the person taking it.

Almost every beating I ever received is stored in my memory. We were never given the luxury of being grounded as a punishment. We weren't told that we would miss our dessert after dinner or asked to go to our room . . . we were told to get the very belt that we were going to get the beating with. We had to bring it to the beating place (which was always a long, slow walk) and then beg for mercy as the belt (sometimes with buckle) was thrashed against our backsides.

I always felt that my dad had it in for me because my beatings seemed much harsher than those he gave the others. I thought this was because I defended my mother more than the other kids did, or simply because I was the big brother, so I should have known better. Whatever the reason, I resented being beaten, and I will defend the right of any child not to be beaten, just as I would defend the right of my mother, or any woman, not to be beaten.

★　★　★

Things came to a head one day. Dad was lashing out at Mum for some reason. My brothers and sisters had all run for cover but I had run to help my mother. Instinct took over and I tried to defend her. There was little me, kicking at my father's ankles and punching his knees. He was that big, and I was that small. I couldn't really hurt him but I did just enough to give Mum a chance to escape. She ran for it and I ran with her. Dad shouted, 'Where do you think you're going?'

I called back, 'You hit me too. I'm going with Mum.'

Everyone else stayed with my dad, even my twin sister. Dad tried to stop me but I got past him and escaped. It was very frightening. It was also the beginning of my nomadic existence, moving from place to place with my mum. At first we tried going to women's refuges, but they wouldn't take us. The women running these places said stuff like, 'We want to take you in, but it's the rest of the women here . . . they're not used to people like you. They won't be able to accept you. There might be trouble.'

The GPO took care of the post, telephones, telegrams and every other form of public communication back then, so my father's job meant he had access to all sorts of organisations. With his connections he could track down my mum any time she tried to do anything official, like claim child benefit. He would phone the social security, get her details and come looking for us. There was no data protection or privacy laws then; certainly none that applied to us.

When Mum went shopping it was my job to hold her hand and look the other way, keeping an eye out for my dad. So she'd be looking one way and I'd be watching her back. It was a really strange thing to do, as if there was a 'Wanted' poster of my dad imprinted on my mind. A couple of times I did actually spot him and would say, 'Mum, quick, it's Dad!' And we'd slide away, leaving the shopping where it was. But there was another time when we bumped right into him. He jumped on her and started to beat her. I cried for help but, although there were many people looking on, no one did anything to assist. I had a little knife in my pocket, a miniature penknife. In those days you could buy them from a newsagent for six old pennies. It was quite pretty, with a pink handle. I jumped on top of my dad and started stabbing him.

As I was on top of him I recalled something I'd heard in the playground about the temple at the side of the head being a weak spot, and that if you stabbed someone through there you could kill them. So I tried to stab him in the temple as hard as I could. The blade folded back on me, so all I did was cut my own hand. I did cut him a little, but not enough to do any real damage, and not in the right place. To make things worse, when the police arrived they held me while my dad simply walked away. Once I was in the station, and they understood what had happened, they decided to let me go, but not after some tough interrogation.

There was another incident when he found Mum walking on Dudley Road in Edgbaston. It was the kind of incident that would be like slapstick if it wasn't so tragic. He'd somehow got hold of her address, so he waited for her to come out; when she did he grabbed her and started hitting her. As he tried to drag her away, Mum tried to calm him down but that wasn't working. A shouting match began. I started yelling, 'Leave her alone!' and my father was shouting, 'Come with me, you wretch!' and my mother was saying, 'No, no, no, let's talk about this. Let's calm it all down.'

I didn't know it at the time but Mum had a plan. She stopped resisting and gave him the impression that she was willing to go with him.

'Okay,' she said. 'Let's go this way.' He wouldn't take his eyes off her, so as she was talking she led him down the road, eventually walking him right into Summerfield Police Station. He didn't realise until it was too late, and when he tried to make a run for it the cops grabbed him and detained him. Mum and I left straight away. After reassuring the cops that this was a one-off, that he was an upstanding member of the community and that the woman had pushed him into it, he was let out.

★ ★ ★

We would live in many places in Birmingham — and also in other cities — over the coming years. We stayed in some places for such a short time that I once went to school in London for just one day. It was Kennington Boys' School in south London, the only all-boys school I ever went to, and I'm glad it was only for a day. They went on and on about how life would be different if they had girls in their school. Every school I'd been to had girls; it was no big thing. But these guys would be going crazy and getting excited every time they saw a girl.

While we were on the run we rented a series of small rooms. They would have a bed or two, a paraffin heater and, if we were lucky, a wardrobe. We would have to share bathrooms and toilets with other people, and use of the kitchen was limited by either space or time and sometimes both. It was all very basic but I didn't care much. When we found a new place I would get

52

instructions from Mum on what my new name was, and what I was to say if anyone asked me where I came from or asked about my dad. Once all that was done, my only concern was where to find new friends to play football with. The love of football and other physical pursuits kept me going; the church kept my mother going.

7

Moving in with the Church

Mum had always been religious but it was during this time that she started going to church to find solace. Like a lot of people, she found friendship, peace and happiness there; it took her away from the dreariness of life, especially when she was being hunted by my father. The church was her escape, her refuge.

Black-led churches were springing up all over the country back then. It was one of the only things that gave people meaning in their lives, and a sense of community. This was the generation of Jamaicans who had answered the call from the Motherland for help, only to find that the Motherland was at best difficult and at worst hostile.

Most didn't have their own church buildings so they used the houses of members of their congregation. The churches did have names, though. Ours was the Triumphant Church of God, and it had branches in Bristol, Burton-on-Trent, Cardiff, London and other towns and cities where there were black communities.

Our church was at 55 Bevington Road, Aston, a place I've been back to many times, and on many of those occasions I've had a film crew or radio producer in tow. The last few times I've been back a Bengali family has been living there. They've got so used to seeing me with my various crews that one time I could hear them saying, 'Oh, it's him again', or words to that effect.

In ye olde England, churches would compete to see who could build the highest steeple; in our churches it was always about who had the best preachers. These were fiery, inspiring, charismatic men who could be on their feet burning energy and sweating buckets as they called upon the Holy Spirit to come cleanse the sinner and reward the faithful. A good preacher could preach for four hours or more, non-stop. Others would call upon members of the congregation to step up and testify, then anyone who had a problem or who had something to say — something inspiring or a psalm they wanted to read — could get up and do their thing. Sometimes they were as good as the main preacher.

It was during one of these moments in church when I did what I call my very first public, or semi-public, poetry performance. It was my mother's turn to testify. She was a good speaker and the crowd was expecting something special from her, but to everyone's surprise, and mine, she stood up and said she was going to take a rest and that her son would read a poem.

Little me looked up at big her with a quizzical expression drawn across my face and shrugged my shoulders. She looked down on me with a 'go on, my son' look, and I felt I had no choice. I got up to perform but didn't know what to say, as my poems up to that point were about playground politics, stupid adults and girls. I had no church poems or going to heaven poems. I did have a great memory when it came to words, though, and in Sunday school I practised memorising passages from the Bible and the order of the books therein.

I suddenly knew what I was going to do. I jumped up and began to chant: 'Genesis, Exodus, Leviticus, Numbers, Deuteronomy, Joshua, Judges, Ruth, first and second Samuel.' I danced as I chanted to a reggae-cum-ska rhythm, and when I got to Revelations I began to do them backwards. When I stopped there were shouts of 'Hallelujah!', 'Praise the Lord!' and 'The Holy Spirit has touched him.' Some even called me a little prophet. It was here that I was first given the name Zephaniah, by one of the pastors in the church, after he who prophesied in the days of Josiah, ruler of the Kingdom of Judah (641–610 BC). A lot of people think Zephaniah is a stage name. It's not. It's the name on my passport and on all of my documents. The name is thought to mean 'he whom God has hidden', or 'treasured by God'. I always felt I was a modern Zephaniah.

From then on I was constantly asked to get up and do that performance, or to perform random passages memorised from the Bible. I was the star turn when we went to conventions with other churches. It didn't matter how good their preachers were; none of them had a Bible-rapping kid like me.

It was nice being a bit special, but what I didn't like so much — and I think most kids would understand this — is that all these women kept coming up to me, rubbing my hair, going, 'Oh, he's such a nice boy, give auntie a kiss', and that sort of stuff. I'd be so embarrassed! I can't understand why aunties think kids like that.

This church, like any other, had its fair share of hypocrites. That may seem a bit strong, but I can honestly say that nearly all the people I knew well were not practising what they preached. Many had secrets and vices, and when I asked them why they were doing the very things they were preaching not to do in church, I was told: 'Shut up and don't interfere with big people business.'

There was one pastor I used to get lifts home from, and there was always one woman he would drop off last. He'd say, 'Sit dere, boy', so I'd sit in his car while he disappeared inside the house with her. He'd emerge around half an hour later saying, 'Praise the Lord!' I never realised until much later what he was up to. I heard little whispers but I never put two and two together at the time.

★   ★   ★

After spending a long time moving around, my mother began to get close to another guy. But he wasn't any ordinary guy; he was the head of our church. Known to everyone as Pastor Burris, he was a legend in his own church time. Originally from Jamaica, he was thought of as one of the best, if not *the* best preacher in England, and his knowledge of the Bible was vast. He wasn't that tall, but he was strong, powerful and muscular, and when he preached it was an event not to be missed. Ladies would leave the kitchen, men would put down their instruments, and children would gather at his feet. He was so charismatic that as he preached and worked up a sweat those listening would sweat with him.

He too had a big family of seven children, and he had separated from his wife, Gwen. His relationship with my mother caused some controversy in the church. Although they weren't living together at first, they kept getting closer and closer. He would help her if she didn't have any transport, he would take her shopping and, if she wanted furniture delivering, he would fix it for her, but most of all, if she wanted company he was there. And he was there for me too.

He was the complete opposite of my dad. He would go to the park and kick a ball with me, and we'd go for long walks over the Malvern Hills. And he taught me how to play dominoes. He was a laugh, and he had real presence. He was always smart and wore big baggy suit trousers of the kind that a lot of black men wear, particularly churchmen. And he would normally wear a hat. At some quite important moments in my development he became like a father. He was the first man to give me proper advice about girls, money, survival and all those other things that puzzled boys. I got on extremely well with him, and he was never afraid to help me try and answer the big questions I was always asking.

He wasn't well off but he was savvy. And he was really keen on saving. He'd say to me,

'Benjamin, when you grow up and start work, say you get five pounds, what you gonna do?'

Of course I'd say, 'Spend it?'

Pastor would say, 'No, you've got to save. Saving's important. Save one pound of every five you make so if you lose your job you've still got some to tide you over.'

I was learning stuff from Pastor Burris — perhaps more than I learned in school, as we were moving around so much.

For a while, me and Mum were living in Stourbridge, just outside Birmingham. We rented a small room in the house of a Pakistani family. Although the room was small we were the only tenants and Mrs Chupty was happy to let us wander all over the house, even into their living space. This is where I developed my love of South Asian food, my favourite being channa, but I loved all types of vegetable curries and would happily devour ten chapattis in one sitting.

We lived next to a pub called the White Horse, which was next to a field called White Horse field, and in the field there actually was a white horse. He would be moved to graze from one corner of the field to another, and whenever he was there we would play football at the opposite side from him. I spent about four months in a school there, which was unusually long for me; I have never met anyone who has been to more schools than me. I normally spent a couple of weeks in a school and then we would be forced to move on.

I was quite happy in Stourbridge, but one day

something came over me. I suddenly had the feeling that I had to get away from the town, away from the house, away from my mother, away from it all. Looking back, I think it wasn't so much about getting away from anything or anyone; I think I was just missing my brothers and sisters, so I ran away from home. Well, let me be precise: I *walked* away from home. In fact, I walked all the way from Stourbridge to Fentham Road in Birmingham, which was some walk. It would have been about eighteen miles door to door, a long way for a young boy of ten. In all those miles, along fast main roads, no one stopped me, not even the police.

I did the journey from memory, with a little help from road signs. I knew the route because I'd done it on the bus, so I walked through Dudley and West Bromwich, and then I followed the signs for the biggest place of worship in north Birmingham, Villa Park — the home of Aston Villa Football Club.

When I arrived in Fentham Road, Dad was suspicious, looking behind me and saying, 'What you come home for?'

I said, 'I just wanted to come home, you know . . . ' but as soon as I arrived I felt like a stranger, even though I was back with my brothers and sisters.

Mum contacted Social Services and they told her I'd gone back to Fentham Road. So I stayed for a while, although I never felt completely at home there or fully part of the family. I always thought they were talking about me behind my back. There was just something about it; it didn't feel like my family. At least Dad didn't try to capitalise on the situation with the authorities, like he was better than my mum or anything because he was looking after all the kids.

A woman used to come in and do domestic things while Dad went to work. Mum came back as well, at one point, to try living with Dad again, but she couldn't take it, said he hadn't changed, and left again. I agreed with her, and was fed up with his interrogations. Not long afterwards — maybe a couple of months later — I decided to go back to Mum.

It would have made sense to return to the place where we were living when I left — Stourbridge — but for some strange reason I was drawn in another direction. It was a guess, it was risky, but I walked for a couple of miles in the other direction, to Pugh Road, where you could still see the Villa ground (but from another angle), to the house of Pastor Burris. There he was, with all of his seven kids, Stanley, Peter, Lena, Brunetta, Jimbo, Kern and Trevor, who were all very surprised to see me, but they couldn't understand why I had come to them. I couldn't understand either.

Pastor questioned me on the doorstep; he kept asking, 'Why do you think your mum is here?' And all I could say was, 'I want my mum.' Eventually he let me into the house and sat me down in the front room. In the back room, where the rest of the family was, I could hear something that sounded like a negotiation going on, and I presumed they were talking about what to do with me. Then Pastor came back, looking rather serious, and said, 'Now boy, who told you that your mother is here?'

I told him nobody had; I just felt that she was, and if she wasn't maybe he could take me to her, because it was a long walk and I didn't want to hurt my feet again. The atmosphere was tense. He stood up, opened the door to the other room, and Mum was standing there. She didn't smile. She looked behind me, as if waiting for something to happen; they must have all thought it was a set-up and Dad was going to leap out. After I reassured her that I came alone and that no one had followed me, she too asked me how I knew she was living there. I could only refer her to my previous answer, but later on in life I put it down to a son's intuition.

So that was it — from then on I would live with Mum and Pastor Burris and his kids and we'd all make a new home together.

8

My Other, Wild Family

Mum and I stayed at Pugh Road for a couple of years and I loved it. I loved the neighbours, I loved the area and I loved the family. It was very lively with the ten of us, and usually there'd be someone else round for a chat as well — perhaps a friend or Pastor's sister, Aunt Maud, who lived down the road with her kids. We'd take turns eating our meals on our laps, as although there was a table, there wasn't room for us all to fit around it.

My biological family was a little naughty at times but on the whole they were pretty well behaved. The Burrises, however, were *absolutely wild*. Every time we went outdoors it was an adventure. We would find hills to climb, canals to explore and people to chase us. We would often get into fights and come home dirty or with cuts and bruises. It was a very rough area. Trevor and Peter were fighting all the time. If somebody gave us racial abuse, we didn't go home and tell the grown-ups, we'd get stuck in and have a fight. If somebody said something bad about a family member, we'd get stuck in and have a fight; even if somebody said something bad about Aston Villa, we'd get stuck in and have a fight. We liked fighting. And if we came home and told Pastor that we'd got into a fight and lost, he'd send us out again to have another go until we won. I fought one boy in Erdington four times before I managed to beat him, and when I finally triumphed, he shook my hand and said, 'Well done.'

I was fighting all the time but I never really got the mob-fighting over football thing. My Uncle Simpson, on Pastor's side, used to take me and Pastor's sons to Aston Villa and put us on his shoulders, but we'd inevitably get racist abuse. I remember one match when Villa were winning 3 — 0 and the white fans were going, 'You're our mascot.' Then, in the second half, Villa lost it, and it was, 'It's your fault!' and the racist chanting would begin.

In later years, when we were older, Trevor and I would go to matches at the Villa. West Ham and Manchester United fans would always come and have a go at us. United's firm once organised to meet Villa fans at Birmingham New Street Station for a battle. The route they took went right past our house, and Mum closed the curtains in daytime — something she had previously talked about doing only if someone had died. And I started thinking, *Why am I going to fight these people from Manchester? If I lived there, I'd probably support them.* I didn't go to another match for years.

★ ★ ★

One of our favourite things was to leave the house and say, 'Right, we're gonna get lost.' We would keep going until we got lost and were hungry, then the adventure was finding our way home, and if we really couldn't find our way home (and that rarely happened) we would simply ask a policeman and, if he wasn't helping an old lady across the road, he would sometimes take us home. Oh, the good old days when the bobby was on the beat and your dinner was in the oven . . .

There was one incident around this time that did involve the police but it didn't involve fighting, and I guess it was the sort of thing that happened to a lot of kids. Trevor and me and a couple of others were playing in Aston Park one day when a boy about our age — eleven or so — came up to us and said, 'Wanna see a wanker?' So we followed him across the park to the toilets, which had those glass bricks that were used a lot in the '60s and '70s. One of them was broken, and we all craned our necks closer and saw this white guy in there down below, masturbating. Of course we made a load of noise, falling about, going, 'Argh, look at him, he's wanking', not really understanding what it was, but knowing it was something 'wrong'.

He heard us and looked up. 'What you doing?'

'We're just watching . . . '

He said, 'Wanna go to the graveyard? I'll give you a shilling each.' That sealed it. So we said, 'Yeah, OK.' And he gave us each our shilling and we stood and watched him do it in the graveyard. He didn't touch any of us, but at some point he mentioned, 'When you're having this kind of sex', and I thought, *Ah, so this is about* sex. I don't remember feeling scared. The only thing I was fixed on was the amazing pair of winklepinker shoes he was wearing. After that, we just giggled and went about our business.

A few days later the police came round with stern faces, wanting to talk to me and Trevor. So we sat round the table with Pastor Burris while the policeman tried to get the story out of us.

'What happened?'

'We went to the park and we saw this man. He didn't touch any of us.'

He was really pushing us on this. 'Well, we still want to speak to him. Tell us what happened.'

So we told him how events unfolded and then mumbled our way through the nasty business, muttering, 'He started . . . doing it . . . '

'Doing what, boys?'

'You know . . . doing it . . . '

'Doing what?'

Long silence. Me and Trevor looked at each other, then looked at the ground.

Finally Pastor Burris shouted at the top of his voice: 'DOING WHAT??!!'

And we answered as quietly as we could: 'Wanking.'

'Right! Why didn't you say that?'

There was another long pause, then Pastor asked, 'What's wanking?'

'Can you leave us for a minute please, boys?' said the policeman.

Me and Trevor left the room and were in stitches, creasing up behind the door. We were a bit scared about what might happen, but then we started imagining the conversation going on behind that door, between the cop and Pastor.

'Is he gonna take it out and show him?'

'Do you think the cop is gonna start wanking?'

We were bent over and could barely speak for stifling our laughter.

A couple of days later they caught the offender — because of the shoes. They drove around until they found him, like the burglar who'd robbed our gas meter in Farm Street. It was still all a bit like the *Beano* to me.

★　★　★

Pastor didn't give us pocket money. If we wanted money we had to earn it. Sometimes we washed windows, sometimes we ran errands, but I then broke with tradition and got a job peeling potatoes at the local Chinese takeaway. All my friends had paper rounds and things like that, but I worked better hours and got a bag of chips at the end of it.

There was something about life back then that really helped me in my future years. I loved the way we were left alone and were encouraged to think for ourselves. Most of our toys were homemade or recycled. If we wanted a bicycle, we would get a frame, find a pair of wheels, then clean them up, get a chain and some brakes — although most of the time one brake was enough — and then we'd put them all together.

Trevor and me loved fixing things, and we started a little cycle repair business in the garden. It was nothing grand; we'd do jobs for a few pence, but we built up a reputation and lots of pennies made lots of pounds. We made sleighs at Christmas, we fixed prams and train sets and we made and mended go-carts. But our biggest earner was minding cars.

When Aston Villa played at home we would stake out a patch of a couple of streets, and as the drivers were getting out of their cars we would run up and say, 'Mind your car please, sir?' If they said yes we'd note the car and make sure no one messed with it. If they said no we would leave it. Sometimes car thieves would come and we would beg them not to touch our cars, but we'd turn a blind eye if the car wasn't on our list.

We were learning how to work and survive. Although we lived in a house, we were really like street kids who were left to our own devices. Mum had gone back to nursing, working all hours, and us kids looked after each other.

We once made the local paper after a minor adventure not far from our house. There was a derelict pub at the end of our road that we used as one of our dens, where we would mess about and learn how to smoke cigarettes. One day a whole gang of us went in there and crept down into the cellar and, like a scene out of a kids' adventure story, we found a couple of old-fashioned swag bags full of money. Somebody had robbed a post office and left three sacks of money there. Trevor and I took £20 in £1 notes, which to small kids back then seemed like a fortune. We ran down to the bicycle shop at Lichfield Road and spent the money decorating our bikes with transfers featuring red dragons and words like 'cool' and 'easy rider' and 'speed monster'. We also got some fancy mirrors and horns and we felt pretty special riding back into town.

When we got home Pastor went mad and started to administer beatings to everyone. Poor Trevor got it the worst. Not because we took the money, but because of what we did with the money. He kept going on about this lawless family we hung out with, who'd been with us when we found the cash, saying, 'You see what the white kids did. They took the money and gave it to their dad. You took *twenty pounds* and went to the bicycle shop! Look how poor we are. Next time bring it all to me.'

A lot of parents would have said, 'You naughty children, you shouldn't have taken that money.' But we got into trouble because we didn't take enough, and we didn't bring it home. Pastor was like that. His approach was, if you're gonna do it, do it good. That's what poverty does to you.

The lawless family took much more money than we did. They bought clothes and food and presents for their girlfriends and gave the rest to their dad. Word spread, the police came, and the money was quickly removed. The next day that family had a big cake with their dinner, and their associated ladies came out onto the streets adorned in the nicest cheap dresses we had ever seen. We just had cool-looking bikes that we couldn't ride because our bottoms were so sore.

9

Learning to Hustle

Pastor's house was crowded. We slept three or four to a bed: two up and two down, or two up and one down if you were lucky. Different kids had different levels of smelly feet, so there were always tough negotiations over who would sleep where. Me and Trevor would steal Pastor's talcum powder to put on our feet, so we thought of ourselves as a sweeter brand of stink than those who were simply sweaty with no talc.

As I've said, Pastor could be a great laugh. He was full of jokes and stories from back in Jamaica, but when he got mad he *really* got mad and, like all Jamaican men of that generation, when he gave his kids a beating you knew about it. I was lucky; after the bike incident he only tried to beat me once. We had all done wrong, so Trevor had to go and get the strap and, one by one, he beat them all, starting with the youngest, Stanley, and working his way up. When he had done with Trevor, he came towards me but I stood there defiant and said, 'You can't hit me, you're not my dad.'

It saved my backside but I've always felt it was a horrible thing to say; after all, he was more like a dad to me than my own dad was, and he treated me no different from the others. I saw

70

the sadness in his eyes, and then I felt like apologising and offering up by backside for some bruising, but I could hear the others crying and I wasn't man enough. After that, Pastor never tried to beat me again, which sometimes made me feel bad when I was told to sit down and watch the others getting a thrashing.

In other ways, Pastor was incredibly relaxed and a real sport. For instance, there was this girl called Anthea; she was bigger than me, and she fancied me. I was about twelve and she was older, thirteen or fourteen. She said to me one day, 'Can I come to your house and see you?'

I said okay and she came to the house one night when my mum was working late. I can't remember how it happened, but she started kissing me and said, 'We should find somewhere we can be alone.'

Somehow we found our way upstairs. Pastor Burris saw what was going on and then locked us in the bedroom and said, 'Gwan boy, do yer ting.'

I sat frozen on the bed while the very forward Anthea said, 'Do you know what roaming hands are? Come here, I'll show you.'

I was going, 'Get away from me! Get me out of here!' I was freaking out. But nothing happened, and Pastor let me out soon enough. It was a sudden introduction to girls and 'heavy petting'. I wasn't ready then, but I'd be ready soon enough.

★ ★ ★

As bad as the beatings were, and as hard as life was, the most important thing for me and my circle of friends was the pursuit of happiness. Trevor and I had a couple of really good friends, one of whom was a guy called Philip Evans, a white kid who seemed even blacker than we were. He had this real love of black culture and a massive collection of reggae and ska records. In the days before skinheads were associated with racism, the original skins were into ska music, and Philip was like a skinhead without the skin head; he liked his hair too much.

By this time we had heard the music of Bob Marley in our homes — at that time he was just another ska musician — but Philip knew Marley was much more than that. He sat us down and made us listen to the lyrics, and then he got us up and made us move to the beat.

We couldn't afford many new clothes of our own; we had to make do with whatever Pastor or Mum bought us. When we did pick up some new threads we'd try and get clothes that made us look like skinheads. We were desperate to look cool, so sometimes we took extreme measures to achieve that. If we saw something we liked, we'd liberate it from a washing line. Ben Sherman shirts were the shirts to be seen in; Wranglers or Levi jeans if you were going for casual/hard, or Sta Prest two-tone trousers if you wanted to look hard and smart. The white skinheads were trying to look like black rude boys, and here were some black rude boys trying to look like hard skinheads. And over the back of where we lived was an entire family of what we called 'greasers'.

None of us wanted to look like them.

Ska had evolved into reggae, and occasionally a reggae record would get in the charts, like 'Montego Bay' or 'Double Barrel' in 1970, or a novelty one like 'Skenga' later on, but some lyrics had started to get very rude. Us young 'uns were already aware of songs like 'Wet Dream' by Max Romeo and 'Wreck a Buddy' by the Soul Sisters, both of which were released at the end of the 1960s. Another song had lyrics like: 'White pum-pum, black pum-pum, every pum is the same pum-pum.' My parents wouldn't have been playing this, although even Prince Buster sang suggestive songs, like 'Rough Rider'.

Judge Dread was around too at this time — a larger-than-life beardy white guy who every year released one of his 'Big' 45s, like 'Big 5', 'Big 6' and so on, and he would chat naughty rhymes about 'pussy' and 'playing the horn'. His records were banned from radio but word would get round schools and the young rudies, white and black, would find places selling them and then play them at home, dancing in their tonic suits and Harrington jackets.

People have asked me if I think Judge Dread was an exploiter, taking the piss. I say no, he was a real lover of reggae. His own stage name was a reference to a Prince Buster song. Years later I saw some footage of a show he did at a festival in the '70s. Dennis Alcapone is there. Judge Dread introduces him and you can see the artists have love for him.

We were starting to grow up. Some of it was

positive, some of it negative. We would imitate some of the older boys around us and I soon found myself in court. Philip Evans, Trevor and me started doing burglaries together. Our parents thought we were at school, but we weren't. We'd go to the nicer parts of Birmingham, find a house, knock on the door and see if anyone was in. If someone came out we'd ask for a person who obviously wasn't there, but if nobody came out one of us would go round the back. A minute later the front door would be open and we'd be in.

By the time I was halfway through my teens, the path to me becoming a full-time hustler was well established. From an early age we knew that if we wanted money we had to get it ourselves. Our parents didn't give us money, and the wrongs and rights of how we got it weren't that important. If we didn't get our own, we wouldn't have any.

In those days most houses had television meters and gas meters. We would break into them and get the 50ps out of them. I was expert at getting into all kinds of meters and putting them back as I'd found them. We didn't go for goods that much; we usually wanted quick cash that we could spend on pinball machines or buying a 50p draw of weed.

There was always shoplifting, and we'd mostly go for clothes. We even went in for a bit of ram-raiding — someone would have a car and smash through a shop window and we'd have the goods away in a flash. One time we took some material and got suits made up from it. Or we'd get women's clothes, coats and things, and sell them to girls in our neighbourhood.

One of the more exciting robberies I found myself doing involved me sneaking into a department store in the Bullring in Birmingham city centre. I did this twice, once with a kid called Paul Davis, who not long afterwards died in the Birmingham pub bombings. We walked into the shop near to closing time, found a place to hide and stayed overnight, filling our bags with everything we wanted. Next morning, when they'd opened and customers were milling about, we strolled out with the swag. You couldn't do that now, of course, as they have sensors and CCTV and everything is monitored.

We were always listening out for opportunities. On one occasion we heard that a local couple had won the 'spot the ball' competition in the newspaper. There were rumours in the neighbourhood that they'd cashed in the money and stashed it in their bedroom wardrobe. They threw a party downstairs and Trevor and I climbed in the back way over fences and through the bedroom window. We were searching the wardrobe and had to hide really quickly when the couple came in to have a smooch.

They were saying stuff like, 'I'm so happy, darling', and having a good, long snog. We were holding our breath and sweating. We didn't find the money and we beat a quick exit once the coast was clear. I was okay, but Trevor fell through the roof of an outhouse and there was a commotion. We got caught after the fact, and then had to admit to loads we didn't do.

In 1972 I appeared in court on one charge of burglary and one of receiving stolen goods. I was given two years' probation and twenty-four hours at an attendance centre. These were places where you had to go for two hours every Saturday morning to make things that could be useful — like an early form of community service. The next year the police caught us robbing a house and they managed to trick us in the station by using what everyone now knows is an old con. We were arrested for one burglary but the police could see by our style that we had done many more. So an officer went to Trevor and said Philip has told us everything. He named all the jobs Philip has 'confessed' to and showed him a false statement. Then Trevor got angry and said, 'Okay. Now what?' Then they went and did the same to Philip and me. So we all ended up confessing to all the charges, even jobs we didn't do because we each felt that one of the others had grassed us up.

★   ★   ★

A move was on the cards, and we were all soon living in a house on Normandy Road, in another part of Aston. Pugh Road as we'd known it didn't last much longer anyway; it was flattened like so many streets at that time to make way for flimsy new council houses. My mum and Pastor were still together, although Pastor had another house in Aston.

My dad's grip on my brothers and sisters was much looser now; sometimes they would come

76

and see us, and when Dad wasn't around we would go and see them. Now there were two families in three houses, and we would move between them (almost) as we pleased.

Normandy Road was much 'nicer' than Pugh Road. In Pugh Road people quite literally seemed to live out on the streets, which I liked because it made it feel like a community. Normandy Road was completely different. Houses had lawns, the street had trees, and the trees had birds singing in them. There was a semblance of order, but no community. I started going to Canterbury Cross School, which later changed its name to Broadway Comprehensive. It felt as if we had arrived on the good side of town, but the problem was we were still bad.

The kids I hung around with would threaten the local grammar school boys, as they weren't very streetwise. All we had to do was go, 'Boo, gis your watch', and they would whimper and hand it over. Anyone with a slight weakness was fair game. Some of my friends would go gay bashing, or 'queer bashing', as they called it back then, and I was with them one time when they started kicking this gay guy, expecting me to join in. I thought, *He ain't done nothing to me.* I didn't want to touch him. I stood there while the others were going, 'Come on, Benjamin, kick the bloodclaat boy.'

I did this token kick that was really soft. I feel terrible about it now, but if I hadn't done that kick they would have made my life hell, saying, 'What? The batty man your friend? Or is you batty man too?' That would have been it for a long time. I'm sure, if you did the statistics, that somebody doing the kicking was probably gay himself, but they had to go along with the aggro to fit in with the crowd.

I'm so glad I never really got stuck in, or did anything to old people. Even in the fair fights I had, where I could've laid into an opponent and possibly killed him, I'm so glad I didn't.

There were lighter moments of bravado, however. Pastor now had a beautiful Morris Oxford car. It was his pride and joy. He looked after it as if it was another member of the family, but it got no beating. He would always park it right outside the house, but little did he know that Trevor and me used to take it in the middle of the night when he was sleeping; we'd pick up some girls and go driving for the night. The method was thus: the family would go to bed, we would wait until everyone fell asleep, and then we'd get up, take a spare key that we secretly kept, push the car away from the house and go party. We would go dancing or just drive around all night, stopping every now and then for a kiss and a cuddle, or a party in the car. Then, as morning approached, we would take our loved-up friends home, before topping the car up with petrol and putting it back. Then we would creep back to bed as if nothing had happened, and wake up late like lazy kids.

One night we messed up really badly. Everything had gone to plan until we went to top up the petrol. We couldn't. Pastor had bought a fancy new fuel cap with a lock and, of course, we didn't have a key, so we were sure we'd be rumbled. There was nothing we could do, so we parked the car with a couple of gallons missing. The next morning when we came down for breakfast we could sense something was wrong. By now Trevor was as big as his dad, but he could still get a beating, and I was waiting for the fireworks.

Pastor came down the stairs, sat in his chair and said, 'You know, it's so strange. I'm sure I had more petrol than that . . . and my car, it smells of chips.'

Trevor and I stood there waiting for him to start questioning us, but he never did. Eventually, about thirty-five years later, we told him what we used to get up to. He said, 'I knew it!' And laughed.

10

Animal Liberation Time

By now I'd become a vegetarian. I'd always been an animal lover and a very reluctant meat eater. Sometimes I hid a bag under the dinner table. I would take the meat off the plate and put it into the bag or, if my mother was watching, I would put the meat in my mouth for a couple of seconds and then it would go in the bag when she turned away. Then I would either throw it away or give it to some wild dogs.

Everything changed the day I had a boy-to-woman talk with my mother across the dinner table around the age of eleven. At first it was genuine curiosity. I asked her where she'd got the meat from and she said the butcher. So I asked where the butcher had got it from, and she said the farmer. So I asked where the farmer got it from, and she said he got it from the cow. I thought, what a clever cow, and then I asked, 'What is the cow doing with meat?'

She said, 'You silly boy, this is the cow!'

I was horrified. I had never connected the meat on the plate with the cow in the field. I pushed all the meat in my reach away from me and said, 'I won't eat my friends', and that was the last day I ate meat. I subsequently learned that George Bernard Shaw had said exactly the same thing, but at the time I'd never heard of him. I wanted to express my disgust at eating dead bodies, and my love of animals.

Imagine a school playground. I think the general sound that comes from a playground is fantastic: the joyous noise of hundreds of kids playing, having fun and seeking pleasure. But if you are alone in a corner of that playground because none of the other kids will play with you, it's the loneliest place in the world. When I was in that place I made friends with animals. A cat came along one day, and we hung out together. He came the next day and we played a little catch, then the next day he brought a few friends along. I also made friends with caterpillars, and by the pond I talked to frogs. They didn't judge me because of the colour of my skin, and they weren't planning to fight me after school.

Although I said I wasn't going to eat animals, people still tried to feed me meat. At school I'd have just potatoes and veg (usually peas), and the dinner ladies would attempt to pour meaty gravy all over it, saying, 'It's only gravy, it's not the actual animal.' But I wouldn't have any of it. I stuck to my principles and only accepted the carbs and veg. I don't remember that as being such a struggle. What I do remember is when I went vegan at the age of thirteen.

I worked it out for myself that mothers produced milk for their children, and not for the children of others, especially others of another species. As soon as I'd sussed that out I stopped drinking milk and consuming all dairy products.

I hadn't been to any meetings; I hadn't read any vegan magazines — there weren't any. I just didn't want to take from animals. I didn't realise at the time that the term for my stance was 'vegan'. That knowledge came soon after, when somebody asked me if I wanted an ice cream. I told them I didn't eat ice cream because I didn't eat any animal products. And this other kid said, 'You're a vegan.'

I thought he was insulting me and replied, 'Who are you calling names? Do you want a slap?' I went for him, and he screamed, 'No, no, vegans are nice.'

When I first heard the word it sounded strange. Some years later I learned that a guy called Donald Watson had coined it in 1944, when he took the middle out of the word vegetarian.

I always loved sweets, but so many brands, especially back then, had animal products in them. I liked things like Wagon Wheels, lollipops and fruit and nut bars, but I gave them up until vegan options became available. Now I can eat them whenever I like as, of course, the options for vegans have never been better than they are now.

I have always been proud of the fact that my choices weren't based on being fashionable or following a movement; they came from my soul, and I was vegan by instinct. Later on I'd meet Rastas who were also committed to this path, although they didn't call it vegan, they called it 'ital'. Some people take that to mean 'nice and healthy', even when they eat fish, but ital should mean strictly vegan.

People tell me they think it's amazing I went vegan at such a young age. It didn't feel 'amazing' to me — it felt right then and it feels right now. I don't eat in places that serve meat and I don't allow meat in my house. At times it has been difficult when I've been travelling, but there's no such thing as *no* vegan option. There's always some rice and veg somewhere. Even if I have to eat bland foods for a while, I always think, *It's only for a week or two.*

* * *

Later on in life I realised there were vegan organisations and groups of people that cared so much about what was happening to animals that they were prepared to do something about it. I became active as soon as I could. As with my attitude to human rights issues, my bottom line is that you can't just be a poet or writer and say your activism is simply writing about these things; you have to do something as well, especially if your public profile can be put to good use.

Since understanding the work of the animal rights movement I have always thought them to be the most dedicated of liberation movements. Let's be honest: most of the people fighting for women's rights will be women, most of the people fighting for aboriginal rights will be aboriginal, many of the people fighting for the rights of low-paid workers will be low-paid workers etc. But all the people fighting for the rights of animals are human. Their struggles have not an ounce of selfishness or self-interest attached; they truly campaign for those who cannot speak themselves. Their struggle is the ultimate struggle, because it is for the liberation of others.

I have supported Uncaged, the National Organisation Working Against Live Exports, PETA (People for the Ethical Treatment of Animals), VIVA (Vegetarians' International Voice for Animals), NAVS (National Anti-Vivisection Society) and many others, including of course the Vegan Society, of which I am a patron and a life member, but the people I most admired were the ALF, the Animal Liberation Front. I told someone this once and, not long afterwards, she invited me to go on an ALF operation, a 'live liberation'. This is where they enter a laboratory, liberate the animals and take them to safe homes or, if needs be, to vets. I jumped at the opportunity.

The ALF film their work and the activists wear masks, but on the night that didn't work for me. Beneath the mask you could still see my dreadlocks and hear my voice, which everyone says is quite distinctive. At one point, when I held a liberated rabbit in my arms, I almost burst into poetry, but the other people on the operation kept telling me to shut up. We were successful but afterwards I was advised to stick to my normal mode of struggle and not go on another operation. I was too recognisable. So I continued to work in other areas for them. But I still think merely writing about it isn't enough; you have to be active.

11

Black Liberation Time

Muhammad Ali was the greatest heavyweight boxing champion of all time. Malcom X and Martin Luther King had both been assassinated but the words of these great orators were reverberating in our spaces and places. Yet in school I was still being told that black people had been 'discovered', and apparently before we were discovered we were uncivilised, unsophisticated and unintelligent.

It wasn't so much the racism from other kids that was bothering me at this time. I was a big kid, and any kid that came to me with racism would have a fight on his hands, and besides, most of the people around me were black. In fact, the white kids feared *us* because in some areas, like Handsworth and Aston, our gangs were much bigger than theirs. Sometimes white kids would be too scared to pass us on the street or walk through one of our areas, but we would reassure them and let them pass. There was no way they would be attacked simply because they were white, but they would be attacked if they messed with us.

Plenty of white boys and girls were hanging out with us because we had cool music, cool smokes and cool style, and they wanted some of that. No, the racism I was seeing at this time came firstly from the police — who were relentlessly stopping and searching us, even right outside the school gates — and that which I came across in school. It's hard to say if the teachers were serious, hardcore or even soft racists, but the books they were teaching from, and their Anglocentric world view, were seriously racist.

While we were supposed to have been discovered, uncivilised, unsophisticated and unintelligent, they were great, civilisers of savages, never to be slaves, rulers of the waves, victorious and right. I can't believe that most of the teachers teaching this stuff really believed it, especially when I consider that all the teachers I've come across as an adult are open-minded and curious, so what was happening back then? I go with the idea that they were just obeying orders, but when it came to the teaching of the Nazis I was told that obeying orders couldn't be used as an excuse. Or maybe they just didn't know any better.

It wasn't the only thing they didn't know the truth about — at the time I was struggling very badly with dyslexia (and so were other kids I knew) but teachers back then didn't know what it was, so I was 'stupid'.

On television I caught glimpses of the heroes of the Black Power movement. Muhammad Ali, Stokley Carmichael and Yuri Kochiyama were all preaching about the condition of black people, and Angela Davis was still regarded as the most dangerous person in the USA. Something had happened and something was happening; I just wasn't fully aware of what it all was — I was too busy trying to survive in my home town — but I felt that my struggle in Birmingham, in the West Midlands of England, was connected to the struggles of people in Birmingham, Alabama, in the USA, and I could feel something calling me, but I didn't quite understand it all.

Pastor and Mum didn't really comment on the Black Power movement. Pastor mentioned it was good that Muhammad Ali wouldn't go to Vietnam, but that was it. I remember Mum coming in one day and being really happy because she'd heard a woman in a restaurant had thrown a cup of tea over Enoch Powell. In terms of the politics of race they'd mention the 'colour bar' and places that were off-limits because they were hostile, but in terms of the politics that was going on in the big world, very little comment. For them it was all about Jesus.

All I knew then was that I didn't like people killing people and I didn't like people killing animals — but all I wanted was a girlfriend who didn't eat meat and wasn't a racist.

12

Here Comes Babylon System

It's dark and I'm running, running . . . like a school cross-country event, except this time it's the middle of the night and there'll be no cake and juice once it's over. The air is crisp and the twigs crack beneath me as I pound across the woodland. On the boundaries of the trees, in the far distance, I can see pinpoints of light from the villages but here, deep in the foliage, it's like a jungle. Bracken and brambles and badger sets and earth. Strange musty smells. Mustn't slip or twist an ankle. Even if they realise I'm missing, they'll never be able to catch me. I'm fleet of foot and good at hiding and no one is on my tail. I'm desperate to sleep, but I know if I do that I'll get cold and stiff and won't be able to run again so easily. I've got to keep moving, got to get away. Stay limber; stay on a straight line that'll take me all the way to Baschurch, where I'll get a bus that'll deliver me back to Birmingham.

Mum won't scold me and Pastor will take me in, even though he said no good would come of my ways, and it's turned out he was right. 'Make your bed and you lie in it,' he said. But at least he didn't come down hard with any preaching or talking about Jesus or sin. But I can't just 'lie in it'. I'm done with being banged up with all those kids going crazy. And all those rules and regulations. Babylon system.

I have to stop for a while to gather myself and rest, even though I won't let myself sleep. I've got nothing to sleep on and no bag. All I've got is the clothes I'm wearing and some loose change. I wish I knew how to survive in the wild. Maybe I'd have learned that sort of stuff if I'd gone to Scouts instead of the stupid Boys' Brigade with all their military marching. At least it's dry. I can lean against a tree for a while and plan my next move.

My heartbeat gradually slows and thoughts about my life flow freely. Some of the tension of the day falls away a little bit, and I start going over what's been happening. I shouldn't have hit that disabled kid, the one who walks with the sticks. I'm usually his back-up. Everyone needs some back-up in that place. I like him. I've even been looking out for him. It's survival of the fittest, though, and if you aren't fit yourself, you'd better find someone who is.

I shouldn't have lashed out at him. All he did was say hello and I jumped up and landed a flying kick on him that was so powerful it knocked him out. I really don't know what came over me. I guess it was the visit from Mum. She'd yet again made that really long journey up here from Aston, with the locals staring at her as she changed buses. They're not used to seeing black people in Shrewsbury, except when the police wagon delivers boys like me to Boreatton Park Approved School.

We're all thrown in together. There's tough

street kids like me who have nimble fingers and who can be in and out of a burglary in two minutes, or who have lifted a purse here and there, but some are a few levels up from that — hardened criminals and kids who have killed their parents. But there's plenty down the lower rungs — lads who have lost their families in car crashes or those no one seems to care about, and weaker ones with disabilities, or the kids who get preyed on and fiddled with.

Take the kid a couple of beds away from me. He's always getting up in the middle of the night to leave the dorm. We know he's going to see that pervert teacher and, one time, I felt I had to do something. I saw he was leaving as usual and I got in front of him, stood by the door and said, 'Listen mate, it's three o' clock in the morning, you don't have to go.' And he said, 'I've got to.' He was trembling with fear, like he was hypnotised; he didn't know how to stop it. I've tried to get him to tell me about it but he won't.

There's some good lads in there, even though it's tough. I guess some of us black kids are more used to taking a stand than the white ones. No pervert teachers are gonna be putting their hands down our trousers — they'd get decked. I told this kid we'd take down the teacher responsible; land some licks of justice on him. We'd even go to court and defend him if it came to it. But still he goes to see him and it drives me crazy. I want to shake him out of his trance. If he doesn't take a stand he'll be worn down, 'cos that can happen really easily in a place like Boreatton Park.

It may be approved but it certainly isn't a school. The first day we arrived they gave us a Maths and English test, but that was it. The authorities would say we're there to be reformed or re-educated, but for us the purpose is survival. That's all any of us thinks about. They impose a house system, like you get in school, with four houses, and every boy has to belong to one. But I don't know any normal school with a padded cell in its basement. This is for the kids who lose it and throw a wobbler, explode or get themselves into a crazy state. The staff drag them down there until they go quiet, so they can't hurt themselves or anybody else, or cause more problems and paperwork. But all the hurt is going on inside.

Me, I can handle it. I'm used to being self-sufficient. I'm healthy and can spot opportunities. But there's never any peace or quiet. In fact, it's usually the opposite. Fighting can break out over anything. One day, a few weeks back, there was a massive riot, blacks against whites. It really kicked off — tables turned over, plates smashed, heads jumped on, TVs kicked in. We were outnumbered but we always feel we're stronger than the white kids. It was such a big deal that the staff couldn't stop us, so they called the police. When they arrived things got more exciting; we all teamed up together to fight *them*. Suddenly the people we'd been kicking and punching became our allies and we let the cops have it. We were really fighting because of boredom, I think.

I am an excellent fighter; a slick kung fu stylist

from watching so many Bruce Lee films. I've been to kung fu classes and I'm ace at kicking. Good luck if you're trying to get close to me. When it comes to fists, though, Trevor is the king. Punches just bounce off him before he knocks you out. He's hard. He was already in Boreatton when I arrived, so I've got back-up and no one messes.

So yeah, today Mum came to visit, bringing with her, among other things, a packet of my favourite Jamaica ginger biscuits. I ate the lot as she sat in front of me. The smell and taste of those biscuits, and watching my mum watching me, was too much like home, and I couldn't take it anymore. I didn't say anything but I decided to make my escape. I left through the back of the school and absconded into the forest. I ran and ran and ran and here I am, drifting in and out of sleep in the small hours, up against a tree. It'll be light soon, 'cos it's summer, then I'll slip down into Baschurch and I'll be free.

Who knows when I'll next get something to eat. I'm really hungry. I burn calories fast with all my running and general activity. I've realised something: I won't be able to blend in with the locals when I get to the village. I'll stick out like a sore thumb. They're bound to know I'm a fugitive from Boreatton. Still, I'm gonna take my chances.

★ ★ ★

As it happened, I didn't make it to Baschurch that morning. It had been a long night, my feet

92

were tired and damp from the morning dew, and I was ravenous. When I finally emerged onto a road, I turned to look at the surroundings and I saw Boreatton Park just a couple of hundred metres away from me. I thought I'd been going straight, but I'd been going round in a big circle! So I went back in time for breakfast and no one was any the wiser.

I suppose it was inevitable I'd come up against the punishment system. By this time, 1973, I'd been suspended from a number of schools for being a rudie, and I also got permanently expelled from a few others for being worse, although most of the time I was quite happy. The first school I got expelled from was Ward End Hall when I was about twelve. Until that fateful day, I'd been doing quite well there. Although lessons like History were still entrenched in teaching Victorian notions of empire and colonialism, one place where I didn't feel so discouraged was on the sports field.

Of the many schools I attended, Ward End Hall was one of my favourites for that reason. Its sports facilities were excellent. It had a long-jump pit, we did rugby and basketball, and it was here that I really flourished as a 100 metres and 200 metres sprinter, as well as doing cross-country running for the first time. I was unbeatable. Not only did I represent the school but the whole region. Certificates of my victories hung on our walls at home, and I became an AAA (Amateur Athletics Association) champion. Running, and later, jogging, became part of my everyday routine from then on.

Then, one day, I was sitting in class minding my school business, when some of the other kids started passing round a porno mag. They were talking and quietly giggling, while I was trying to come to terms with some algebra. Being a boy the magazine eventually came to me, but I didn't even get a chance to look at it before the teacher spotted me and shouted: 'You, boy, what have you got there?' She came over and took the offending publication from my hands and marched me out of the class to the headmistress.

The headmistress took one look at the magazine and said she would not tolerate it. That was it. I was expelled. As I was leaving the office, I turned back and said, 'I'm being expelled for looking at a magazine I haven't seen. Could I at least have a look at it so the punishment can fit the crime?' She did the angry teacher shout and told me to get out of the school and never return.

I was glad to be out of school but I didn't understand how damaging it could be and would be to my future. The last time I got expelled was from Canterbury Cross, or Broadway Comprehensive, as it had become. I had been given lots of warnings for fighting, misbehaving, truanting and not paying attention in class, but when they realised there was no hope for me they told me to go forever.

As I left the school a teacher told me I was a born failure and that within a short time I was going to be dead or doing a life sentence in prison. I know that sounds a bit harsh but I didn't take it badly; a few people had said similar things to me and there was a small part of me

94

that thought they could be right.

Not long after I was kicked out of Broadway Comprehensive, I was arrested again and this time it was for one robbery with fourteen others to be taken into consideration. The judge considered everything and then sent me to Boreatton Park. You were never actually sentenced to an approved school; your sentence was to be put in the care of the local authority. If the local authority was imaginative, you could end up in all kinds of interesting places but most of us were simply sent to approved school.

After my secret escape, Trevor and I were put on a course to learn about car mechanics. I did that for a while and found I had quite an aptitude for it. My most vivid memory of being at Boreatton Park isn't the fights — it's of me and Trevor stripping down a Ford Corsair engine and rebuilding it. I loved it, and although I never fancied myself as a car mechanic, I'm quite proud of being able to understand how cars work, and being able to fix them. When it was rebuilt it was used for pumping water rather than as a car engine but I didn't care — I'd learned something that might come in useful.

Later on I apologised to the disabled kid I'd knocked out. I begged him for forgiveness, and told him I couldn't explain what I'd done. He was so cool about it. Somebody had told him that I'd seen my mum earlier and wasn't feeling good, and a couple of weeks later he told me that I'd saved him from much worse beatings, so he didn't mind one kick getting through, especially from me!

Throughout my time there, Mum and Pastor never gave up on Trevor and me. They never abandoned us like some parents did to their kids. They knew how tough it was trying to survive on the streets, and they knew the police were corrupt and racist. I found out later the police said some terrible things to them. They'd sometimes take a couple of days before telling them we'd been arrested. She knew they should've done it immediately, as I was a minor, but there was no point complaining. The way the police were back then, it would only have made things worse.

Although approved school was a tough place, it wasn't like you see in films; there wasn't really heavy stuff going on *all the time*. Boredom was the worst thing, although we did have a record player, and by this time I was getting into a more righteous sound that would have a major influence on my life. I had this album by Big Youth, called *Screaming Target*, and I'd play it all the time. Some older teenagers in Handsworth had brought me into contact with a thoughtful and revolutionary black sound. Burning Spear had just released his first album and black youth in the UK, including me, were starting to grow dreadlocks and learn about Marcus Garvey and Africa. Black consciousness was rising.

13

Dancing the Blues

I was discharged from approved school, my formal education was officially over, but I was still just fifteen years old. With no school and lots of time on my hands, I started hanging out on the streets with other kids who had been expelled. We would spend time in cafes, playing pinball machines, or find girls who were playing truant, and then we would play together, if you know what I mean.

Around this time my name was made official by an elder of the Rastafarian Twelve Tribes of Israel church (not to be confused with the country Israel). There was a simple ceremony of burning ganja in a chalice, some drums being played, and the elder reading from the book of Zephaniah.

Most Rastafarians take names that are biblical or African. The important thing is to not go by a name passed down from slave owners. Bob Marley's tribe name was Joseph; musician Trevor Sutherland became Ijahman Levi, and one of my favourite artists, Michael Williams, is better known to the world as Prince Far I.

At night we'd go to blues. This is how blues parties worked: someone would find an empty house, or a house that was between tenants.

They would make sure it had electricity, or they would run some illegal electricity into it. Then they would buy drinks and hire a sound system, if they didn't have one already, and spread the word. But the word, or more precisely the music, would spread itself. These sound systems weren't just big stereos; they were powerful homemade rigs with speaker boxes the size of double wardrobes and amplifiers that looked as if they'd come from Dr Frankenstein's laboratory.

The parties were illegal, but I'm sure the amplifiers were also against some kind of law; after all, the bottom end, i.e. the bass, was designed to blow you away. The people running the blues would move in around 11pm. The party would start an hour later and go on until about six in the morning. All night there would be hardcore reggae, reggae with very few lyrics, dub reggae, with very little on the top end of the auditory scale but plenty of bottom end. The point was not to just listen to the music, you had to feel it, and when a sound system was good you could feel it if you were down the road or a couple of streets away.

The police would raid the parties every now and then, but not as often as you might expect, considering how loud the music was and how many 'herbal' cigarettes were being smoked. Sometimes they'd put informers in — black guys, or the occasional white woman. If you were sussed out, my God you got a beating! If someone came to the dance and left soon after, and then half an hour later it got raided, then we'd have our suspicions. But the white kids who had won our trust and loved the music were made very welcome and were protected.

I had performed poetry in the school playground, I had performed poetry at the breakfast table, but it was in the blues dances that I really learned how to use a microphone. It was here where I learned to freestyle, and it was here where I learned that if I was different from the crowd, and had something important to say, people would listen to me.

There was always someone ready to grab the microphone and be the 'toaster'. The toaster's job was to be a social commentator — to use wit and verbal dexterity to talk about one's roots and culture, or to lampoon politicians or the police. We were taking a style that had long been used by Caribbean entertainers and making it our own, adding a revolutionary edge that was pertinent to the times. The best thing about it was that it was a scene we created for ourselves; it wasn't something invented by record companies. And the money we made from the door fee went back into our own communities.

At various times over the coming years I would toast with many different sound systems including Duke Alloy, Sir Christopher, Quaker City and, my personal favourite, Mafiatone Hi-fi. Most of the time these systems played on their own, but occasionally there would be a sound clash, when they would take on a system from London, such as Coxsone or Shaka, or head out with all the equipment in huge vans to other 'frontlines' in cities like Bristol. It was hugely competitive and fiercely territorial, with each system looking to outdo the other. Dubplates, exclusive and straight from the recording studio, were the thing. If you turned up with an exclusive pressing — not just a dub version but one with a special message from that artist, name-checking your crew — the place would erupt and whoever brought the dubplate would be the king.

Sound systems were always looking to get an edge on the opposition. The scene was exciting, full of expectation, and would instil loyalty in a crowd similar to that of following a football team. But you had to be good to hold the crowd and ride the rhythm. Only the fittest would survive. I'd been practising toasting around people's houses and in youth clubs, where table tennis was going on at the same time, and I'd had a bit of space to learn the craft.

But when I first took up the mic in a blues it was like I'd been in the Championship and was suddenly plunged into the Premiership. All eyes were on me, and my main concern was not to be put to shame. My strategy was to chat about something positive and inspiring. The majority of guys who took up the mic would be referencing Jamaica, which for me felt a bit phony, as many of them had not even been there; no one thought of chatting rhyme about Handsworth or Aston. In later years Steel Pulse would mention Handsworth in their songs, but that was a different style of music. Toasting and dancehall and, later, ragga, were rougher and faster, and if the guy that followed you could verbalise better than you, then you could lose face.

I didn't want some guy to slam me down. I wanted to stand out and be different. I'd always been fascinated by what was going on in other parts of the world, and I started chatting about South Africa and the Vietnam War, rather than about girls and hustling. The person who followed me at the mic that first time said something like, 'Wise words, brother,' and then did his thing, and I knew I'd survived at the turntable. I had not been put to shame. I would never have said it at the time, but I wanted to bring poetry to the dancehall in a toasting style.

★　★　★

By now Trevor was living with a girlfriend, so I moved in with them. Now there was nothing to stop us; we could go to blues every night of the week. We became creatures of the night. Sometimes we ventured into other cities like Manchester, Leeds, Nottingham, Leicester and, one of my favourite places, Wolverhampton. We would be heading home when everyone else was waking up, which made us feel a bit superior. They were working themselves to death, and we were having one big party.

The police were arresting us all the time, though. Sometimes for nothing at all, sometimes to get a reaction, sometimes because they were bored. We all know that cops get away with things now, but one copper once said to me, 'Most of us are hardworking racists with the power of arrest.' I'd been roughed up by the police a few times, so I was getting toughened up, and there wasn't much they could do to scare me. But one officer did manage to scare the hell out of me without raising a finger.

I was in Thornhill Road Police Station, being questioned about some robberies I genuinely knew nothing about. When he realised he wasn't getting anything out of me he took me into a room that had a mixture of hats in the Rastafarian colours of red, gold and green, and people's dreadlocks pinned on the walls. They were like scalps. The officer stood there and, with great pride, he named the victims one by one and then he looked lustfully at my newly grown dreadlocks, warning me that I'd be up there soon if I didn't co-operate. I didn't co-operate, even after he offered me a 'rewarding' deal if I were to turn informer for him.

On the street they would come up and ask what we were doing. If you said you were doing nothing they would tell you that you weren't allowed to do nothing; that would be called Loitering with Intent, and if we walked around our postcode we were told that to walk around in circles is suspicious. It was a game of cat and mouse.

Among our own community, though, apart from the police, it was an exciting time to be young. A film had just come out of Jamaica that blew everyone's socks off. It was the first time the rude boy lifestyle had been committed to film on a general release around the world. It was *The Harder They Come* and it starred reggae singer Jimmy Cliff as Ivan Martin — a Jamaican musician forced to live like a fugitive.

The soundtrack was a landmark in music history, and some of the tunes made the UK charts. It helped to establish reggae music as a serious force in Britain, and attending the cinema when it played in Birmingham was an incredible event.

I can't think of another Jamaican film before that, and when we went to see it there was some thirty or forty of us. Everyone was saying, 'Haf fi see *Harder They Come*, man.' A lot of big Handsworth names went to watch it, sporting the fashions of the time, like long leather coats and smart shirts with wide collars, and velour hats. In recent years, young people have talked about 'representin their endz' — well, that's how it was for the Handsworth delegation back then.

I don't think the cinema was quite ready for this audience, though. Instead of sitting in their seats, maybe going 'Oooh' quietly when something happened on screen, you had guys standing up, roaring, 'Yah man!' If they'd had pistols they would have been firing them in the air. Can you imagine, thirty or forty of us doing that while in the aisles there'd be these old white ladies selling ice creams, who had probably been at *Carry On Matron* the previous week.

The atmosphere was amazing. We British-born kids would go 'Yeah, Jamaica . . . ' but there were also Yardies from JA in the audience, who actually recognised the places on screen. With that film you heard, for the first time in the movies, people speaking the way we spoke. I saw it again years later and it was subtitled. And a lot of subtitles weren't correct. They're often wrong when it comes to subtitling Caribbean dialects and slang. I'm not sure if it was that film, but I definitely saw one where a character said, 'I shoot you to pussyclaat' and the subtitle was: 'I'm going to shoot your cat.'

★ ★ ★

I don't want to be accused of glorifying crime, but around that time I loved pick-pocketing. I was able to bump into someone and take their wallet from their inside pocket. I could empty the money from it with one hand and, if I felt like it, I could apologise for bumping into him and, when so doing, replace the wallet. Or I could throw a note on the floor and tell someone they must have dropped it. If they were greedy enough to pick it up I could relieve them of money they had in their pockets. It was slick work; it took confidence and quick thinking and I had a great technique.

I was never a snatch-and-run merchant, but one morning a large group of us were coming from a blues, bragging to each other about the bad weed we'd smoked and the bad girls we'd been with. I had done so much with these guys, we were close, but most of us still only knew each other by nicknames. There was Bunny, Badfoot, Snappa, Ruggs, and a few more. There was also Cheesey, whose real name I did know. He was the kind of person that, if you met him, you would never forget him. He was tall, incapable of standing still, and he spoke in a very nasalised, high-pitched voice: 'Mi name Cheese,

104

Ronald Cheese. Come, we go look fe some gal.'

When people first met Cheesey they would think he was playing some kind of game, showing how long he could speak through his nose for, but they'd soon realise this was what he really sounded like. The pitch of his voice was so high that at first you simply wanted to laugh, but you couldn't, because if you did he wouldn't hesitate to drop you to the floor.

As we walked down Witton Road at five o'clock that morning we saw a woman on her way to work. Cheesey then said, 'I'm going to snatch that woman's bag.' Some of us told him not to and we started to disagree. Half of us were saying no and the other half were saying yes. I was completely against it, and I said: 'No, don't do it, that's not cool, what's she going to have in her bag? She's just a cleaner.' But then Cheesey went and did it. When something like this happens you all have to run, and we scattered in different directions. The police caught us later and we were arrested and had to appear in court.

14

Borstal Boy

I was sentenced to borstal training. This time it was the big time. Well, big time for little me. When you get sentenced to borstal you're actually told the sentence is eighteen months to two years. That's the minimum and the maximum. First you're sent to an assessment centre, where they determine how mentally stable or dangerous you are, and then you're allocated a borstal. When I was sentenced I was told that all the assessment centres were full, so my assessment had to happen in prison, in Winson Green. I was there, in G Wing, for about four months. G Wing was supposed to have been a remand wing, but because the prison was full there were long-termers and even lifers in there. Down in the basement were the Rule 45s — prisoners who had committed crimes that even the other prisoners wouldn't approve of: sex offenders . . . and six men called the Birmingham pub bombers.

Going from approved school to prison was like leaving junior school and going straight to university — a really bad university, with bullies that could kill you or rape you. I went from being up with the top dogs to being pretty small fry. I never got beat up though. Fortunately, coming from Handsworth gave me status, and my family was seen as fighters, so I was never a target. What prison had in common with approved school was the racial segregation. It was black and white, straight down the middle, so in effect if somebody started on me I'd have a rather large posse of black guys to back me up. Once you had a posse you were cool.

But if I was okay with the rest of the prisoners, I wasn't prepared for an onslaught from a man of the cloth. When I first went in, I was waiting at the reception, the place where you get kitted out with your uniform, and some kid had said to me, 'Say you're Catholic. It's easier to get weed,' so, without thinking too much about it, I did.

A couple of days later a priest came to my cell. Now, this guy wasn't what you might expect. We're not talking a gentle humanist. He looked like he'd spent his whole life on a chain gang. He was huge, thuggish, with a head like a block of concrete, and he spoke in this rough cockney accent. He took one look at me and bellowed, 'You're not fackin' Catholic. Alright, if you're Catholic, I want to hear you recite ten Hail Marys.'

Of course, I was at a loss.

He comes up really close, jabbing his stubby finger in my face. 'You fackin' nigger. Answer me or I'll fackin' thrash you, you bastard.' And he starts pushing me around the cell, threatening me — all this with his dog collar on. The next time someone asked me my religion, I told them I was Hindu.

A surprising and much more rewarding

relationship developed with an Asian officer, or 'screw', as they were called. He was unusual in that he was the only non-white screw I ever saw, and one night we got to know each other. He peeped through the spy hole in my cell door late one night and saw me stretching and doing my martial arts workout. He opened the door slowly and I addressed him aggressively. As far as I was concerned he was black, so if he was a screw he was on the wrong side.

'What the fuck do you want? I'm not doing anything wrong,' I shouted.

'I just wondered what you were doing,' he replied.

So I replied in rhyme: 'Kung fu, so what's it to you, and what you going to do, screw?'

I carried on training and he stood watching, almost drooling, like a perverted gym instructor. I jumped to me feet. 'What's your problem?' I said. Almost as if confessing, he replied, 'I do karate. Do you want to fight?'

We went to his office. He was on night duty, so there was no other staff on our landing. We cleared a space in the office, and then we sparred. After that first time we did it every time he was on duty. It was the best thing that happened to me in prison, apart from visits from my mum. Our styles were very different. The Japanese art of karate is rigid and low; Chinese kung fu is a lot more fluid and light. Sometimes we would spar for hours. In the morning he'd tell the other guards to leave me because I was tired. We both had a passion for martial arts and we weren't going to let our prison statuses dampen our enthusiasm.

I soon got into a routine to help make the time go quick. I had a transistor radio, so I could listen to BRMB and some of the pirate stations. I also set aside time to do nothing but think about life, to think creatively, or about poetry. Then I had my exercise, which included meditation. I felt I had to occupy myself, and I had to keep myself sane.

This was fine until echoes of my outside life would sometimes literally filter into my cell. Winson Green Prison was located right by the community centre on the same street, where my friends and associates would set up their sound systems on a Friday or Saturday night. Winson Green Community Centre was one of the best locations for sound clashes. I would hear the bass reverberating from across the road as I lay on my bunk. One night I even heard people calling to me: 'Your girlfriend's here.' Followed by her shouting, 'You alright?' I shouted back, 'Come and see me at the weekend.' That was really painful.

I occupied a cell for two people, and I saw a couple of cons come and go. First there was a lifer, who looked at me as if he wanted to rape me. All he seemed to do was cough and masturbate, and then there was a really funny, red-haired guy from the Black Country. He also masturbated a lot, but he was full of jokes. He told them non-stop and never repeated himself. For weeks I laughed at his jokes, and then I laughed at his escape plan. It was the craziest escape plan ever. He'd heard that if you lose your memory in prison you have to be set free because you cannot do a sentence for something you can't remember.

I had no idea if this was true, but this is what he believed. So one night he pretended that he'd fallen and knocked his head. I rang the emergency bell and he was sent off to the hospital wing. After a few days I thought he really was pulling it off. They came and took his belongings and, after a couple of weeks, I thought he had done it. Then one day the door opened, his clothes were thrown on the floor, and in he walked. He told me it was all going well until an officer had told him that he received a letter from his girlfriend but he couldn't see it because he can't remember her. The officer also said that his girlfriend was 'leaving him for John', and then the pretender stopped pretending and said, 'I'll kill that John Fry when I get out.' Game over.

* * *

I don't think being locked up in prison did me any good at all, not in the way the people who sent me there would have liked. It just made me angrier and more rebellious. I used to dream of killing a police officer, which might sound like a contradiction, because I was a peace-loving vegan, but I always retained the right to self-defence, and I thought I had to kill one of them before they killed me. I was now becoming even more aware of the struggles of people all over the world, and I began to fantasise about being a freedom fighter.

I looked up to the great intellectual C. L. R. James, a truly international thinker, who expressed a revolutionary vision of what we could learn from history, and what was possible. In London, the activists Darcus Howe, Olive Morris, Mala Sen and the Black Panther movement were inspiring me. Being in prison didn't reform me, it gave me time to think; so I thought, and when I thought, I thought I should blow the place up. But I couldn't do that because I was in it.

I was eventually sent to Glen Parva borstal — a brand-new establishment built on an old army barracks outside Leicester. We were the very first inmates, and whereas borstals were known for their tough, no-nonsense regimes, Glen Parva was to be different. Officers would wear plain clothes; they would also act as counsellors — they were to be friendly and approachable, so we could talk to them about our problems. Unlike in other borstals, the cells in Glen Parva had sinks, toilets, mirrors and real wooden furniture, not just an iron bed. Everything was brand new and everything worked. Everything except me.

Just a few weeks into my stay we were preparing for a gymnastic competition. The idea was that we would form a team, devise a display, and then girls from a girls' borstal would come in and we would show off to each other. Well, I was happy to look at girls' stuff if they were happy to look at mine, so I joined the team. Among other things I was working on a trampoline routine, but I noticed day after day that I was getting weaker. Then one day I went to do a somersault and I was in so much pain that I forgot the whole technique and went out of control. I landed partly on the trampoline and partly on the floor. The landing wasn't as painful as it sounds, but the internal pain I was feeling was unbearable.

I was taken off to the hospital wing, the first inmate to be taken there, and the borstal doctor thought I just had a bad case of the flu. After more than a week my condition wasn't improving, and they started to ask if there was any way I could be faking it.

'Faking it?' I said to the officer questioning me. 'I'd rather be looking at girls' stuff than faking it here.'

After three weeks and no improvement I was taken to a doctor in Leicester. He took one look at me and, without hesitation, insisted I go straight to hospital. I had a form of tuberculosis. After weeks of treatment involving drinking foul potions, partial isolation and a minor operation where liquid was drained from my lungs, I was able to leave.

Now here's the good bit. It was thought that I'd contracted TB when I was in Winson Green, from the lifer who had been continually coughing. Being so young I should never have been in prison, so a deal was struck. I went back to Glen Parva for one night and was then discharged. As part of the deal I promised to say nothing. I wasn't paying attention to TV or radio news back then, but I'm guessing overcrowded prisons were in the news and they didn't want my story to be thrown into the mix. So I was told

112

that if I was let out a few months early I could boast, with some pride, that I was the first person to ever be discharged from the newly open HMP Glen Parva.

★ ★ ★

Not long after I came out of borstal, Trevor appeared in court. We thought he was going down for a long time but, to our surprise, he got off. As he left the court I approached the officers who charged him. They were feeling pretty low, as cops do in times like these, and I began to mock them. I laughed at them, pulled faces and told them what I thought of them. One of them then said, very calmly, 'I'm going to do you.' And he did. A few weeks later he arrested me for the robbery of a woman — a robbery I hadn't done.

I pleaded not guilty, but in court a woman stood in front of me and identified me as the person who had robbed her. She described how I was supposed to have done it, and told the court how she had been scared to go out in public afterwards, and how her life was ruined because of her lack of confidence. It was very convincing, but I knew I hadn't done it. I was remanded on bail, and while waiting my solicitor suggested I change my plea to guilty. I didn't want to, but he reminded me that I had not long done a borstal sentence, and so the judge was going to send me down, but he thought that if I pleaded guilty he could then ask for a lenient sentence. Reluctantly I agreed, thinking he knew best.

On 19 July 1976 I went back to court.

Proceedings started and I changed my plea to guilty. The victim was called once more to let her feelings be known, but she didn't appear — in fact, she didn't even come to court. Then, suddenly, the police dropped the charge, so I was told to leave the court, but as I turned to go the judge stopped me and pointed out a little problem. I had pleaded guilty and now, regardless of the circumstances, he had to address that.

The look I gave my solicitor told him I wanted to kill him. I could see him already gathering his papers and getting ready to run. The judge thought for a while and then gave me the minimum sentence possible for the charge, which was eighteen months' imprisonment, suspended for two years. I was just glad to be free. I left the court and went home with my mum for a big dish of butterbean stew and some cornmeal pudding.

I did some streetsearch (street research) and found out that the girl I was supposed to have robbed was a prostitute who had agreed to work with the police to fix me up. This was not such an unusual thing. Girls who worked the streets had an incentive to cooperate with the police because they knew that if they played ball they'd be left alone for a couple of weeks. Apparently the copper who was out to get me had got to this girl and struck a deal. At first she agreed to speak out against me, but after she saw me in court she felt sorry for me and changed her mind. She knew people who knew me, and she knew I was going down if it went the copper's way, and she couldn't live with that. So she backed out, but it was too late for me. Now, this didn't surprise me that much, and I was free, so I didn't dwell on it, but little did I know that this episode would come back to haunt me much later.

★ ★ ★

Trevor and me began to drift apart somewhat. From time to time we would check each other out, but we were surrounding ourselves with new friends. Trevor was into cars and money. I went the other way, and tried to live as naturally, as organically and as independently from the system as possible.

This lifestyle was inspired by Rastafarianism. I had been growing dreadlocks since I was fourteen, and I'd always thought about politics, culture and, of course, the big questions — where did we come from, where were we going, what was it all about, and why did white people hate us? — but now I was reading (or trying to read — my reading and writing was never good) and reinterpreting the Bible. Having grown up in an actively Christian household, I already knew the Bible really well, but it was all about the past, and not applicable now, and did I really want to live in the past?

But Rasta said no, this is the new way of looking at things. You did this thing, like a game, where you would interpret the book of Revelation. You'd look at the beast with seven heads, perhaps saying, 'That's Russia, that's America' etc. It allowed us to be political and spiritual at the same time — something that seems lacking today. I had tried desperately hard

115

not to believe in God, but I always felt there was something greater than us. The Rasta thing was great because it put me on a path. The thing about Christianity is it's like Shakespeare. It is so deeply entrenched in our culture that you don't realise that every day you're probably quoting from the Bible. Rastafari updated it and started to answer some of those big questions.

I went to live in a squat in Handsworth for a while, known as the House of Dread. It was a couple of houses with the dividing walls removed to make one big dwelling. Everything was owned collectively, duties were shared and, as much as possible, we tried not to use money. Money had the Queen's head on it, and we didn't like the Queen. It was a great way to live for a while. It made me appreciate the things we really needed in life, and consider less the superficialities that we fill our minds and lives with.

It was good to be part of a group by feeling connected to Africa — the homeland. Britain was a small place, JA was a small place, but to the Rastafarian the whole world is Africa. Better to say you were African than say you were Jamaican or English. We had a message to spread. White people had the hippies, but Rastafari was a black thing; but it was also about peace — bringing people together, black and white unite. If you wanna fight, fight Babylon rather than fighting each other. I'm from the Malcolm X school of non-violence. I'm non-violent to people who are non-violent to me. We have to defend ourselves, but killing each other is not good. I always felt that.

116

A big event for me was the release of a new Bob Marley album. I would always get one on the day of its release. Most people around me were into Burning Spear, Pablo Moses, Prince Far I, and a much harder sound than that of Marley; he was considered a little too commercial, and too radio-friendly. But I loved the poetry of his writing, the meaning behind the words, and I felt he would understand me. So I got about ten of my poems typed up and sent them to him in Jamaica. For a long time there was no reply and then, one day, there was a reply. It was handwritten and it didn't say much, just, 'I love the man works. Keep it up. Britain needs you, so forward on.' But that's all I needed. It was as if I had the seal of approval from the master. But I was stuck in Birmingham, trying to find food and stay out of jail. How was I going to 'forward on'?

For a long time I tried to go straight, looking for paid work — but this wasn't easy for a Brummie Rasta in the mid-1970s. Then, somewhat incongruously, I found a job making whistles for the police. It's hard to imagine now that a whistle was an important part of a police officer's kit — it's more like something from the 1950s, *Dixon of Dock Green* and all that. If the modern copper is in trouble, she or he calls for armed back up, or they pull out their truncheon, pepper spray or Taser, but then they simply pulled out a whistle and blew it. Anyway, I did that job for two and a half days. On Monday I started as a welder, on Tuesday I was a tester, and on Wednesday I was a cleaner. I could see my career trajectory was going in the wrong direction, so I left.

My longest job lasted four months. I worked as a painter and decorator. We were painting large buildings, mainly factories, and day after day I would listen to stories of previous workers whose lungs had been messed up by inhaling fumes, or the men who'd fallen off ladders or scaffolding and died. I started to notice that every time the boss came round to inspect our work he had a different car. I'm talking Jaguars, Rolls-Royces, Ferraris and Lamborghinis. I asked one of my fellow workers where he got the money to buy all those cars and he said he got it from us. When we do the jobs, he gets lots of money, then he gives us a little money, and we go on to paint the next building while he goes to buy his next car.

I felt I was being exploited, and that the boss didn't really care about me, so I left. I tried to find more reasonable work, but I couldn't. It was hard enough back then being black trying to find a job, but having a police record made it even more difficult. Eventually, sadly, I went back to a life of crime.

15

Cars, Money, Girls

I really did try to go straight many times. I tried my hand as a self-employed painter and decorator, advertising my services among friends. One evening, a classy-looking woman approached me in a blues and asked if I could decorate her flat. I said, 'Yes, of course.' When I turned up to give her a price she said something very strange: 'It's a deal, Benjamin, but what I'd like to do is double your price. I will pay you twice as much on one condition: you must agree to decorate in the middle of the night.' I thought that was strange, but I was keen to make all the money I could, so I agreed.

On my first night I found out why I'd been offered a nocturnal job: she was on the game. In those days many girls worked the streets but this woman worked for herself out of a flat. I'd often hear her with a punter. Most of the time it would be straight sex, but sometimes I'd hear the more theatrical stuff: 'You naughty boy! Say sorry to Mummy!' and the sound of some guy's arse being slapped. One day she was a strict nurse: 'You haven't taken your medicine!' Another day someone would be crying like a baby. 'You wet your pants, didn't you?' Imagine me in the next room, halfway up a ladder with my roller, trying to keep my mind on the job.

It wasn't only about the painting. I had to be trustworthy and keep my mouth shut. She could rely on me for that. In fact, she was so pleased with my work that she recommended me to other girls. Those girls would recommend me to other girls, and I'd soon created a niche market. It was so niche that I drafted up a business card that read:

Benjamin Zephaniah.
Painter and Decorator to Pickpockets,
Hustlers and Concubines.
Discreet and Well-Hung Papering.
Specialist in Late-Night Services.

But they were never printed. Still, it was good work and I was the only one doing it. The girls trusted me with their gear and they were confident that I wouldn't speak about them or grass them up.

I knew a fair few girls who worked the streets back then. They approached it like career women, determined to do it for a while and then retire. It was very rare that anyone was being pimped, and I didn't know anyone doing drugs other than smoking a bit of weed. If something went wrong the girls had to have someone in the background, like a minder, but they weren't pimps like you'd see in American films; it wasn't Miami. I didn't know anyone who was being forced by another person to be on the game. These women were pretty tough hustlers in their own right. I lived in places where rooms were operated by these girls and much of the time we'd have a really good laugh. There was always gossip and activity.

★ ★ ★

It was during this time that I first went to Jamaica. Someone paid for me to fly out and do a little business in the capital, Kingston. I didn't tell my mum I was going, as there would have been all sorts of questions and demands. I was barely in contact with my family at this time, in any case; I thought them too soft, too well behaved and not very streetwise. Very occasionally I would call my mum from a phone box, just to check in, and if there had been any emergencies I'd have heard about them on the street grapevine, but I was very much a free agent.

In a number of early interviews I told people I'd spent a lot of my youth in Jamaica. That was true enough, but what I hadn't explained was the reasons why. Let's just call it underground business. I guess you could say I was in an import and export situation, and I used to visit the country to see my suppliers. Yes, the British and Jamaican authorities would have disapproved of some of the things I got up to in Jamaica, but it was survival, and I was doing my little bit for globalisation long before them. Nuff said.

Although it's a bit of a cliché to say it, what struck me on arrival was the wall of heat that hit me as soon as I stepped off the plane in

Kingston. I'd never felt anything like it in the UK, and I spent some time trying to work out what clothes to wear to stay cool. Although the environment was new to me, at the same time it felt familiar. I was recognising all the places mentioned in records, like Orange Street, the Gun Court and Constant Spring. It was like stepping into a film or a song.

If you look at a lot of reggae album covers from the 1970s, you'll see photos of the artists hanging out in the street or at record shacks and recording studios with people in their neighbourhoods. Big Youth was always outside his local record shop. Doctor Alimantado would walk down the road looking as he did on the cover of *Best Dressed Chicken in Town*. I'd barely arrived in Kingston when I saw Gregory Isaacs outside his record shop.

I heard many tales from people whose chair Bob Marley had supposedly sat on, or whose cup he'd drunk from or whose yard he'd played football in. I thought they were being fanciful but, when I checked out their stories, they were true. That's how it was — it was the thing to be seen with your people. Not like in the UK, where famous musicians would hide away in posh houses with the elite.

I was very aware I was English, though. First couple of days I'd have kids giggling at me in the street saying, 'Why the man walk so fast?' When I spoke to them they understood: 'Ah, you from a Inglan.' People found it highly amusing when they saw someone moving at what I thought was a normal pace, but seemed comedy-quick to a local.

122

Another thing people found curious was my bedtime routine. I'd make myself a little bed, put my alarm clock beside me, get a drink of water — things that seemed normal to me but which came across as incredibly mannered to the young men I was mixing with, who were more like Ivan from *The Harder They Come* than I'd ever be. If a Jamaican man wanted to sleep, he would fling himself any which way on a chair or sofa, or even a log, no covers or anything, and snooze away. 'Jus sleep, man!'

The Rasta culture was huge in JA at that time. It had grown out of an increasing awareness of black history and black cultural identity that looked to Africa as the homeland. The Rasta experience was being broadcast via the lyrics of numerous reggae artists, and was reaching huge audiences. I was looking to Africa via JA, but they were just looking to Africa. I was thinking, *If things are this basic here, what's Africa going to be like?* I realised at such times how English I was.

★　★　★

I didn't have many possessions, money came and went, but the most expensive things I had back in Birmingham were my cars, the best of which was a Triumph GT6 — a great little sports car with amazing coupe styling, but it brought me too many problems. I hadn't taken a test, so I had no licence and, besides, the red beast had been bought with money raised by ways and means that didn't involve working nine to five.

The police stopped me — nothing new, as I was always being stopped — and this time I provided enough papers for them to let me go: an MOT certificate, an insurance note, and the car was taxed, but when one of the officers saw that the receipt stated I'd bought the car for cash, he wanted to know where I'd got the money from.

He walked around the car, looking at it admiringly, and then stood in front of me and said: 'I'm a white man, this is my country, and I work hard to make a living in my country. I've worked all my adult life and I can't afford a car like this. I couldn't buy this with cash, so I want to know how you can.'

I thought it was ridiculous — they could have easily done me for not having a licence — but there was no law that said I had to show how I got the money to buy the car. I stood my ground, telling them it was none of their business, so they took my car away from me. I was furious but I walked home and the next day I bought another car, one that wasn't so flashy.

I forgot about the GT6 but I mentioned it to Mum on one of the rare occasions I visited her, and she wouldn't let it lie. She kept on at the police, demanding they return my car, and when they did it was a wreck. They'd destroyed the interior looking for drugs. Mum wouldn't let that go either. She demanded they fix it and pay compensation. She battled with them, without any help from me, and to my amazement she won. I got a call from her one day, telling me she had some money for us. We split it fifty-fifty, then

I sold the car and the police left me alone — for a while.

★ ★ ★

During this time, in my late teens, I was living in a suburb called Northfield. It was a nice, mainly white working-class area full of newly built maisonettes and high-rise flats. I had a girlfriend there named Yvonne. She was extra large, extra dark, extraordinary and always smiling. She loved cooking and reminded me of those women we used to see in books about Jamaica — the ones who have their heads wrapped, wear an apron and always carry a basket. She had a young son called Horace, with whom I got on really well. I would try to impress him with my record collection and kung fu moves, and he would try to impress me with his maths, and when we'd both had enough of that we'd gang up and give Yvonne grief. I could say I treated Horace like a son but in reality I treated him like a friend, and I taught him a lot of bad habits.

Yvonne thought she just had two bad kids, but she was amazingly tolerant. Sometimes I would disappear for days and then turn up at her flat and expect my dinner to be on the table. Incredibly, it was. The most she would do is jokingly tell me that it didn't matter which girl's bed I'd passed through as long as I came back to her for real food. That woman would do anything for me, and I could never work out why.

Living in Northfield was a lot different from

living in Handsworth or Aston. If a crime was committed in north Birmingham, and I knew how the job was done, I could usually tell who'd done it and be able to find him or her within a few hours. To put it simply, Handsworth and Aston had a lot of outlaws; Northfield didn't. When I told other outlaws that I lived in Northfield, they'd say: 'Oh, you live uptown.' It wasn't really 'uptown'; it just had a lower crime rate.

Yvonne's home became a safe house where all my friends could go, any time of the day or night. At any one time I would have at least five girlfriends on the go, and if you'd have asked any of them, 'Where does Benjamin live?' they'd have all said, 'With me.'

In reality I didn't have a permanent base, but that didn't seem to matter. I could rest up with one of my many girlfriends or, if I felt like a night off, I could stay at friends' houses. Living under the radar meant a permanent address was unnecessary. The kind of people I was dealing with didn't write letters. I never ordered things from catalogues and none of my girlfriends were Avon ladies.

16

How Crime Paid

The painting and decorating work began to dry up and I didn't want to go back on the frontline of crime, so I started my own 'firm' and took up a more managerial role. I had a gang of about ten young men — whom I called my boys — who would go out and nick car tools for me. I would then sell them on to mechanics or backstreet garages.

This is how it worked: most garages operated in one of two ways; either a garage boss would let his mechanics use his tools (which they'd clean and put back carefully after use) or, as was most often the case, a boss would employ mechanics to bring their own. Sometimes I'd talk to the boss, and sometimes the mechanics, and occasionally the boss would tip me off about mechanics that needed tools. And it'd be, 'What've you got?'

Most of the time it would be screwdrivers and spanners, but it would be a very happy day indeed when I could say, 'I got a hydraulic jack.' A hydraulic jack was the big one — along with an engine lift. Occasionally you'd find one in a parked van or lorry, and they were worth thousands. In cars you'd mostly get bags of tools. In those days motors were always breaking down, especially in winter in the Midlands. People needed to keep a tool bag accessible for the inevitable snowy morning when their car wouldn't start and it'd be 'crunch crunch' down the path with the bonnet up.

We tried to live by a Robin Hood principle, though. I never stole from Aston or Handsworth; I always went to the more affluent areas. And then I'd sell the tools to smaller garages. Certain places would only deal with me, no one else. I was their exclusive tool guy. Occasionally we'd find tools in their boxes with the price stickers still on them. If something was £5, I'd say, 'Gimme three', and everyone was happy.

My boys would bring their stuff exclusively to me. Sometimes I had to tell them where to go because if they worked too hard in one area the police would go out in plain clothes to wait for them. It also helped that I knew so many prostitutes. They would be exchanging favours with cops, and they were always overhearing things. For instance, they'd know if the law was going to have a blitz on an area and they'd pass that information onto me. I would then tell my boys to find new territories.

I'd moved higher up the food chain and it felt good. I'd grown tired of being out on the street, stealing and dodging cops. I could have gone into a different line of crime and made much higher profits, enabling me to live a more lavish lifestyle and show off more, but after the trouble with the GT6 I wanted to blend in and adopt a low profile, so I bought a Ford Escort.

My 'job' wasn't completely straightforward

though. Sometimes my boys would come back with all kinds of stuff. They once turned up with a load of music gear — amplifiers, speaker boxes and the like. Being the creative type, this made me very angry. 'What did you take that for? Some poor guy just wanted to play his guitar,' I shouted. But I knew I could never find the owner, so I sold it anyway. Another time they returned with a load of bras — I mean hundreds and hundreds of bras, all shapes and sizes. I had no problem getting rid of them, they made me a good bit of money, but more importantly they made me a lot of female friends. I sent the lads back to get some knickers but they came back with boxes of bow ties. So quite a lot of clothing came my way and it was never difficult finding somebody to buy it. I had good contacts with working girls, taxi drivers and a newly emerging class of citizen: the Asian shopkeeper.

A typical day would start at 11pm with me briefing my boys, telling them where best to operate and what best to look out for. They would then bring me goods throughout the night, until about 5am. Then I'd need to sell them on. Sometimes buyers would come to me in the early hours of the morning, but usually I'd sleep and get up at lunchtime or during the afternoon. I might then visit a couple of mechanics to off load some tools, but apart from that nothing much really happened for the rest of the day. The cycle would then repeat itself day after day, night after night. It wasn't very glamorous, it wasn't even very dangerous, but it was very boring.

I wasn't being creative, not artistically anyway.

I was no longer performing poetry on the streets for my friends; I was no longer chatting on the sound systems. It was as if my poetry facility had been disconnected, just turned off. The only thing I was doing was hustling.

Nothing was really typical in terms of my income, but fortunately I wasn't receiving tax demands. Occasionally I'd go a few nights without earning anything, but those times were few and far between. Cars didn't have alarms then and my boys were well equipped with bunches of car keys. They were also happy taking the risks. They didn't have the contacts to sell things on, and if they'd tried they'd have come undone: I had my spies. That's why they brought things to me. I had people sitting waiting for goods, people who would give me money without asking questions. As soon as I got the stuff, I sold it. I'd give the boys some money and I'd take a share. It was my firm, but I didn't want to turn into a version of the boss at the painting and decorating company I'd worked for, so I made sure the boys were well paid.

It was 1978 and we could make £300 some nights. On a really good night we might make £400 or more, but it had to be split many ways. If somebody came back with high-quality tools — branded stuff from a respected manufacturer — we'd all celebrate because we knew we would make a lot of money, but it wasn't exactly the big time. No one was buying luxury homes in Spain.

I was once offered a very lucrative deal that would have involved stolen cars and international clients, but I wasn't interested. If I'd accepted it and got caught I'd have gone straight back to prison, and I didn't want that to happen. My operation was at a level that was just under the radar of the big-time cops. If I'd started to do more serious crimes, I'd've had the vice squad or serious crime squad after me. But still, gradually, things began to heat up. On one occasion a couple of guys went too far, and instead of stealing tools they actually stole the cars. They took the gear from the vehicles and brought that to me but then they sold the cars to a rival gang. This caused all sorts of trouble. Stealing cars was a more serious offence and I knew it would bring unwanted attention from the law.

I was once asked to take on a new recruit, so I took it upon myself to 'train' him. The first thing I had to do was to let him know that he was part of the team, and that we would do whatever we could to protect him, but if he crossed us, or worse still, double-crossed us, there would be trouble. He had stolen cars before, but he used the 'roll then stole' technique, which meant getting into the car, making sure the key worked in the ignition, and then quietly pushing it away, starting it up only when it was a good distance from its sleeping owner. What we did was to search, and if necessary strip, a car right where it stood.

I took him out to show him how it was done, found a Ford Cortina, and opened the boot. It was packed with boxes and random packages that made me think the car belonged to a shopkeeper. Cars could contain strange things, so I wasn't surprised to find the leg of a mannequin — but it wasn't a mannequin, it was a man. I shut the boot and we ran. And that was it. I told the new recruit to say nothing, and used it as an example of how he should expect the unexpected.

A few days later one of my boys got shot. He was only seventeen. A rival gang shot and killed him. I sent a threatening message to the people who did it and then one of my boys tried a revenge thing on them, but it went wrong. My guy tried to shoot one of their guys but he missed. That led to repercussions and the rival gang sent out a message that they wanted to hit back, and they wanted to hit back at me. The word went out that I was next in line. If the gang couldn't get the guy who attempted the revenge shooting, they were going to shoot me. I had to buy a gun for protection. I slept with it under my pillow. I felt I had to protect Yvonne and Horace, and I also had to be seen to be willing to defend myself. But it was all getting too much and I wanted out.

People were dying, street wars were going on, gangs were marking out their territory and individuals were talking about killing me. In return my mindset was that if they were coming for me, I would have to take them out before they took me out. It was as simple as that. I couldn't go to the police and say: 'Look, I've got an illegal operation here and I need some protection.' So I had to take care of myself. It didn't make it any easier that I wasn't the only one in the firing line. I knew two other guys who were killed around that time for things unconnected to me. There were even little wars going on over sound systems; people actually fought over who had the biggest and the best. And fights also erupted over women. There was lots of testosterone needing to be got out of the system.

One of my friends from Handsworth went to a dance in Balsall Heath on the south side of Birmingham, got into a fight with a youth who followed a rival sound system, and that youth cut off his ear. My friend retaliated, going back soon afterwards and stabbing to death the guy who did it. The court gave him a life sentence and it had a big effect on me because we were so close. It didn't stop there. Somebody from Balsall Heath came over and killed a close friend of his, who was also a friend of mine. So in a short space of time I was close to three killings and also lost one of my friends to a life sentence.

My pistol was easy to get. It came from a friend who'd got it from his friend, who'd got it from another friend who'd indirectly got it from a bent copper. For a while I really did believe it would give me protection. I was no stranger to guns. Some people I knew had robbed post offices, and I'd handled their sawn-off shotguns once or twice, but I hated them. They were big and clumsy. I had never fired one in anger but a couple of times I did go out late at night to the Lickey Hills, on the outskirts of the city, and fire one among the trees. When you fired one of these things you didn't just hit the person you were aiming at; you hit anyone and anything that was in the general area of your aim. I was into self-defence, not murder, and certainly not mass murder. Even though I had one, I always hated guns. I think they are one of the worst inventions ever, manufactured with the sole purpose of taking life.

★ ★ ★

Things were getting shaky in the world of hustling, but also closer to home. Although I wasn't in regular contact with my mum, her own sense of continuity and companionship was about to come to an abrupt end. She had persuaded Pastor Burris that they should be properly married. They had been together a long time and the traditional way of things felt like the right thing to do, as she was getting older. But it wasn't to be. Just a few days before the wedding, Pastor fled to the US. Apart from the occasional visit to Birmingham, to see his family, he would stay there for the next three decades, until ill health forced his return to the UK. Trevor said he'd called round and found him in the process of loading suitcases into his car, saying 'Don't tell anyone, but I'm leaving.' And that was it, he was gone.

Mum was devastated, of course. Nobody could understand why he left. I think he just chickened out. It was a real shock to everyone, not least his seven kids. The only, very small, saving grace was that he didn't jilt Mum on the actual day.

17

London Calling

One summer night in 1978, I lay on my bed looking up at the ceiling, wondering what life was all about. The ceiling (with its adjoining walls) seemed to represent the limits of my ambitions, but these ambitions were related to the circumstances I found myself in, some of the bad choices I made, and some of the bad people I followed. It was time to really think for myself. I recalled the teacher at Broadway Comprehensive telling me I was a born failure, and that I would soon be dead or doing a life sentence in prison. I didn't have to be a mastermind to see that if things carried on the way they were going the teacher would be proved right.

When I was eight, I told everyone, even the big moustache in the Boys' Brigade, that I wanted to be a poet when I grew up, and there I was looking at a ceiling that belonged to Birmingham Council, with a gun under my pillow, thinking I was some kind of triad gang master don or ghetto godfather. Just as the eight-year-old me had done, I spoke the words out: 'I want to be a poet. I want to prove that teacher wrong.'

I reached under the bed and pulled out a big folder containing some of my poems and the letter Bob Marley had sent me. I read the letter again; the last words were 'Britain needs you, so forward on.' Right then I thought only the police needed me, and I wasn't forwarding on. Something had to change.

The next day I told everyone it was over — that I wasn't doing this anymore, and they should stop too. I told my boys I had no bonus money for them, no pension, it was now every man for himself. And then I told them I was going to London. I can remember that day vividly. They all protested. A normally quiet guy called Testa said, 'Come on, man. You know you can make good money here. Why do you want to leave us?' The guy almost had tears in his eyes.

I reminded them of how good I used to be on the sound systems, that that was where my heart was. I told them I wanted to be a revolutionary poet, thinking about the big questions, talking about human rights, peace and the things I used to care about. I looked at Testa and said, 'It's crunch time, mi breddrin. Me a go kill a man, or a man a go kill me. Or we can just stop now.'

They looked at me stony-faced, and I ended by saying, 'What I'm doing right now is like saving your lives. So set up yourselves and do another ting.'

I paid them what I owed them, told them to leave, and that was that. When another of the group asked me when he would see me again, I said, 'Next time you see me, it'll be on TV.'

Of course, the moment I'd made the decision to pursue my dream I began to wonder how I would actually do it. What would it involve? I had so many questions and so few answers. I knew I had to get away from Birmingham otherwise I'd be drawn back into crime. London felt like the logical place to go. I'd been down to the capital many times with various sound systems, but I felt there would be opportunities for me there that weren't possible in Birmingham. It's hard to reinvent yourself when you're surrounded by familiar things and familiar people.

To add to my troubled mind, the police had started looking for me. They were just behind me all the time. On numerous occasions I found that places I'd just been to would be raided shortly afterwards. I thought the police were investigating my business affairs, until I visited Cathy, another girlfriend. After leaving her house she was also raided, and she got a message to me: 'Disappear,' she said. 'The police want you for murder.' I made some enquiries and found out they wanted me because my fingerprints linked me to the murder of a man whose body had been found in a car. I instantly knew which car, and which body, they were referring to: it was my night of training the new recruit, when we'd gone looking for tools and found a man's leg in the boot of a car.

I didn't tell anyone about this, not even family. The only people who knew were the ones tipping me off. I was chewing it all over, thinking on the one hand it was surreal, and on the other that this was really serious and was upsetting other people. Even though the pressure was on, I was reassuring myself that the police would soon find the real culprit; they must know that I hadn't committed murder.

Looking back, that confidence was probably optimistic. In the late 1970s the police were fitting people up left, right and centre if it suited their agenda. It was like the TV series *Life on Mars*, but with much more racism and brutality. They wouldn't have cared if one more black man with a history of juvenile crime was banged up for a murder he didn't commit.

A friend gave me the address of one of his ex-girlfriends in London. Her name was Clara. I had met her only once, when she came to visit him in Birmingham, so I hardly remembered her. I packed up a few things, jumped into my Ford Escort and started driving across Birmingham in the direction of the M6. On the way there, I stopped off at a music rehearsal space in a cellar in Moseley, where a band was rehearsing. The band didn't have a name then, but they went on to call themselves UB40. I didn't know them particularly well, but I knew a couple of guys they knocked about with. I also knew Astro, the percussionist; we'd been around the same sound systems.

When I arrived, there was a girl watching them. She was very glamorous and interested in Astro. I walked up to her and told her the band was going nowhere. I said they sounded too white for a reggae band and that I was going to London to be a famous poet, so she'd be better off with me. I remember thinking I'd have to spend some time chatting her up and working on her, for at least half an hour, but she said, 'Yes, I want to go with you.' She just got in my car and we headed off to London.

I can't even remember her name, but she had nothing with her, not even a change of clothes. I had a bit of money and a few clothes, but that was all. I was also worried about my old Escort; it wasn't in great shape and I wasn't sure it would make it. It was halfway through being sprayed and had been rubbed down with patches of body filler and primer, so it was quite conspicuous. Also, I still wasn't a legal driver because I didn't have a licence, so I was quite nervous about driving to London, but we did it anyway and of course I kept my worries to myself.

A few hours later we arrived in south London and knocked on Clara's door, but she wasn't there. In fact she didn't show up for two days. So there I was; this was the big time . . . well, at least the beginning of it. I was in London with a beautiful girl who I'd promised a life of fame and the bright lights, sleeping in a Ford Escort in a car park in New Cross. 'Well,' I told her, 'this isn't too bad really, and things can only get better.'

When Clara finally did show up, she was happy. She was in the money. She was a 'clipper', fleecing gullible men of their cash. She would go through the routine of soliciting for sex, but once she got the man in a vulnerable position, usually with his trousers down, she would take his wallet and disappear. Or she would find tourists or an out-of-towner looking for an illegal smoke, and take him somewhere that looked like a dealer's house, tell him to wait around the corner, then she'd disappear with his money. So, after two days of hustling, she'd come home to find us waiting for her. She was very welcoming, even though at first she had a bit of a shock because she wasn't expecting guests.

Me and my new girlfriend shared a bed with her. That may sound a bit strange but that's the way it was, and nothing happened. Honest. We had to sleep where we could. All kinds of ladies of the night and men of mystery were passing through Clara's place, so she thought if we slept with her it would guarantee a place for us, and the others could fight over the remaining beds.

One night, about four weeks after we'd arrived, my new girlfriend had a telephone conversation with one of her mates in Birmingham who told her that UB40 were beginning to get noticed. The friend talked them up and said she should have stayed because they were really going places.

So that was it. She upped and left me. She didn't even have things to pack. I was told that she went back to Birmingham and, although I never saw her again, her mother once turned up to one of my performances, where I told that story. She came to me after the show and said, 'That was my daughter, that was. She was a right one. But she's doing OK now.'

★ ★ ★

One day Clara told me a reggae toaster called Dillinger was coming to stay, along with a singer called Horace Andy. I jumped off my seat with

140

excitement. I didn't particularly like Horace Andy's music. He'd done a couple of rootsy tunes but I thought he was a bit too sweet and loverboy-ish, but I was mad about Dillinger. He was a militant Rasta who'd released a legendary album in 1976 called *CB 200*, a massive hit with the title track being about a couple of Rastas flashing their dreadlocks as they rode on a then-popular Honda CB200 motorbike.

From the moment Clara told me they were coming I could hardly control myself. I was going to meet the great Dillinger. I'd come to London to mix with the stars and now it was going to happen. But when it did happen it wasn't as I'd imagined. Dillinger was very arrogant and show-off-ish. He dressed like Elvis Presley, in a shiny jumpsuit, and all he did all night was talk about his gold rings and money. Horace Andy was totally different. He was a very humble guy, and charming, and I'll never forget how he sat me down and spent hours showing me how to play a few tunes on an old guitar.

I'd picked at the guitar a little since the days of going to church with my mum, when I'd been given an old instrument by one of the musicians who played there. Although it was a rhythm guitar, I played it like a bass. Horace Andy was amazed that I could do vocals and play at the same time. I don't sing, but doing vocals and playing bass (to reggae) at the same time is very difficult, because the bass is going in a different direction from the voice.

Horace also gave me some really good general advice about the music business and how to get on in it. By the time they'd left I'd completely changed my view — I didn't like Dillinger anymore and Horace Andy had become a true brother. And the time I spent playing guitar with him inspired me to keep practising the instrument.

★ ★ ★

By then I was starting to think like a poet, and I was looking for ways of making myself known. I wasn't writing much but I was resurrecting some of my old poetry and performing it to people. Most importantly, when people asked me what I did, I told them I was a poet. I had to, to get myself in the right frame of mind. I now had no interest in crime. Some of the people Clara mixed with were good pickpockets and occasionally they'd follow her to the West End. I was on the periphery of that, and they'd ask me if I wanted to go with them, but I never did. As much as I loved pickpocketing, and as good as I was at it, I resisted the temptation because I didn't want to go back down that road.

18

Kilburn and Other High Roads

Clara was a godsend. She never asked me for a penny in rent, but the longer I stayed, the more I thought I should register as unemployed to get some money to help her, but for reasons unknown she didn't want me to do that. Maybe the money she made from clipping was enough. Still, I knew I couldn't stay at her place forever, and my opportunity to move on came when I went to hear a sound system in Brixton called Soprano B.

I was in the darkest corner of the dance floor, doing what could loosely be called dancing with a Jamaican girl who was as sweet as chocolate. As we rubbed our groins together and she started to melt, I felt a tap on my shoulder. When I looked around I saw one of my good friends, Pops, from Wolverhampton. A couple of years earlier, when he'd needed somewhere to stay, I'd taken him to Birmingham to stay at Yvonne's. He was amazed by her place. It was the first time he'd seen a really plush carpet. This time, Pops returned the favour. He said he could get me a place of my own that was rent-free.

I looked at him and said, 'What kind of place is that?' He said it was a squat, a licensed squat, so it was legal. There was a row of houses in north London that was there for the taking. The local council owned them but didn't know what to do with them so they were gradually being occupied by creative people who needed the space to work on their art and music. Some arrangement had been made with the local council and the squatters were allowed to stay. I thanked Clara, said goodbye and moved into a squat on Princess Road, Kilburn. The only problem was there was no bath. But it had everything else: a toilet, bed, cold running water and so on. There was a public baths nearby, so we would go there, pay 50p and shower or bathe for as long as we liked.

It was an amazing place. I had my own large room and most of my furniture was recycled from builders' skips. I even made a table from old coat hangers. Like a number of places in London at that time, the whole street was occupied by creative people. The place was a magnet for musicians with an alternative edge. Some guys who hung around were in the reggae band Aswad. Ian Dury and the Blockheads were also knocking about. I saw Elvis Costello there, Joe Strummer from The Clash (on an excursion north from his west London scene) and Annie Lennox. The houses were big Victorian buildings and most of them doubled up as rehearsal spaces for bands. We always lived in fear that one day we would be told to get out and the houses would be destroyed, but every now and then I drive past and they're still there — albeit now privately owned and worth a fortune.

As well as the house in Kilburn, I spent time

in East Finchley, also in north London. I'd met a woman who lived there called Sheila. She was much older than me, and although I didn't really think of her as a girlfriend, she sometimes allowed me to stay at her place. It was as if my place was one star and hers was five stars — a little luxury. She was also a twin, and much better educated than me but, more importantly, she was interested in my poetry, and she encouraged me to start thinking creatively again.

She explained what she knew of the publishing world. And, because I still had difficulty writing, she helped me by typing out my first book, *Pen Rhythm*. We didn't talk about it much but I suspected she had been a groupie when she was younger. In conversations she would casually slip in the name of a singer or actor; they were usually locals, but one day she asked me if I wanted to go with her to meet Peter Tosh.

'What, you mean Peter Tosh, Peter MacIntosh, from Jamaica?' I shouted. Peter was one of the original Wailers alongside Bob Marley and Bunny Wailer. I loved Bob for his song writing ability and his poetry, but I admired and respected Peter for his militancy. He was uncompromising and had been arrested many times by the Jamaican police, beaten and imprisoned, but he would come out, put his band together, and carry on where he left off.

Sheila took me to meet him at the Holiday Inn in Swiss Cottage. As we travelled there I was waiting for her to say she was joking, but she wasn't. When we arrived he was doing an interview in the lobby, and he was as militant as ever, even with the journalist. He had a reputation as a very difficult person to interview, and I could see why. As the journalist questioned him, he questioned the journalist.

After the interview Peter invited me to his room and we spent a great day together talking about politics, kung fu and herbs, but I wasn't to know that this was going to be the start of a special relationship. On the strength of that meeting he invited me on his tour around the rest of the UK. Of course I jumped at the chance. I didn't get involved in the performance side of things; I was just there as a young Rasta feeling the respect and watching how the man went about things. Good times.

★　★　★

I began to make homemade books of poetry, to see what a book of my poetry might look like. The first one I did was *Pen Rhythm*, the collection that Sheila had typed out for me and, like much of my early writings, the poems were very serious and heavily influenced by Rastafarianism. I was still working out how to write about Rastafarian spirituality and politics. I wanted to address the injustices I saw around me, and felt there wasn't much room for humour. I tried to inject a bit here and there, but there wasn't much.

After watching a news report on television that was full of war, death, kidnappings and rape, I wrote a poem called 'It Happens Every Day', and then I went to bed. When I read the poem

146

the next day I couldn't believe the words that had poured out of me. It was as if there was some greater power working through me and controlling the pen. It was the first time I had ever experienced anything like this. Pure inspiration.

The good thing about making my homemade books was that it helped me begin to understand the publishing process. I wanted to do as much as I could by myself. In those days, before computers were used to design books, I would pay for them to be typeset. I would lay out the pages myself, cut them to size with scissors, and stick them together. I made a few prototype books with titles and even credits. I loved working on them. After *Pen Rhythm* there was *Calling Rastafari* and *City Psalms*. I wanted the poems in *City Psalms* to sound like psalms in the Bible but with a modern spin. There were a lot of words like 'Kush' (a biblical word for Ethiopia); there was a lot of brimstone and fire and Babylon burning. As my friend the linguist David Crystal would put it, it was just a phrase I was going through.

Hey, I was just thirteen when I wrote some of those poems, and in certain places I was more concerned with the style than the content.

19

Rocking Against Racism

One of the great things about being in London was that it opened up my mind culturally and politically. For the first time in my life I went to rock gigs — gigs full of white people where I really was a minority but where I felt absolutely no fear at all. I once even bought a ticket to see 10cc play at Wembley, which was a strange experience. I had never paid so much for a concert ticket, or attended a gig with so many people to watch a band I could hardly see because the arena was so huge — there were no big screens then.

One of my true pleasures, though, was going to punk and post-punk gigs. The Ruts, X-Ray Spex, Siouxsie and the Banshees, Sham 69, the Slits and the Dammed were bands I would see again and again. The energy that came from the stage would go though you, and if you couldn't dance you had to jump. These bands would sometimes play on the same bill as reggae outfits like Aswad, Misty in Roots and Birmingham's own Steel Pulse. You had punk music thrashing out 125 beats per minute, and reggae, which could be as little as 90 beats per minute, but they had so much in common. These poor white kids lived on some of the same estates as the poor black kids; they felt persecuted by the same politicians, hated by the same bigots, and they felt as alienated as the black youth, so it made sense to share the same platforms.

A guy called Red Saunders, along with a few of his friends, had formed Rock Against Racism in 1976, not just as a reaction to the racist skinheads terrorising our streets, but also in response to comments made by Eric Clapton and David Bowie. It's extraordinary to think that back then Eric Clapton (aka God) said he agreed with Enoch Powell and that Britain was in danger of becoming a 'black colony'. And then there was David Bowie saying Adolf Hitler was the first superstar. Who'd have thought it?

Rock Against Racism gigs were a mixture of political rally and rock concert. There was always a good mixture of punk and reggae bands, but there were also poets. At one of these gigs, held at Alexandra Palace one hot Saturday night in April 1979, I had just seen the Ruts, one of my favourite punk bands, who had ended their set with 'Babylon's Burning', which I think is one of the best punk songs ever written. I had been dancing like a crazy pogo stick with a funky punky girl from Billericay. We poured with sweat as we waited for another of my favourites, Sham 69, to play. Then a strange-looking poet emerged on stage. He was tall and really skinny, wearing dark glasses with jet-black hair, and he stood up so high that he almost touched the overhead stage lighting. His name was John Cooper Clarke.

He was a mess. His suit didn't fit, his arm was

in plaster and he looked as if he had come off worst in a fight and escaped from hospital to get to the gig. He said, 'Hello, London', and then he began to rant. I remembered having heard someone play a record back in Birmingham of a punk poet called Patrick Fitzgerald. Patrick was a white poet with Irish roots, living in east London, but he talked about living in the same conditions as we were living in, and his favourite music was reggae. But I'd only heard Patrick; John Cooper Clarke was the first punk poet I saw in the flesh. He fired off words so quickly but so effectively that it made his Mancunian drawl sound like music. Every punk and Rasta in that hall stopped to listen to him as he performed '(I Married a) Monster from Outer Space'. As I watched John, I thought, *Yeah, that's where I want to be. I want to be on stage with that freak.*

★   ★   ★

It was less than two weeks later that some of the same people who had been pogoing to the Ruts were fighting the extreme right-wing National Front (NF) on the streets. The Battle of Southall started when we marched against racists under the banner of the Anti Nazi League (ANL) on 23 April 1979. The racists had been intimidating the people of Southall and the police were doing nothing, so we were going to do something — we were going to show the National Front that we would defend the people of Southall. We wanted to show the police that if they wouldn't take on

150

the racists then we would.

The police showed no mercy that day. Very few people who were there or who saw film footage of that demonstration doubted that they were doing the work of the National Front. That day the police killed Blair Peach, a gentle teacher and ANL member, and a martyr was created. On that day, too, the band Misty in Roots had their headquarters smashed up, a friend of mine was hit so hard with a police baton that she lost part of her memory, and someone took a photograph of me in that so-often-seen position: struggling as I was being arrested. Unfortunately I've never seen the photo and I've often wondered if someone still has it. Nose bleeding, my arms forced behind my back, I was bundled into a police van and beaten even more once inside it. And for good measure the police ripped out a handful of my dreadlocks as a trophy. The police at Thornhill Road, Birmingham, would have been proud.

These were politically volatile times. I don't think Mrs Thatcher actually said it, but you were either with her or against her, and I didn't know anyone that was with her. There were of course lots of people who *were* with her, but they didn't live in the areas where we lived, and if we ever strayed into real Tory territory we were soon made to feel unwelcome. When she came to power she sold a lifestyle to the aspirational working-class voter, but she was only ever addressing her vision to white people. We were the ones she'd mention in other conversations as swamping the country.

She said what she was going to do and she got down and did it: she privatised everything she could; she clamped down on trade unions; she despised feminists and the politically organised working class, and she openly supported the racist apartheid regime in South Africa. Unsurprisingly she wasn't doing much about the racist skinheads on the streets of Britain. We were left to defend ourselves, which was pretty hard when you also had openly racist police who would sometimes arrest us when we told them we had rights too. All this meant that the music, poetry and comedy of the time were highly politically charged.

Different strands of youth culture were coming together to take a stand against oppression. The Midlands had always been a hotbed of musical talent but something special was beginning to happen there. They came out of Coventry and they really were the Specials. This band was a mixture of black and white kids who, in the midst of all the punk and reggae music around at the time, looked even further back, to ska. Ska had always been popular with non-racist skinheads, but the Specials injected new energy into it. I got to know them quite well, but I was closest to Neville Staple.

Neville sang a little, but most of all he danced. He danced everywhere: on the lighting rig, on the speaker boxes, on the heads of audience members, and sometimes he even danced on stage. He was an energy ball, full of life. I was with Neville after one of their early London gigs. Their EP, *Gangsters*, had come out and they were doing okay. As we watched the punky stragglers leave the hall, Neville told me of their grand plan. They wanted the punks to tidy up — to throw away their bondage trousers and safety pins and get smart suits with razor-sharp creases, and pork-pie hats. He wanted to transform that subculture and start a new craze. I'd heard people say things like this before, so I didn't take much notice, but less than six months later the two-tone craze was in full swing. Some punks kept their bondage gear, and not all Specials fans wore razor-sharp suits, but overall Neville got it right.

20

Publishing the Unpublishable

Any writer who has tried to get published will tell you it can be very difficult, and every published writer has a story (usually a long one) about how they got published. Mine was a little unusual, though thankfully it didn't take too long. With encouragement from Sheila, I started to seriously look for a publisher. At first I tried the traditional way of sending the poems with a letter by post, but I much preferred taking the poems to the publisher myself. I didn't know that wasn't really the way to do things — I was just enthusiastic, and I knew my poems worked best when performed. With that in mind, I thought it best that I turned up with the poems, and if necessary I would perform them.

Many publishers glanced at the poems and said no, and when I suggested that I perform them most of them looked at me as if I was mad. A couple of them said to my face, 'Sorry, we don't do black or Rastafarian poetry.' I would try to tell them that my poetry was for everybody, not only blacks and Rastafarians. I told them I had white friends who liked them, but they weren't having it. I think it's too simplistic to say they were just being racist, however. Mainstream publishers in Britain knew nothing about black

154

poetry, or dub poetry, or rap poetry back then.

In Dalston, east London, there was a bookshop called Centreprise. It was also a community centre, a meeting place and a small publisher. When I heard about them I thought this must be the place for me. I arrived early one Monday morning and met a colourful woman who welcomed me in . . . and then rejected me. Many years later another friend, who is also called Benjamin, went there with his poems and saw the same woman. She turned him down too. He walked out of the bookshop to the bus stop, and as he was waiting for his bus home the woman came running after him and she said: 'You know what. I said no to Benjamin Zephaniah about twenty years ago and I've regretted it ever since. Why don't you come in and have a talk?' I met her again in 2007 and she was very good-humoured about it. She said her colleagues had never let her live it down.

Around this time I found another old friend from Birmingham called Raggs. He had come down a bit before me and was living in Leyton, east London. While we were all into hardcore reggae, he'd always been into funk — Parliament, George Clinton, Bootsy Collins. He made his own clothes (hence his nickname) and sported an Afro three times the size of his head. He had an extensive record collection and all he did, all day and all night, was dance to this funky stuff and design clothes. He was a great dancer. He had long, skinny legs that were like rubber. They would twist and turn like a rag doll's legs, but he had great balance. He was totally in control when he looked out of control.

Raggs understood the Dread and Rasta movement but he never jumped on that bandwagon simply to be fashionable. He never got into the hustling life; he was always an honest, hardworking funkateer. At first the funky thing wasn't my bag but it began to grow on me, as Raggs's zest for life was so infectious. He was earning a living by making clothes that appealed to the funk and soul crowd — flamboyant shirts and shiny fabrics. He'd run them up on a sewing machine in his home.

I'd stay at Raggs's house sometimes. I was working on my poetry and beginning to think about my first real public performances. On one of these occasions I was on a nearby street when someone suggested I visit another bookshop where they also did publishing. I found the place — called The Whole Thing — in nearby Stratford. It was a bit like Centreprise but more holistically connected. Part of the premises was used as a vegetarian café, another part was a wholefood store, and the bookshop was as radical as they came. Along with the *Morning Star*, they sold every feminist, gay, Irish Republican and black publication going. It was what was called an 'alternative bookshop' — a term I'd not previously heard used in that way — and it was a workers' co-operative.

The staff was made up of the happiest, hippiest people I had ever seen. There I met a bearded man called Derek Smith. He was a thoughtful, humble man, but he had the kind of face that didn't really do smiles. When I told him

I was a poet, and I'd like to be published, I could just about see his lips move, as if to indicate a smile, then he told me I had come at the right time. They had recently formed a publishing co-op and received a grant. Their brief was to publish somebody who was unknown and represented a minority community. Gill Hay was another worker there. Tall, and the complete opposite of Derek, her eyes were always alight and she seemed to be forever smiling.

They both read my poems and straight away told me they would like to publish me. But there was a catch. It was a co-operative, so it wasn't just a case of me leaving my poems and then waiting for the book to arrive through the post. I also had to get involved with the publishing process. That suited me fine; after all, I was always trying to understand that side of things, so we had a deal. Over the next few weeks I helped with the layout of the book, and then the pages would arrive at the shop and we had to staple them together. I loved it.

I had been in London almost two years when, in 1980, *Pen Rhythm* was published. It was a very small book, more of a booklet, really, and it was a slightly different version from the prototype I had made, but helping to put the book together was a great learning process through which I also met interesting people.

These days I'm not that keen on self-publishing, as I think a writer always needs an editor, and a lot of self-published books are full of spelling mistakes and use terrible typefaces, but I always tell new writers, especially poets, to

157

imagine their first collection and, if possible, to create a model of what it would look like. Not necessarily for others, but for themselves. You must think about the order of your poems, and your mock-up book must have a title, dedications and as much information as there would be in the real book. Then you should put it away and read it later. You will then notice changes you might want to make, and you can begin to imagine what it would be like in the hands of someone who doesn't know you.

I was told that *Pen Rhythm* was well received, but I didn't know what that meant. I don't know how many copies were sold, but it very quickly went to three editions. A few months after it was published, an independent filmmaker called Simon Heaven came to see me in the bookshop. He told me about a new TV station that was soon to go on air. It was going to make films about marginalised and minority communities, and it would give a voice to people like me. The station was to be Channel 4.

Simon had won a commission from the station, and his brief was to make a series of documentaries about alternative poets. He wanted the first one to be about me. I said yes. I had a book out, people were talking about my poetry, and I thought it made sense to do a documentary, but I was very nervous. As far as I knew the police were still looking for me in Birmingham. It had been in the back of my mind that they might have found me after the publication of *Pen Rhythm*, but they didn't, which convinced me that the police didn't read poetry.

It took about three weeks to make the documentary. The filming process was all new to me. I would say all the wrong things — things that were right for me but wrong for television. For example, in reply to a question about why people needed to fight, I began to talk about liberation movements in Africa, that felt they had no choice but to fight their oppressors. As I spoke, Simon nodded, as if to say, 'Very good.' But then I said, 'The people of Africa must fight for freedom and equality, like the Catholics of Northern Ireland.'

The filming stopped, the crew looked at each other, and Simon said, 'Very good, Benjamin. Can we do it again and be a bit less specific, a little more general?' That was the moment I realised how cautious the British media could be when talking about the government's interference in Ireland. Thatcher didn't call her war a war — not when it was at home; that was what foreigners and dark people did. The British establishment and their friends called it 'the unrest' or 'The Troubles'.

I wasn't diplomatic, my poetry was raw and so was I, so that kind of thing would happen many times. I began to understand how much self-censorship there was in the British media, and how much the British people (especially the English) censored themselves. Still, the programme got made and was called *Pen Rhythm Poet*, and it was one of the first documentaries to be shown on the new channel — which had begun broadcasting in November 1982. The original idea was to screen it as part of a series about emerging talent, but by the time it was ready for transmission the book and my performance had raised my profile so much that Channel 4 decided the film should stand alone, and so it was shown in its own right.

Looking back, it's a very strange film. Many people say I don't look much different from the way I look now, in my late fifties, but I actually sounded much older and more Jamaican when I was younger. My performance style was more static, and I tended to get on stage and blast poems out without really introducing myself or my work. I just wanted to blow people away with poetry; I wasn't really interested in 'stage craft' or making friends. I would learn that in the coming years.

21

A Bard of Stratford

I left Kilburn and moved in with Raggs in Leyton. I was being called the Bard of Stratford, so I thought I should at least live in the area. Things were really changing. I had experience of chatting on sound system microphones, and I'd done a few performances in small community centres, but now I was doing gigs on bigger stages. I even did one accidentally. I went to watch a benefit event for the Troops Out (of Ireland) movement. The fighting in Northern Ireland was very hot at the time. I was watching the bands and, although I was passionate about justice for the Catholic minority, it was a pretty, dark-haired Irish girl who caught my attention.

I whispered some stuff in her ear about how good I thought we'd look together, and how, if we got together, we could represent the struggles of the black and Irish peoples. Then, in order to show her I was really on her side, I gave her a close-up, personal, whispered recitation of a poem I'd written called 'Troops Out', and I thought I was in.

She said she had plans for me and she wanted me, then ten minutes later I watched with a sense of shock as she took to the stage and said: 'I've just met a really nice guy and he's going to come up here and do a poem for us. Give him a round of applause!'

I was stunned, but I had no choice, so I went straight up on stage and did it. It was only one poem but that was my first gig in front of an all-white audience. I know it wasn't 'my gig' — it was only one poem after all — but there was something liberating about performing in a place where absolutely no one knew me.

After my Troops Out debut, things moved quickly. I was soon to top the bill at an event organised by Gill and Derek from The Whole Thing. It was to take place in a room above the shop, but I needed a support poet. I didn't have to look far. Raggs's brother was known as 'King' and had been writing poetry as a hobby. He said he was happy to warm up for me. He was a real wheeler-dealer and had a look based on what you might think of as the classic pimp style — the way he walked, spectacular hats, a girl on each arm. He always talked with a very posh accent, which was put on, but he developed it.

His real name was Alexander Gordon, but I thought that sounded like someone from a soap opera, and he agreed with me. So I looked at his name, moved a few letters around, took a few letters out, and came up with the name 'Da Zanda'. He now sounded like a magician, but he liked it, so I went and designed a poster. I wrote the words on the poster myself. It said:

Come hear local poets in a revolutionary style. Featuring Benjamin Zephaniah and Da Zanda. All who have ears, let them hear:

162

voices from the city, on Saturday 31st January 1981. 1 o'clock at The Whole Thing, 53 West Ham Lane, Stratford, east London.

So that was my first real gig, with my own poster and my own audience. It had an immediate impact. I remember somebody stopping me in the street the next day saying, 'You're that poet. When are you doing another reading? Everyone's talking about you.'

I didn't have another performance planned but I could feel them coming. Then Derek suggested I work with them in the shop or, to put it correctly, that I should fully join the co-operative and not just the publishing operation. So I did. I started working in the bookshop and café to earn some money on the side. They ran a housing co-operative there too, which was a vital and thriving alternative to the traditional rental market. Once I began to understand how co-ops worked, I got a group of people together and we started our own housing co-operative.

Back then, before the days of the internet, and before everything became a corporate 'revenue stream', like-minded people still had ways of finding each other and spreading information. Most cities had their own alternative scene, and it often congregated around wholefood cafés that doubled up as bookshops and food stores. These places weren't like Holland & Barrett — they would be alive with left-leaning activists hanging out, talking about philosophy and the Green movement and organising resistance. Radical ideas would circulate and there would be flyers about the Greenham Common protest and CND, and noticeboards where people would advertise events and look for others with whom to share their co-op or squat. It was the perfect environment for my message.

The buzz was going around and people were asking for more gigs, so I obliged. I was big in Stratford. People were starting to look at me differently; they called me 'the poet' and my audiences were typically a mixture of alternative types and Rastafarians. One day, a very well-respected and quite religious Rastafarian woman called Claudette said to me, in a very matter-of-fact way, that I was going to be around for a long time. When I asked her why she thought that, she said, 'I don't know anything about poetry but I know there is no one else like you. You've got intelligence, you've got reggae in you; black people and white people and youth can understand it.' She was a very no-nonsense, to-the-point woman, so I knew she wasn't just trying to impress me.

My day-to-day life was spent working in The Whole Thing. Helping to run and maintain the housing co-op also took up a lot of energy and time and required members to attend regular meetings. Being very left wing and ethical, there were endless debates and democratic votes. The community was running things for themselves and feeling a sense of autonomy that people these days don't seem to have, unless they're rich. It was an alternative existence with excellent principles that empowered people to learn about co-operation. We got paid, although it wasn't very much, but we all had food and shelter. If something went wrong you could draw from the people around you in that caring, sharing collective.

I was chatting to Derek one day and he told me that most of the phone calls coming into the shop were about me. If someone wanted to book me for a gig, that's where they'd find me. This is when I thought, *I'm busier than the shop. I can be a poet full-time.* I looked at my earnings and they were higher than the shop's. I was wary about leaving the safety net of The Whole Thing — the co-op movement had really helped me — but I had to do it. I was beginning to build a name for myself.

Stratford was a very run-down part of east London back then, with lots of unfinished building projects, or buildings that were falling down. On a wall of corrugated iron on Stratford Broadway someone had spray-painted the words: 'Beware Babylon, the poet has arrived'. I didn't feel that Babylon was going to fall in the very first term of the Thatcher government, but it was uplifting to know that the poet was me.

22

From Page to Stage

I managed to get somewhere of my own, a housing co-operative place in Stratford. Although I had been out of touch with my family for some time, my mum started to visit and this gradually eased into her living with me. She would complain about the London air, and that the water wasn't as good as in Birmingham, but after being abandoned by Pastor Burris I think she wanted a fresh start and some familiar company in the form of her firstborn son.

Around this time I frequently performed at weekend fairs in community centres, in mid-sized venues at African-Caribbean cultural events, at music gigs and at large political rallies. At one particular anti-racist gig, the band Aswad were getting ready to go on stage. I went to the side of the stage and asked their manager, Michael Campbell, if I could 'drop' a poem before they played. He asked the band and they said okay, so I went on stage with no introduction.

Most people just carried on talking. I could hear others saying, 'Who's this?' and some saying, 'I think I've seen him somewhere before.' But I told myself not to be distracted by anything in the crowd; this was punk, so anything could happen. I began to chant a poem called 'African

Swing' and slowly the background noise faded as everyone started to pay attention to me.

It's a great feeling when you begin to turn an audience around, but it's a feeling you must ignore because you are there to deliver the poem and not to congratulate yourself. Then I delivered the last line: 'And look at me now, I'm an African', and the crowd went wild. It was time to get off, but they wanted more. I looked to Michael, who was now surrounded by members of other bands who had come to see what all the noise was about, and then they all started to encourage me to do one more. I ended up performing another three poems, and I could have done more. Now I knew I could perform alongside well-known bands, and not just other poets. I'd managed to hold an audience on a big stage and I started to think, *Yeah, this is gonna happen.* I wasn't arrogant about it; I just knew.

I began to do this often. I would go along to a gig, stand at the side of the stage and ask a band member or the stage manager if I could do a poem between bands. Or sometimes the bands would hang out in the audience watching the support act and I would have a word with them there. Soon they started to approach me and ask me to go and turn the crowd on for them. This was before rap was big in Britain, and before the appearance of spoken word gigs. Crowds had never seen or heard anybody like me. There was John Cooper Clarke and a handful of punk poets, and there was Linton Kwesi Johnson, whose delivery was more relaxed than mine, but they had never heard the fast reggae version of dub poetry that I delivered.

Not only were the audiences shouting for more, sometimes the bands would encourage me from the wings, urging me on, telling me to 'give it to 'em'. Bands would never be concerned with me eating into their time; they thought of me as complementing them, and I was easy to work with. I had fire in my belly, and all I needed was a microphone, so roadies could change the bands' gear as I performed, and I didn't ask for any money, although many bands were happy to get me a little something for my time.

I felt at home at these gigs. I had admired the Rock Against Racism movement and now I was part of it. I used to watch groups like Buzzcocks, Subway Sect and Matumbi, and Birmingham's finest, Steel Pulse, and now I was playing with them. Their fans had become my fans.

23

The Punked-up Reggae Party

My other skill was being able to introduce bands, or being the MC. If I was introducing Black Uhuru, I wouldn't just say, 'Ladies and gentlemen, welcome Black Uhuru', I would tell them what Black Uhuru represented. I would say why they needed to make some noise for this band, and why this band was making some noise for them. I wanted the audience to express themselves, to join in or chant along.

Rastafarian audiences who liked what you were saying didn't just clap, they made gunshot sounds or stamped their feet; some would even shout biblical passages that would praise the poet or remind people of the importance of the poet. Punks, on the other hand, would spit at you and throw beer. I was never spat at, and I was never wetted with ale. I think they respected the Rastas and knew they weren't keen on this kind of cross-fertilisation. Nevertheless performing for them was always a good test. If I could win over the punks, I wouldn't have much problem with people who were sitting down to listen to me with tea and biscuits.

My poems got angrier and angrier because I was so eager to get my message across; my community was desperate to be heard, and I wanted to politicise my audience. We were living on the edge, and gigs could turn nasty at times. Sometimes, to get into gigs, fans would have to run the gauntlet of National Front supporters hanging about outside. The police wouldn't get involved; they would tell us to let things take their course and call them if there was trouble. There was lots of trouble, of course, but by the time the trouble started it was too late to call the police.

There were two informal organisations from that time that I had a great love and respect for: Red Action and the Sari Squad. Both would protect our gigs and events when the police wouldn't. Red Action was almost exclusively young left-wing white kids. Their politics were all over place. I remember two of them having a big argument about what Karl Marx did or didn't say, but the one thing they were united on was their hatred of racism. Then there was the Sari Squad, who were quite incredible. They were a group of Asian women based in east London — each one a wicked kung fu fighter, each one willing to defend their community to the end, and some of them did actually wear saris. They started by guarding women's gigs, but would then guard any gig where fans might need protection from racists.

Both groups deployed themselves like a cross between bouncers and police — they would put a couple of people on the door, others around the building, and then some further away from the event, looking out for any racists or fascists making their way to the venue. If any were seen they would send messages using their then state-of-the-art walkie-talkies, and then go and confront them. There were times when National Front thugs managed to get in to a venue and all hell would break loose. They would smash up equipment and attack artists and audience members, regardless of their size or sex, but most of the time we would chase them off. Red Action and the Sari Squad were life-savers, and I have no doubt that without them the NF and their supporters would have had many more victories than they did.

Performances were part of a mission to recruit militants and make people aware of what was happening on the streets and in the corridors of power. I was aware that, to a certain extent, I was preaching to the converted, but that didn't matter if some of those converted would bring along non-converted friends. I could then encourage the friend to get involved. Very often I would challenge individuals. I would look into the audience and point people out and say, 'You, you and you, are you coming to the demo on Saturday?' They'd invariably say 'Yeah, we're coming.' So I'd give them stuff, like a book, and say: 'Alright then, read this and then give it back on Saturday at the demo.' That way I would know whether they had turned up.

I once promised a girl a kiss; she turned up as I was about to do my anti-Nazi rant in Brockwell Park, so I kissed her on stage in front of the assembled multitudes. The word got round that I was up for such exchanges, and I began to get many similar requests, but I always kissed in public, sometimes with the girl's boyfriend (or girlfriend) present. It was a tough job, but it was all in aid of the revolution.

★ ★ ★

An organiser I often worked with was a brother called Jah Bones, who was also a great personal friend. He was based at an organisation in Tottenham called RUZ, which stood for Rasta Universal Zion. This was a strictly Rasta group, which would hold regular speaking events and publish a newsletter, *The Voice of Rasta*. Bones was a lovely, lovely, really large Rasta elder, whose dreadlocks truly resembled the mane of a lion. I became one of their regular poets but you have to look hard to find me credited in the newsletter or on their posters. Very rarely would they call me Benjamin Zephaniah. It would usually be something like Ras Benjamin, Benji Dread, Zephaniah I, Rasta Zephaniah or even Zephy. I spent a lot of time hanging around Tottenham, where the community would hold cultural events in hired church halls, or in parks on sunny days.

Like the hippies of the 1960s, we really thought we were going to change the world for the better, and at that time I would have said my poems were in aid of the revolution. Poems like 'Dis Policeman Keeps on Kicking Me to Death' or 'I Don't Like Mrs Thatcher' may not have been great examples of creative writing — they were far from what most people would call literature — but they expressed my anger and

172

the anger many others were feeling. Poems like 'Fight Dem Not Me' were written as if to be performed directly to the National Front. I was trying to tell them that I understood what they felt about housing conditions, unemployment, poverty and other social ills, and that we had those problems too. I was urging them to see beyond race and to understand that if working-class people could unite we could then deal with the politicians who were exploiting us all.

★ ★ ★

If you have no understanding of the oral tradition, it's better to think of these poems as songs rather than literature. People would chant along with me to the best known of them. At Rock Against Racism gigs, for instance, or Anti Nazi League events, thousands of people would be jumping up and down, shouting: 'Dis policeman . . . dis policeman . . . dis policeman keeps on kicking me to death'. It was an amazing feeling to see all those people chanting my poems back at me. It was probably more amazing because I was doing it with just words and no music. It was just them and me, with nothing in between. What was even more moving was knowing that many of these poems had never been written down; these were people who followed me from gig to gig to learn the poems, or they picked them up from a friend.

The ability to get so many people to chant your words is a sort of power — a power one could easily manipulate. I've always loved watching those preachers in the United States that have churches like mini-empires, where it seems the audience doesn't just worship God, it worships the preacher too. I don't like them — actually I can't stand them — but their followers are happy to give them their money and, in some extreme cases, their lives. It amazes me what people can do with a bit of charisma and a well-delivered promise of something better than this earthly existence. I'm astonished by such preachers' ability to perform, even when they themselves don't believe the ideas they preach.

When I stand on stage and tell the crowd to shout, or be silent, or 'say after me', and they do, I realise the power we have, even more so when they are connecting with an idea I had one day when I was doing something as arbitrary as getting dressed. I've never thought of myself as someone with my own manifesto. I've never wanted to start a political party or launch any kind of movement. I want to inform people about what's going on, and I don't mind throwing in a few suggestions as to what can be done, but most of all I want to inspire people to think for themselves. Even if I say something in my poetry that I believe to be fact, I say it because I want them to think about it and not simply take my word for it. Power can easily be abused, but I've never been interested in that kind of power, or the abuse of it.

Having said all that, there was a time when, mainly to shock people (who needed shocking), I would say that I'd started a revolutionary movement called the IRA — the Independent Rasta Army.

24

Babylon's Burning

Another struggle we had was against the 'sus' laws, or the law of suspicion. Police officers could arrest you merely if they thought you were suspicious. She or he didn't need a witness or a victim, a complaint or an order from above — an officer just needed to not like the way you looked and you could be arrested. It was supposed to be used for crime prevention, but the police used it as a way to discriminate against our community, and they didn't hide the fact that they used it in a racist way. I remember one officer saying that, as far as he was concerned, every Rastafarian was suspicious. If he wasn't wearing a hat and his locks were out, he was probably high on marijuana, and if he was wearing a hat, he was probably concealing a gun up there.

I'm proud to say I took part in political actions against this law. Yes, I did a few awareness-raising concerts and performances at demonstrations but, it has to be said, our most effective action was rioting. But we didn't call it rioting; we called it uprising.

In 1981 uprisings spread across the UK, and I travelled all over the country to be a part of the action. In St Paul's, Bristol, in Brixton, London, in Toxteth, Liverpool, in Chapeltown, Leeds, in

Handsworth, Birmingham, and many more towns in many more cities, people had had enough of the injustice, racism and subjugation that was entrenched in police and state.

Tensions between the black community and the police had been a fact of life from the mid-1970s (well, they had been a fact of *my* life since then), but black history tells us they went back way before then — to the Notting Hill riots of 1958, for example — but when my generation rose up in the early '80s, the whole country sat up and took notice. The soundtrack of 1981 was provided by the Specials, who had a number-one hit with the brilliant 'Ghost Town' — and it still sounds fresh over thirty-five years later.

My first major uprising could be seen coming very clearly months in advance. The police would drive around London in SPG (Special Patrol Group) vans, shouting insults and taunting us. Or they would stop their vans then surround and search us. One night, I was in Coldharbour Lane, Brixton, and I heard somebody shout that the talking was over; the time had come for war. We were playing pool in the Atlantic, the big pub on the corner of Railton Road, when we heard some commotion. Somebody ran in and shouted, 'Man! Babylon's burning!' So we went out and were soon caught up in it.

The frontline in Brixton was a community under siege. There was corrugated iron every-where, poor housing, and something like 50 per cent of black youth was unemployed. Constant police harassment and Thatcher (along with the then Home Secretary, the aptly named William Whitelaw) talking about people feeling 'swamped' only ratcheted up the tension.

I still have a very strong sense of the smell of that uprising. I wrote a poem with the line: 'Bonfire night in the middle of summer; fireworks smell like burning rubber'. And that's what I remember — the smell. And the sound of the police sirens, which were different back then — more of a drone and not as high-pitched as they are now.

The air was hot and sticky and the youth were out on the streets arming themselves with bricks. There were so many of us. I remember wondering where all these young people had come from. They just appeared. In those days, if you walked past another black person, you tended to nod to each other. It was like an unspoken knowledge that in the future you might need to rely on that person. Well, that time had come. There was no question over whose side you were on; and in an uprising you found yourself working in co-operation with someone you'd never met before.

There was real solidarity. Me and another guy rescued a youth from the clutches of the police. They almost got me, but there was so much excitement going on that I evaded capture. I got hit in the mouth by another guy aiming at a cop, who immediately apologised, saying, 'Sorry, brother.' Basically, when you're in the thick of it you don't analyse it, but looking back it was about venting years and years of pent-up anger.

People in the media would have their cosy debates in TV studios, not understanding the reality of life on the frontline. We were angry; we wanted to hit back at Babylon and burn it down. Some people asked, 'Why downtown?' as in, 'Why riot in our own neighbourhoods?' The truth is we had nowhere else to go. The police had come to us using constant intimidation tactics and racism, and those areas of those cities where the uprisings happened were our space. We couldn't say, 'We're gonna pool a load of people together and go to another part of the city' — uprisings are not organised like that. If Babylon was going to come into our area, using state-sanctioned brutality, we were going to fight back. People were sick of being beaten down, beaten up and picked on.

When I look at what people have to put up with from their governments, I'm surprised they don't rise up more often. When you live in a community under pressure, where the living is hard and the policing racist and uneven, you can feel the tension build and build, and it can take just one incident for it all to kick off. The most recent uprising in August 2011 started because of police being cleared of shooting dead yet another black man, but it quickly descended into looting. I never looted, but I can see how disadvantaged and unpoliticised young people might see an uprising as a chance to accumulate stuff any which way they can, especially if it has a label on it. I think it's all part of the legacy of Thatcherite greed — the privileged class will do their tax swindles and shady banking but the people on the streets, that's their version of it.

But back in the 1980s, after all the times we'd

been stopped and searched and slapped in the face by the police, this was our opportunity to let it all out. We wanted to get back; we wanted to vent our anger. After the riots of April 1981 the government was forced to set up an inquiry, which was headed by Lord Scarman — a judge and fully signed-up member of the establishment — who found that the sus law, and the way we were being stopped and searched, were just two of the contributory factors that caused the uprisings.

We had to rise up. Conversations and inquiries weren't going to do it; debates on television and paying educated black people to tell us to calm down weren't going to do it; we had to protest, and take 'actions' on the street to get this law abolished, so that's what we did, and that's how we won.

We rose up again in September 1985 after police shot Cherry Groce in her home in Brixton. They were trying to arrest her son, my friend Michael Groce, on firearms charges. Michael wasn't there when they raided, but the way they brutalised his mother meant that she was left crippled and spent the rest of her days in a wheelchair. When this uprising started I was in the East End, but the message got to me via some political activists.

A couple of friends and I jumped into a car and drove to Brixton. We were stopped on the way by police who said we couldn't go any further, so we parked the car and went by underground. In order not to bring attention to ourselves, we bought return tickets, but when we reached Brixton station the ticket office had been abandoned. As soon as we hit the streets the police hit us, and we resisted.

On another occasion I was arrested and taken in for questioning before I was able to reach the frontline. The police said they had intelligence and they knew that I knew who had organised the riot (their words). I didn't know, of course, and the uprising was not organised, but as a way of making me talk a policeman put me in the corridor and said, 'Would you wait there for a moment, please?' Then these other policemen came past and, one by one, they stamped on my feet. It was torture; they would say things like, 'Sorry, young man' or 'I didn't smell your feet there', but every one of them did it.

At one point I saw a woman coming towards me in civilian clothes and I thought she must be a probation officer or a visiting magistrate. She looked so innocent, so I thought she wouldn't do anything, but then, *crunch*, her stiletto came down on my toes. It hurt more than the men's shoes and, unlike the men, she stayed in position for a while and twisted her heel. She looked right at me and said, 'Is it true what they say about the size of men's feet?' and 'Is it true what they say about the size of black men's feet?' I could hear the other officers laughing in rooms off the corridor. I stayed silent.

She went, and a few minutes later I was called into the interview room and was asked if I was ready to talk. I couldn't talk, I knew nothing, but every time they stepped on my toes or slapped my face I stored up the anger and, when they let me out, I went downtown and let all that anger out.

The problem was that the more 'famous' I got, the less I could actually do. One night in Brixton a policeman was coming towards me; he had pulled out his truncheon and his whole demeanor told me he didn't want to stop for a chat. I looked around for a brick or some kind of weapon with which to defend myself, but there was nothing, and then he shouted, 'What are you going to do now, read a poem to me?' At that moment I realised that when it came to actions on the streets I had to know my limitations and understand that I couldn't disappear into the night anymore.

25

The New Variety

I did many gigs at North East London Polytechnic, or NELP, as it was called then, but one was memorable for two reasons. The first was that the guy who was supposed to pay me disappeared with my money. He also disappeared with the door money, the cloakroom money, the beer money and the money of my supporting artists. And second, I met Roland Muldoon. He sat me down and told me about an idea he had. He wanted to get away from all the bullshit that other comedians were doing at the time, with their racist, sexist, mother-in-law gags, and he wanted to create something new. He called it New Variety.

He told me he had a pool of people to work with, among them Dawn French, Jennifer Saunders and Tony Allen. The a cappella group The Flying Pickets were also in, at least a year before they had their number-one hit. Then there was Arthur Smith, Ade Edmondson, Alexi Sayle and Rik Mayall. Another performer was Pauline Melville, who went on to become a respected novelist. These comedians were already performing in the Comedy Store in central London, but Roland wanted to get them into the working-class areas of London. I listened to him telling me all this and I thought, *This is a great idea, but he could just be mad*. It turned out to be a great idea, and he was mad, but we did it.

On a New Variety bill there would be a wide range of performers, each performing for 20–25 minutes. We would all get on stage and do our own slots, and sometimes we would combine. In July 1982, when Michael Fagan climbed into the Queen's bedroom and woke her up to ask for a cigarette, me and Pauline Melville did our take on it. She played the Queen and I played the intruder, but I was looking for a spliff and a little conversation.

These were big gigs in great venues and my slot usually followed the comedians. The audiences were really open-minded, so it was great to be part of another artistic movement where we all had similar ideas. There were no gags about blacks, Englishmen, Irishmen and Scotsmen going into pubs; no jokes where women were called 'birds' or 'her indoors'; in fact, we poked fun at the people who told those jokes, and of course, at the political establishment.

The people on the New Variety circuit were a breath of fresh air. A year or two earlier, when I'd been in the bookshop, I was surrounded by people who'd read books and were full of ideas. There was a lesbian, or maybe two; there was a gay guy, or maybe three; a Jewish guy (or a guy that said he was Jewish), and a few black folk. We all talked about our experiences and the books we'd read, and we went on marches together, but with the New Variety family I felt that we came together to express ourselves politically through creating and not just reading. We were bringing the words to life and influencing one another. No one was trying to outdo anyone; there was no competition; we didn't care who headlined, we just did whatever would make the show work and, backstage, well, there you could feel the love.

Roland Muldoon was, by his own estimation, militant. He was anti-police, anti-establishment and anti any authority. He was always smoking a spliff and wearing a hat, and would talk to me for ages about where to find the best weed. He was also part of a theatre group called CAST — he and his wife Claire told me it stood for the Campaign Against Shakespearian Theatre. One of his plays was called *Sedition*, with the subtitle *Living off an Arts Council Grant*. He'd actually got an Arts Council grant and had to write a play to justify it, but he didn't know what to write, so he bought some weed with the money. When he (and the company, I guess) had smoked the weed, he wrote a play about smoking the weed. He'd done another play where they'd chopped off the Queen's head. I don't know where he got the money for that, but it wouldn't surprise me if was from the Prince's Trust . . .

Like most poets, my work went through different stages. There was a time when it was more about the ranting than the work itself. Ranting punk poets like Steven Wells (aka Swells), Porky the Poet (aka Phil Jupitus) and Attila the Stockbroker had the ability to perform at a fast pace and not lose the audience.

Alongside them was a movement of radical black poets, whose main source of inspiration was reggae, and they were called dub poets. I could rant as well as I could dub, and because I was able to cross over so well and perform to both audiences it was very natural to call my first EP *Dub Ranting*.

26

That First Album

I recorded *Dub Ranting* with a small label called Radical Wallpaper, run by Red Saunders. As well as being a founding member of Rock Against Racism, he was also a well-known left-wing operator, photographer, dedicated anti-racist and someone who could get things done. He stood out at gigs; he would come on stage in a bright boiler suit and introduce the acts, but again it wasn't just about introducing the bands; it was also about reminding people of the cause.

He wanted to record some of us ranting poets, so he signed Swells, Attila the Stockbroker and me. I can't actually remember signing anything — we just trusted each other. *Dub Ranting* was mainly poems, with only one track that was a poem with percussion accompaniment. It was recorded by the well-known, soon-to-be-legendary south London reggae producer Mad Professor. The recording didn't really capture the way the poems were performed at gigs, but it still worked.

Around this time I met a guy called Spartacus R. He'd had minor fame as the bass player in the Afro-funk band Osibisa, and was once a friend of Eddy Grant's, but he didn't really make it. He tried going solo, but that didn't work out either, and by all accounts he became a little bitter. He started doing a one-man-band thing, with bells around his ankles and his guitar in his hands. We started hanging out and doing a few gigs together, and soon he became my informal manager. One day we went into a small studio and recorded a musical version of 'Dis Policeman Keeps on Kicking Me to Death' — the poem that'd had the crowd joining in at the Anti Nazi League gigs.

It was just a little version for ourselves but it ended up on a tape for the massively influential music paper the NME (New Musical Express), which was putting out compilation cassettes of indie recording artists. The cassette was called Racket Packet and it went out in '83. John Peel heard it and asked me to go into the BBC studio and record a session for him. So we did. We were given a date for the broadcast of the poem, then on the night we waited and waited but it wasn't played. When I contacted John Peel he told me it wasn't his fault and I should talk to his producer, John Walters. When I got John Walters on the phone he told me that it wasn't played because I'd said the word 'fucking' in the middle of the poem. I argued with both John Peel and John Walters, saying it was always in the poem and nothing had changed since they'd first heard it, so it was crazy for them to now say they couldn't broadcast it. It didn't matter what I said, they weren't going to play it, and they never did. That tape must still be hidden in a BBC vault somewhere.

Despite our initial disagreement, John Peel and I became good friends. He thought what I did was in a world of its own, and would always advertise (or plug) my performances before they happened, and after the gigs he would always ask me how I'd got on. One night, as I was driving to a gig in Harlow organised by Attila the Stockbroker, I was listening to John on the radio doing his gig guide. He mentioned my gig and said he hoped that I would get on all right there and get home safely. He sounded really concerned, which made me worry. I began to wonder what kind of a place Harlow was.

It turned out to be a great gig, with one of those moments on stage I would never forget. Attila introduced me and, as I arrived on stage to a roar from the crowd, they were right with me and I was ready to give it to them. The first poem I was going to perform was 'African Swing', so I said to the crowd, 'I'd like to dedicate this first poem to the all the Africans in the audience.' Suddenly the place fell silent, everyone looked around to see if there was an African in the house, but not one could be seen. Attila looked at me, smiled, and the audience burst into spontaneous laughter. I later reported to John Peel that it all went well, but it was nice to know he was concerned about me.

★   ★   ★

I was soon approached by record labels asking me to record a whole album, or LP, as they were called back then. The biggest offer came from EMI. One of their A&R people came to see me. He offered me a lot of money but he wasn't sure how to deal with me; he said they wanted to give me studio machinery, like drum machines, and I was to go away and work on some tracks, which would be recorded later, but he didn't seem to know what my poetry was about. I had the feeling that someone had sat at a desk, read about me and sent this man out to offer me a deal.

There were other offers, but one label stood out above the others. This was Upright Records. They were probably the smallest label that had approached me, but I immediately took to the owner — a bearded family man called Bill Gilliam. He ran two labels, Upright Records and Workers' Playtime, which had names contracted to it like Dead on Arrival (aka DOA), Jello Biafra and the reggae duo Laurel and Hardy. Bill offered me a deal and, to everyone's surprise, I chose him over the others. I liked the intimacy of the label, and I liked the other bands on it, plus Bill had been watching me as I'd developed and we had a similar political outlook. Although he was offering the smallest financial deal, he seemed to be the most sympathetic to my ideas and what I was doing.

When it came to recording the album, I wanted to do something different. I wanted to use two producers so we could work as a team. I had never heard of anyone doing this before. If an album was credited with two producers, one of them would be a band member, but I had this idea that I would bring people together on the project to move away from the common reggae sound that was around at the time.

I approached Spartacus R and asked him to

work with me on the album with another producer, and he said, 'Absolutely not.' He said he wanted to do it on his own or he would walk away. I tried to convince him to stay on board but he refused to work with anyone else, so I told him to walk away. He then told me that if he wasn't working on the album, then I couldn't use the track 'Dis Policeman Keeps on Kicking Me to Death', at which point I laughed, but so did he, telling me that the track belonged to him.

I did some research and found that he was partly right. This was a lesson I learned the hard way, and I tell young people about it as often as I can. How it happened was that when John Peel asked me to do the session for him, Spartacus R was producing the track and was therefore also taking care of the paperwork. This was at a time when, for the first time in my life, I was making a lot of money. I was in a hotel room, living it large with my big entourage, a couple of brothers to back me up, and a few girls to massage my aches and my ego. Spartacus R came into the room and said I had to sign some paperwork for the John Peel session. I was in front of my crew; I didn't want them to see that I couldn't read or understand the contract, so I made it look like I knew what I was doing and signed it. I didn't know then that I was signing away some of the rights to my own creation.

So my message to young artists is that if you feel you don't need to be able to read to rap or bang out a tune, the bottom line is you should at least be able to read your contract. When I recorded the track, for legal reasons I had to credit Spartacus R with some of the writing, which is odd. I remember once challenging him by saying, 'If you have any part in writing that track, then perform it for me, just a bit of it.' And he couldn't. That track, in fact that album, keeps selling, but every time I get a royalty statement next to 'Dis Policeman . . . ', I see his name, and it doesn't feel good.

★ ★ ★

The album I recorded with Upright Records, my first full album, was called *Rasta*. I ended up producing it myself because I didn't want to repeat the experience I'd had with Spartacus R. What I did find out was that even if Spartacus R wanted to work with me, nobody wanted to work with him, such was his reputation in musical circles for being difficult. All the tracks on the album were ones I had been playing for a long time. I would write the words and then, with a basic idea for the bassline, I would jam with a few friends — people I'd got to know since moving to London, who shared my view of the world.

Most of these jam sessions happened at the flat of a friend called Jerome. The block of council flats where he lived is no longer there, but I remember the place so well: number 111, on floor 11, Drinkwater Tower, at the top of Leytonstone High Road, east London. An informal gathering of musicians would hang out there, and we would play a few tunes, philosophise for an hour or so, play some more tunes, and then philosophise some more. It should never have worked, really, because me and Jerome were both bass players, but this was all about love. He played some, I played some and, as long as Jah was happy, we were happy. As it turned out, Jerome kept playing the bass and I didn't, but he was always a much better player than me.

I wanted my jamming regulars to contribute to the album. Angela Parkinson was a long-time girlfriend, a good organiser (well, she organised me) and a reasonably good singer. Patsy was Angela's friend, and an even better singer. Together they were known as the Sisters of Rant. Steve Parkinson was Angela's brother, and a great drummer, and Tony Ash (aka Tony 'Ganja' Ash) had been my long-time collaborator. I couldn't play rhythm guitar, but I could hear what I wanted in my head and then mimic the sound. Tony was always able to recreate that exactly, but in the studio something very strange happened.

I called Jerome in — it seemed the obvious thing to do, as he knew my tunes inside out, and he knew most of the other musicians I was using. He put on the headphones, began to play . . . and couldn't. He tried and tried, then he tried again, but he couldn't feel the vibe. I could feel his frustration, and I'm sure he could feel mine. He was downhearted and shocked. We could only put it down to the studio environment; it was the first time he had been in one. Just like singing in the bath is different from singing in front of a microphone, jamming with your friends, and even playing live, is very different from playing in a studio. You are in a room, alone, with headphones on. It doesn't feel natural.

After two days, I had to say, 'Sorry, man, I really want you on the album, but every hour is costing me money and, let's face it, it's not happening.' He agreed and bowed out graciously and, because I knew the basslines to every track, I took over and played on the whole album. Bass players tell me they look up to that performance of mine, but I've never played on any of my recordings since, and I never intend to; I much prefer to pay for a real bass player's imagination.

The *Rasta* album was one of the few examples of recorded dub poetry in existence. There weren't many of us who had gone into the studio. Linton Kwesi Johnson — the best-known dub poet, and some would say the father of our movement — had recorded, so had Mutabaruka and Jean 'Binta' Breeze, but that was about it. Dub music was all about taking reggae, breaking it down to its minimal elements and adding sound effects — what clubbers went on to call a remix. Then the dub poet would speak on top of the music. Dub poetry combined words and music, but if there was no music the dub poet simply used her or his own sense of rhythm to make the verses ebb and flow.

To me, music and the spoken word are indivisible. With the album, I took the concept a little further. The foundations were reggae but I also used a sitar player and an oboist, alongside a mandolin player and African drummers. Many years later, one music journalist said it was the first 'world music' album, not because it came from somewhere exotic but because the instruments and musicians came from all over the world. But then again, who's ever listened to music journalists?

27

Solidarity

I'm proud to say that I was involved in one of the biggest British political events of the last century: the miners' strike. The strike lasted for just under a year, from March 1984 until March 1985, and was a defining event in British industrial relations. Margaret Thatcher targeted the mining industry to try to break the powerful National Union of Mineworkers (NUM). Ten years previously, industrial action by the NUM had contributed to the downfall of the Conservative government led by Edward Heath, so she had them in her sights and was determined to destroy them.

Before the strike I don't think I'd ever met a miner, I'm sure I'd never seen a coalpit, and I'd certainly never heard of Arthur Scargill, the leader of the NUM, but all that changed the moment I understood how the future of mining families would be torn apart as mines — and therefore mining villages — were closed down.

Roland and other promoters organised benefit gigs around the UK to support the striking miners — many of whom, by the winter of 1984, were going hungry. Creative people were lending their skills to the cause, and a whole army of performers were willing to go wherever they were sent. I was one of them.

As part of my miners' solidarity work, I agreed to do a gig in a working men's club in Scotland. As I walked in, I noticed the women were on one side of the room, talking about children and baking cakes, while the men were on the other side drinking beer. The children were just playing. A man who looked as if he had just come from below ground said, 'Oh, the poet's here.'

He checked the microphone for me and the men began to leave, the idea being that I would entertain the women and the children with my nursery rhymes while the men went and did manly things. Halfway into my first poem I noticed the men slowly coming back. They stood and listened. When I had done that first poem, they all clapped, and one of them said, 'Bloody hell, this guy's good, order some more beer.' They did, and then they sat down and listened to me.

At another gig in a Nottinghamshire mining village, I got on stage and some of the miners in the audience started shouting racist remarks. One said he wanted to know what a black guy was doing talking to miners; some of his workmates agreed with him, shouting out stupid jokes about golliwogs, but one miner jumped on stage and stood next to me, and he really had a go at them. He delivered a diatribe against racism and urged working-class people to stick together, pointing out that I was the person who in the previous week had sent them a donation of £1,500 (a lot of money in those days) from an

African-Caribbean association, and they, the miners, were happy to take the money and feed their kids. He stressed that this money had come from mainly elderly Caribbean people living in a poor part of east London, but they had gone round and collected money for the miners to show solidarity with them, and to help them to victory.

He told them how I had been travelling around the country doing benefit performances, and that on that very night I was performing without a fee or expenses. The mood of the hall changed immediately as they realised how wrong they were. Then I did a great gig. That type of thing happened from time to time, but I was always able to deal with it by letting them know I had come a long way and that I hadn't travelled the length and breadth of the country to hear racist remarks or fight against people I should be fighting with.

The miners' strike changed white men's attitudes to black people; it changed men's attitudes to women, and women's attitudes to men. A lot of the miners' wives stopped being people whose only domain was the kitchen; they were no longer subservient or beholden to their alpha male husbands — they became organisers, they became union workers, they were empowered.

The miners realised they couldn't win the fight on their own; they needed the solidarity of their wives, black poets, Chinese chefs and Bengali factory workers. They needed all the help they could get, and we were all the help they could get. Alas, even with us they lost, but those who were involved in that strike, many of whom were not even miners, will never forget the picket line battles, the workers' solidarity, the lessons learned through struggle and the dark forces of police and state that were unleashed upon those workers. And those women will never be the same again.

28

To the Art of the Struggle

I was fired up with creativity; it was running through every vein in my body. I had completely put my life of crime behind me, and instead of focusing on making money I wanted to make revolution. In London I could have got into even worse trouble — the gangsters down there were much more gangster than the gangsters of Birmingham — but now I had changed the type of gang I mixed with. We are pack animals, so it's natural to mix with people of a like mind. Gangs are not only made up of young people hanging out on the street, those who follow a particular type of music or ride motorbikes. The most dangerous gangs are made up of politicians. They call themselves 'parties', and the problem is, when they argue among themselves they send people who are nothing like them to fight for them. I could operate on my own reasonably well, but now I was dropping it with gangs of people who were speaking out against injustice, and using poetry, music, performance or painting to convey their feelings.

From time to time I'd hear news from my former life, usually about someone dying or going to jail for a long time, which would remind me that I got out just in time. I was convinced that if I had stayed I would have died. Even though I had an album in the shops, plenty of gigs under my belt, some legitimate money coming in, and people were calling me the new rock and roll, I was still angry. I really felt I had failed.

My biggest failure was that Nelson Mandela was not free, Palestine and East Timor were not free, and the people of the Chagos Islands still wanted to go home. I felt it was my personal responsibility to free the world. I don't know where that feeling came from, maybe I put it upon myself, but I was continually saying, 'We are not free until our family are free.' I took Mandela's incarceration personally. My intensity didn't always go down well, and I probably lost a few girlfriends because of my inability to focus on relationships, but I couldn't turn my political button off, and so I didn't allow myself to have too much fun. I was living and breathing politics; it was all-consuming.

My public performances were coinciding with the fact that apartheid was beginning to be understood and hated around the world. Every weekend there would be a demonstration about it somewhere in the UK. My performances worked in between political speakers just as well as they worked in between bands, and I had a real sense that my poetry had arrived at the right time. People needed someone to express their anger at injustice and racism without then going on to ask them to vote for him.

I didn't see apartheid as an exclusively African problem; it was the unofficial reality for many black people around the world, and even for people like me living in England. I lived in east London, and although I was able to walk around Stratford, Mile End, Walthamstow and Leytonstone, I couldn't cross the line and go to Canning Town or Barking, as these were known National Front strongholds — not only in the political sense, in that the NF were standing in elections there, but in the real sense that groups of these thugs would violently attack black people whenever they had the chance. They would sometimes make incursions into what we considered our territories, and we would defend ourselves and send them home, but crossing the dual carriage way known as the A13 meant risking our lives.

I was so keen to see what this mystical thugland called Canning Town was like that I once asked a white taxi driver to drive me through it, but he wouldn't. I offered him double the fare but he still wouldn't take me. He said he didn't care about me, and he wasn't worried about my safety, but he was worried about his own. If certain people saw him with me he wouldn't be able to work anymore, and he risked his house being torched.

In 1980 a young Asian man called Akhtar Ali Baig had been murdered by a group of racists on the streets of East Ham, not far from the A13. The police, the local authority and the media thought this murder of little importance, and the family of the murdered youth didn't know where to go for help. There were marches and protests on the streets of east London, but that wasn't enough. So a group of people got together to form the Newham Monitoring Project. I admired this organisation so much that after getting involved with many of their campaigns I became their patron.

When the Newham Monitoring Project was originally set up, our job was to monitor the many racist attacks happening in our area, and see how the police were responding to them, but we then noticed a lot of them were actually being perpetrated by the police. Our remit broadened to helping families of victims, getting legal representation for those who needed it. We had a 24-hour emergency helpline, and we also policed the police.

A lot of the far left of the time were active within unions and supporting strikers, but more could have been done to take their principles to people who weren't organising in their work-place. For instance, we'd see them selling their newspapers at train stations on Saturday mornings, but they'd soon be gone — most likely to the pub to talk about Karl Marx. Then I'd go to somewhere like Bethnal Green and find that the NF were setting up youth clubs and pensioners' groups. They were saying, 'Nobody cares about you, but we do.' So you'd get all these kids going, 'Yeah, National Front. They're standing up for the white man.' The far right was penetrating communities where the left wing should have been.

If you tried to tell people in other parts of Britain about the blatant racism we were suffering, plenty would not believe you. They might have heard about such things in the news but many thought these were exaggerations, or that savage black youth deserved what they got because they were all thieves, pimps and drug pushers, and if they weren't, then they were still doing what Margaret Thatcher had said they were doing — swamping the country with an alien culture.

Some actually knew how brutal it was for us, but they turned a blind eye to police brutality, discrimination and racism because they believed that it could never be as bad as in some of those foreign places. It was very bad for us, but the government-sponsored racism of apartheid South Africa was of a higher order. It represented the extremes of what could happen. There were times when, after speaking up for Nelson Mandela and doing benefits for the ANC, the British press and other commentators called me a communist and a supporter of terrorism, but then, during the 1980s, it became very fashionable for educated people to support the anti-apartheid movement. The image of Mandela behind prison bars became a popular symbol, so popular it was on car windows and refrigerators, and people started making records and speaking out. Mandela had quickly gone (after many years of resistance) from dangerous terrorist to the most loveable political prisoner in the world.

★ ★ ★

Around this time I got serious about trying to brush up my reading and writing. Ken Livingstone played a big part in that by setting up easy-access adult education services during his time as leader of the Greater London Council (GLC). My classes cost only £1. I was immediately tested for dyslexia, and the woman who ran the test was the first person in my life to properly explain why I had been having trouble with literacy. Her explanation made sense and, from gaining an awareness of the condition, I was able to overcome it. Nowadays the government has indirectly abolished those services, imposing huge budget cuts on councils and closing down the libraries where such courses would take place.

After she'd effectively destroyed the miners, Thatcher's next target was the GLC, which she abolished in 1986, making thousands of people redundant and obliterating countless community initiatives and resources that acted as a safety net for London's disadvantaged people. With the help of the Tory press in the form of the *Sun* and the *Daily Mail*, the right wing were able to drip-feed propaganda about the 'loonie left' spending rate-payers' money on ventures they deemed too militant — such as anti-racism concerts or language classes teaching English as a second language. The monetisation of everything was underway and our struggle against the Thatcherite mindset was relentless.

29

The Dread Affair

1985, the year of the Cherry Groce uprising, was also memorable for a couple of other reasons. My book *The Dread Affair* was published — although it was my second book, it was my first with a big publisher — and I also became a star in the Eastern bloc.

The Dread Affair came about after I was approached by a woman who worked for a publishing company called Arena. They wanted to produce a collection of my poems, and they would give me a real contract and a substantial advance. I didn't have a manager, so Arena explained to me that if I signed their contract I'd get my advance, and when I delivered the manuscript I'd get paid a second time, and then, on the day of publication, I'd get my final payment.

I signed on the dotted line there and then and went away to write down all my work as best as I could, by hand. It was easy; I had years of poems in my head. I went back the next day, showed them the contract and the results and, eager to get my payment, I said, 'Right, that's two thirds of my money now due.'

They wrote me a cheque and they published my poems but I think they, and I, made a big mistake. The book was well received but I think it was detrimental to me artistically. Arena published the poems just like that — no editing, no revisions, no feedback. Looking back now, I needed an editor — someone to help me think about how the poems could work on the page. All I did was write down performance poems, but 'stage to page' doesn't always work.

I soon ended up not liking *The Dread Affair*, which is a sad thing to say about one's own book, but I have to be honest: it's a book of poems that lacks poetry, and it could have been so different. It reads like a first draft, or worse. I'm writing this in 2017, and all my other books are still in print, but not *The Dread Affair*. I have been asked to republish it but I keep saying no. As a compromise I have taken some poems from the book and rewritten them, but that's as far as I'll go.

I was later told by an ex-employee of Arena why they had published the book in its raw state. They thought I was some kind of god — the god of dub poetry — and they wouldn't dare tell a god how to edit his poems. They were scared that if they told me something I didn't like, they'd get a bad reaction and I wouldn't let them publish the book. So they left me to my own devices. I'm sure I would have written a far better book if I had received some feedback or criticism, or had someone to talk to.

*   *   *

All this time there was something hanging over my head. The police were still looking for me. I expected them to catch up with me at any time. I couldn't understand why they hadn't arrested me yet. I was arguing with police officers all the time on demonstrations, my books were everywhere and I was regularly on television. I could only put it down to a lack of communication between different police forces.

I would appear live on Channel 4, and I so feared being arrested that once the programme was done I would leave the studio straight away and run like mad. But the fear was getting to me. I knew I couldn't go on like this. So I went back to Birmingham and gave myself up, but they wouldn't arrest me. They said they had enjoyed watching me on TV, and they could have arrested me any time, but they'd already found the real killer of the man in the car and they knew it wasn't me. They didn't tell me because they enjoyed seeing me in public spaces, knowing I was living in a state of paranoia.

Actually, by now, I was living quite contentedly in another housing co-op place in Ruskin Avenue, East Ham. I wasn't at home very often, as I was constantly creating new music and being active in the political protest movement, but Mum was still with me and life was throwing opportunities my way.

30

The Empire Strikes Back

One day Roland Muldoon came to me with an idea. He had seen a building he thought would be perfect to revamp as a home for alternative comedy away from the centre of London. It was called the Hackney Empire. Although it had once been a notable venue where music hall stars such as Marie Lloyd and Charlie Chaplin performed, by the mid-1980s it was being used a bingo hall.

I went along to see it. The first fifteen rows were being used by the bingo people but the rest of the building was gathering dust. It was owned by the games company Mecca, and it was obvious they weren't sure what to do with it. Roland was excited, and so we formed a company with me as the chairman and put in a bid for the building, which was under threat of demolition. After going to and fro for a few months and pushing some papers around, we did a deal. We bought it for a token price — I think it was £1 — but we were committed to paying the rates and raising the money needed to restore it. We wanted to make Hackney Empire the home of New Variety. The Theatre Royal in Stratford was good at connecting to people in its community but we wanted Hackney to achieve even more.

The building had been left in a terrible condition: the seats needed replacing, structural work was required and the top gallery needed complete refurbishment. So we started fundraising and putting together plans to restore it to good order. After a long campaign that won the hearts of the public and local people, we opened.

I was occupied for much of the time with practical matters, like overseeing the building work. In some ways the organisation was similar to the collectives I'd been a part of. It was run by a great group of people who were dedicated to providing excellent egalitarian entertainment. Many of the performers who played there were about to break into public awareness as huge stars, including Ben Elton, Dawn French and Jennifer Saunders, Paul Merton, Julian Clary and Harry Enfield, whose character 'Loadsamoney' perfectly lampooned the brash and greedy attitudes of the era.

I only played there a couple of times. I didn't play there more than that because I didn't want to abuse my position as chairman. I got my satisfaction from knowing that the theatre belonged to the people and served the community with a diverse range of acts and performances. It was always a struggle to keep it going, but it survived against the odds and maintains its place in London working-class history, showcasing everything from community choirs to panto.

31

The Yugoslavian Affair

In keeping with what was becoming a very interesting and at times bizarre life, I became big in Yugoslavia. My poems became anthems and my *Rasta* album really took off there. Initially the Yugoslavs imported copies, but then I was contacted directly by a guy called Igor, who worked for a local radio station and was a fan of reggae and punk music. In spring 1985 he invited me over to do a one-off concert, and I immediately said yes.

My band then comprised a great bass player called Jeff Merrifield, my ever-faithful guitarist Tony Ash and two backing singers, or backing poets, as I preferred to call them: Deborah Asher and her twin sister, who sang in perfect harmony, as if they had sung together in the womb. Then there was a drummer called Joseph, who on a good day was great but, like so many drummers, was as miserable as sin on others.

I ended up doing everything for that band. I was the writer, front person, manager, stage manager, accountant, travel agent, babysitter and marriage guidance counsellor. When we were rehearsing and preparing for the tour, Igor sent me some money in advance. It was a large amount, half the fee, but I somehow managed to lose it. I called a meeting and told the band. There was a grim look on all of their faces, so I just gave them a grim look back and said, 'I don't want any of you to say anything. If you choose to leave it all to me you should expect that at some point something has to give. You're all stoned and lazy. I've lost the money and that's it.' They couldn't argue with me and off we went to Yugoslavia.

All of the disappointment of the lost money was forgotten when we arrived. The first, and biggest, gig was in Ljubljana. There were thousands and thousands of people. From my view on stage there were people as far as I could see, and it felt great to be alive. To stand on a stage and say 'Yeah' and hear thousands of people shouting 'Yeah' in return is truly awesome. I don't want to get technical, but on a stage like that you have to really control yourself. There is a temptation to shout louder to reach the people at the back and, of course, that's impossible; you have to trust the equipment.

This was also the first big gig in communist Yugoslavia, and it was their first ever reggae gig. People from all over the country went to it; it was their Woodstock. I went back there to do a television show twenty years later; it was a chat show with people phoning in and sharing memories of that day, and I was amazed to hear what people had to say. Many had absconded from the army to get to the gig; hermits came down from the mountains, and one young man said he'd been conceived there. The *Rasta* album had such an impact in the country that, after the tour, it was released by a local label.

Many years later, a long time after the old Yugoslavia collapsed, the album was rereleased. There is also a live recording of the gig that I've been asked to release but I won't. The overall performance on the recording is good, but it didn't start well. The first note we struck was awful and the drummer messed up. I fumed. But on the day the band managed to get it all back together and it was really, really incredible. The atmosphere, that is, not the playing; we only just got away with that.

32

Benjamin Zephaniah and the Wailers

Soon after the Yugoslavian tour I told Bill
Gilliam of Upright Records that I wanted to
record in Jamaica, where there was a proper
reggae vibe. He was happy to back me. Well, all
he had to do was give me the money. Recording
was a completely different proposition back in
those days. There was no such thing as
computerisation or even digital audio tape; you
had to lug 24-track, 10-inch analogue tape reels
around, and I had to be extra careful because
some of those old X-ray machines in airports
would wipe tapes clean.

I'd been visiting the Caribbean frequently
since that first time when I was still living in
Birmingham, being a painter/decorator. More
recently I had been visiting the island to get to
know my grandparents and extended family. I'd
travel to St Elizabeth, about sixty miles outside
of Kingston — and spend time with cousins,
second cousins and third cousins twice removed.
I'd got used to the way of things in Kingston, but
I'd been warned how basic things were in the
countryside — especially the lack of flushing
toilets. It would be the dreaded 'hole in the
ground' and no electricity. After a couple of
trips, I got the whole family to club together and

we installed a flushing toilet; then my family was the talk of the area.

Even in England people with a Kingston heritage would talk about the country folk — the 'red' people. What struck me when I first went to St Elizabeth was the number of people who looked like me, or were even lighter skinned. The black community in the UK is all kinds of shades, but if you go to St Elizabeth it's easy to see how everyone is blended from about ten families, with the majority being 'red'. A few names crop up all the time: Honeyghan (my mother's maiden name), Moxam, Ebanks.

When I first saw the way they had to live, I realised how it could so easily have been me. I'd hang out with my mum's sisters' boys, who were the same age as me. Next time I'd go back and ask for them and be told, 'Oh, him dead in a hurricane' or 'Him go fishing and never come back.'

When I look at the people I'm related to in JA, who've made it to my age, there are only a few left. Women tend to fare a little better, as they aren't on the high seas or so exposed to the elements. One of my female cousins has owned a little corner store since she was about eighteen. Many become midwives, learning on the job, as used to be the way in the UK.

On this visit to the Caribbean, I was also going to Barbados before I went to Jamaica. I had decided to go and see my dad. I didn't really know him, I hadn't seen him for years, but he had retired there after being told by his doctor that he had only a year to live. He emptied his bank account, withdrew his pension, and six years later I felt I had to go and make peace with him.

When I first arrived in Barbados, customs officers took me aside and quizzed me about drugs, saying, 'You're well dressed.' At that time Rastas were taken in by the police and made to cut their hair and all sorts. But after holding me a while they let me go. The airport was quiet and my dad was waiting outside. When one of the airport staff saw us together, she said, 'Oswald, it your son, dis? You never said you had a son that is a *Rasta*!'

For the first time in my life I enjoyed my time with him. He seemed younger. Every day he went for a dip in the sea, and he was happily entertaining three girlfriends. He had a Ford sports car with the wildest sounding horn I had ever heard, and he spent a lot of time and energy trying to find a girl for me to have sex with. I spent a lot of time and energy telling him that I didn't feel the urge and I just wanted to hang out with my dad, but he didn't see the sense in that.

He set me up with one girl who said she would give me the sweet thing if I went to church with her. I told her that my body is my temple and she should come to my church, then she called me a Jamaican devil and threatened to kill me. Every now and again he would want to talk about Mum, but in the most negative way, so I kept telling him to shut up and let bygones be bygones. I had to do that to agree to visit him in the first place.

I'd always known him as this very conservative

guy, and there I was telling him to control himself. It was like returning to Barbados had given him a new lease of life. At one point the island had the most up-to-date telephone system of any Caribbean nation, and my dad was one of the people who sorted that out, from his time with the GPO, so he was well known. I considered the idea that he must have felt he had to act strait-laced when he came England — stiff upper lip and all that. He was certainly making up for lost time, especially where women were concerned.

⋆ ⋆ ⋆

I left Barbados and landed in Jamaica in summer 1986, where I wanted to work with the legend known as Burning Spear, but when I went to his house in St Anne's I found he was away touring in the USA. With no Burning Spear I decided to go and see the mighty Fred Locks, who I'd always admired. Fred Locks was a Rastaman who had given up on the material world and lived in a cave near a beach. He had a reputation for living very naturally, and although he made one of the best reggae albums of all time, he wasn't that interested in the music business. I couldn't find him either, so I was racking my brains about who to approach next.

I was staying in the house of a well-known Canadian-Jamaican woman called Honor Ford-Smith, who was involved in an all-woman theatre group called Sistren, who toured around Jamaica. She lived in Stony Hill, a leafy mountain on the outskirts of Kingston, along with another woman called Hilary. One day they sat me down to talk about my plans. They knew that my search for a producer and backing musicians wasn't going too well — everyone was either away on tour or meditating in the hills. Suddenly, out of the blue, Hilary said, 'Hey, Benjamin, why don't you work with the Wailers?'

'Are you joking?' I asked.

'No,' she said, 'they would like you.'

I was doubtful. The Wailers were the best reggae band in the world and I was just a street poet from Birmingham with a few extra fans in Yugoslavia; they wouldn't want to work with me, not after working with Bob Marley.

Honor and Hilary were sure they could make it happen but I didn't think it was possible. The Wailers had endured internal problems and had split up but Honor said she'd talk to Aston 'Family Man' Barrett for me. The next thing I knew, there was a message for me from Family Man saying that the Wailers would reform for me. They had gone through many incarnations, but Family Man said he'd get some of the original guys, like the keyboardist, Earl 'Wire' Lindo, who didn't tour much but played on all the early albums. He also said he'd get his brother, Carlton Barrett, and we would record in Bob Marley's Tuff Gong Studio.

I couldn't believe what I was hearing. I went to see them and played them the rough demo tapes I had. One track, 'Free South Africa', was already on the *Rasta* album, and Family Man knew it, but I wanted to record a new version of

218

the poem, with a completely new tune. The other poem was called 'Stop the War', a call to end the cold war and for nuclear disarmament. The guys liked it, and they were particularly happy I had a song that called for the release of Nelson Mandela.

Family Man told me there'd been lots of people who'd wanted to record with them following the death of Bob, in 1981, but they were all doing imitations of the man, all trying to sound and move like him. The reason they were happy to work with me was that I sounded nothing like him. I wanted to perform spoken word rather than sing, but I was also as politically aware and had a message similar to that of the Wailers. So, although they were divided, they came back together because this was about freeing Mandela. As Family Man put it at the time, 'We'd be hypocritical if we didn't do it because of our own personal apartheid.' It made me think back to the letter I wrote to Bob and his reply to me, and then, there I was, about to do it with the Wailers.

On the day of recording, I had a freak accident. I was at Honor and Hilary's place when Family Man pulled up outside the house. He didn't knock on the door; he did what all Jamaicans do: beeped on his horn and called me. When I heard him I jumped up and started to run for the door, but as I was hurrying along a huge flying cockroach came towards me. I tried to move my head away from it, but as I did I smashed my head against the wall and fell to the marble floor, bashing my head for a second time.

I was out cold for a few minutes. When I came round I could hear Family Man getting more and more worked up, shouting, 'Zephaniah, Zephaniah. Come man.'

I got my dazed self together, stood up and went to the car outside. I said nothing to him, but in the studio I recorded the poems with a bit of a headache. All the recordings, including the music and the mixing, were done in a couple of days. I had my poems and music in the can, but what saddens me slightly is there aren't videos of that session, and I only have one rubbish photograph that I took of the two Barrett brothers. I remember saying this to Bill Gilliam, who rightly replied, 'You have the recording, and that's what counts.'

The tracks were released on the 12-inch single, 'Free South Africa'. We didn't publish words with it because the poems already existed and it was pretty obvious what I was saying. Not long after the release I heard a story about a couple of young guys in South Africa who got hold of a copy of the record. They transcribed the words and printed them on a design that looked like an album sleeve. They got loads of them and then went up in a helicopter and dropped them over townships and in some of the more uptown parts of South Africa.

I was told the lyrics fluttered down onto the homes below and the police were ordered to pick them all up, but there were too many of them and the people got to them before the police could. When I first heard the story, I thought it must have been an exaggeration. They would have been shot down and, anyway, my fans over there were poor and wouldn't have helicopters.

But a few years later, when I was back in South Africa, I met the guys who'd done it. I'd assumed they would be African National Congress activists, or hardened warriors from the Black Consciousness Movement, but they turned out to be skinny, middle-class white kids who were quite rich; at least rich enough to hire a helicopter. I thanked and praised them for what they did. I had to. After all, they spent two years in jail for my poetry. I'd also been to prison, but never for my own poetry.

I think that incident, and a few other things, brought me to the attention of Nelson Mandela. I was told some time later that he had been given a parcel containing some of my printed poems and musical recordings when he was still in prison, and that he had very carefully listened to the music and read the words. The thought that the great man would be paying attention to what a working-class boy from the Midlands had written spurred me on. It brought me the realisation that finally, in Bob Marley's own words to me, I really was 'forwarding on'.

33

A Job at the Council

Around this time I came to the attention of the
British Council. Like many people, when I first
heard of their existence I thought they were the
British embassy. When I was told they were
attending one of my gigs, I did an angry, heavy
performance, ranting poems about Thatcher,
war and capitalism and, as I walked off stage, I
thought the men in suits from the British
Council would ignore me and never want to see
me again. How wrong I was. The men in suits
jumped up, saying, 'Well done', 'You tell 'em'
and 'We have to use you again.' And so we began
a long relationship.

At that time there was a lot of positive, fresh
thinking in the British Council. They wanted to
promote the new image of Britain. They were
still sending opera singers and Morris dancers
around the world, but they were now also using
reggae and Asian music, modern dance and
literature, and even modern sports to show all
aspects of the new British culture.

It would be easy to think that the people
behind this progressive thinking were all young
funky things. Some of them were, but there were
also a lot of older workers who for years had felt
restricted to promoting what some (including

me) would consider a colonial relationship. They now felt they could break out. One of the old guard told me that on the day he started work at the Council they gave him his retirement date and told him exactly how many working days and holidays he would have leading up to that date. He was basically told what he would be doing for the rest of his life.

There were rumours that the British Council spied for the British government, and I personally thought that was highly likely, or at least the local knowledge the staff had of a country could be utilised in times of war, or even in times of peace. I have noticed that the British government always seems to think of peace as a space in between wars . . . still, what I really loved about working with the Council was that they would send me to places that weren't on the standard touring map.

Most European countries were easy to tour, as was the USA, Australia, New Zealand and Canada. These countries had promoters who could fly you there and pay you, so it was easy to tour them independently. Where the British Council really came into its own was in sending me to countries that normally couldn't afford to get me there — places like Papua New Guinea or the Seychelles, or locations where political communication wasn't good but being worked on. So I would go into countries like Libya and begin to build cultural ties with likeminded people.

Travel has always been key to what I do. Not having had a good formal education meant I worked hard to make up for it by meeting people and learning from them. I love reading books about how people live around the world, but I prefer to go and meet the people myself.

Soon after I started travelling the world to perform, I had a conversation with my mum and we realised I was the most travelled person in the entire history of our family. She kept asking where I got the money to afford it, and I kept telling her that my flights and hotels were paid for. She found it very hard to believe and, at first, so did I. But for me it wasn't about flights, hotels, or even fees. What I found amazing was the fact that I would turn up at a venue in India, Colombia, Zimbabwe or Fiji, and it would be full of people who had read my books or listened to my music. I was always very humbled by this and so, whether I was at home or abroad, I never took a single member of my audience for granted.

There is a common idea that when you go to a new country you can get a good feel for the place from taxi drivers, but I disagree; you get something from them, but it's usually a very male-centric view. If I want to understand a country I talk to the women. Better still get to know the women. I have been to so many countries where the taxi drivers say, 'Yeah, it's great here, we've got freedom, we can do what we like', and then you talk to the women and they tell you the truth: 'Oh no, we're not allowed to do this, we're not allowed to do that, and we have no freedom.' So I always say, talk to the women. In fact, I think you never really know a country until you've had sex in it and got arrested in it. If you're on a quick visit, you could always have sex with the person who's arresting you. But what do I know? This is only a theory, of course.

Travelling is how I got my education, but more importantly it's how I got my compassion. As well as being able to speak to prime ministers and presidents, I've also spent time with homeless people and drug addicts in places like the streets of Johannesburg. In India, I spent a day with the deputy prime minister, then later that night I was on the streets of Calcutta talking to the poorest people I have ever seen about their dreams and nightmares. I always felt I had the ability to move in and out of different worlds.

If I was minister for education I'd make it mandatory that children have to travel at least once as part of their education, either paid for or highly subsidised. And I'm not talking about trips to France or Germany; they should go to Africa or Asia or to a completely different culture, where they eat differently, where they go to the toilet differently, where their houses are built differently. They should go somewhere their 'normal' will be challenged; somewhere they can really see and learn how different people function, and how much different people are the same.

34

Dread Poets' Society

In the late 1980s a number of British universities began to get interested in me. At first they wanted me to talk or do interviews in student magazines, and there were always university gigs, of course. But then I had a visit from a group of people with connections at Cambridge University, who wanted to talk to me about standing for the post of Fellow at Trinity College. Apparently some bigwigs in the university had found out that a story was going to break in the press about how the post (like the university) was regarded as elitist. Since Henry VIII's time, it had gone to Professor So-and-So's daughter, or the son of a friend of a friend, and it had never really been used for its true purpose.

The original idea was to reach out and allow somebody who didn't have a university education to use the premises. It was for people who wouldn't normally mix in those circles but who could benefit from raising the profile of themselves or their art. My initial response was that I would go for it. I went to Trinity to speak to the powers that were, and they explained that the idea of being a fellow was to add life to the college, to use their rooms and encourage students to engage in creative work.

I spoke to the college at length and was open and honest with them, saying I could definitely assist in initiating creativity. Everyone was sworn to secrecy in that meeting, but someone was talking. I left Cambridge and by the time I reached London it was in the evening paper. Then the *Daily Mail* printed a cartoon of me on stage surrounded by spliffs on the floor, with some hanging from my mouth. A don leans across to the students, and in the speech bubble it says: 'If you hear any rumblings, it's Keats, Shelley and Byron turning in their graves.' The *Sun* then ran a headline on 23 April 1987 saying: 'Would you let this man near your daughter?', as if I was some kind of rapist.

Certain elements of the press began hanging around outside our house in East Ham, trampling over the garden and trying to get stories. I was confronted by one hack who said she'd spoken to a woman I'd supposedly been at school with in London, who said I'd got her pregnant. I told her truthfully that I'd only been to school for one day in London, at an all-boys school. It was nonsense. They were using provocation to try to scrape up all kinds of dirt. And all because the most shocking thing for their readers was the idea that a black man with dreadlocks might be allowed a position in some hallowed part of the educational establishment.

Mum and me were in the process of moving to another house in East Ham when a young, upper-middle-class female journalist for one of the broadsheets found out where I was moving. She turned up looking what she thought would be the part to lure me into an interview. Her blonde hair was braided in red, gold and green beads and she was driving an MG sports car. She asked me for an interview and I declined, saying I wanted to wait for the college decision, but the car caught my eye and I asked her for a drive. She agreed. When I looked in the glove compartment, to put on a cassette, the reggae ones were in the front — Bob Marley, naturally — but hidden behind them was the Dire Straits, U2 and Rolling Stones.

I told her that before she wrote her piece, and while I was waiting for Trinity's decision, she should come to the spoken word gig I was doing in Brixton that weekend. To be fair to her she did come along, and later said she'd had her mind opened by the power of performance poetry. She hadn't known what to expect but was really glad she came, as she had been moved by it. In the end I gave her the interview and she gave the gig a rave review. She'd been under a tough deadline. She told me that if she hadn't persuaded me to speak, the newspaper would have run a piece she'd already drafted before she'd ever spoken to me — with little regard to its accuracy.

In the end, the negative campaign by the tabloid press made the clever folk at Cambridge back down. The dons had felt that if they appointed me, they could never be accused of being elitist. I was interested in the appointment because I felt passionately about education, and I also knew it would have been easy for me to add to the life of the university. The college had wanted to get a 'normal' person in, which is why they approached me, but it turned out I wasn't so normal after all, and they didn't want a fuss made. It wasn't to be; the tabloids had won the day. One unnamed member of the university staff said, 'I like the idea of Benjamin Zephaniah coming to Cambridge. Every time he comes here a buzz of excitement goes around the university . . . but I want him to go home at night.'

That wasn't the end. I had the last laugh. Based on an idea by an independent producer called Rodger Laing and myself, me and the writer David Stafford wrote a screenplay called *Dread Poets' Society*, where I meet Shelley, Byron and Keats on a train, en route to Cambridge. On this journey we exchange notes, read poetry and have a go at the establishment in an old Romantic poets kind of way. It was made into a short film for Channel 4 in 1992, starring me (as myself) with numerous actors, including Timothy Spall, in costume. It was a big hit, and people talked about it for years afterwards.

Intellectual and cultural theorist the late Stuart Hall used the film to illustrate to his students how racist the establishment can be in tandem with the media. Those newspaper cartoons were used all over the world to illustrate the same issue, and although the film was only shown on TV once, it has been shown at festivals all over the world.

35

The Liverpool Years

When the *Sun* slandered me in 1987, people all over the country complained, but people in Liverpool complained more. The people in Liverpool got really angry; many wrote letters to newspapers and to the media watchdog, but one group got so angry they lobbied their local arts council demanding that I do a residency there. It was agreed and, as a guest of the city, I took up residency managed by the Africa Arts Collective. When Liverpool University heard of the residency they offered sponsorship but I declined — there were now so many universities trying to claim me that I wanted to stay clear of them all. I worked in Liverpool for two years but stayed for three. While there, I did performances, visited schools and kept an open house so that writers could see me at (almost) any time of the day. I also published a (very) small book called *Inna Liverpool* to celebrate my time there.

Liverpool at that time was like no other city in Britain. When you heard the term 'Liverpool politics', it meant a different kind of politics to what was happening in the rest of the country. The poverty in Liverpool was like nothing I had seen in the UK, and when someone described themselves as a 'Liverpool black' it could get confusing. They could be Irish, they could be Scottish, they could be white and dating a black person, or they could be black — they just had to be an outsider. To add to your oppression, if you lived in Toxteth (L8) you were probably unemployed and your every move was being watched by the police. Police vans in Liverpool were like armoured tanks, and this was the first place in mainland Britain (not Northern Ireland), to have a helicopter that didn't just chase cars around but would hover over you as you walked home, shining its spotlight on you to see what you were smoking or reading.

Liverpool 8, or L8, as it's known, is right next to the city centre, and is full of black people. When I first arrived I was told to walk from L8 to the city centre. I did, and I noticed how the black people magically disappeared. The dividing lines were clearly defined. Liverpool city centre had very few black people in it, by day or by night, but there was still something about that city that I loved. There's just no one like a Scouser if you want a laugh; no one like a Scouser if you need a hand; no one like a Scouser if you want a drink, and no one like a Scouser if you want a fight. They are amazingly loyal, but if you cross them they'll kill you.

Many theorised about the struggle, but the people of Liverpool lived the struggle. I connected with them, and they with me. The establishment in Cambridge (and London) were having meetings and posing questions on TV to work out if the poetry of Benjamin Zephaniah had any merits; the people in Liverpool didn't

231

need to ask. I had written a lot about the place and defended the people who lived there a long time before I took up residency. I felt a strong affinity with the city, and when I came under attack from the right-wing press, the people of Liverpool stood up for me.

I was called a 'writer in residence', but I was effectively a guest of the city and was able to work for whichever organisation needed me. I would work at the university, in schools or for other grassroots initiatives. My expenses were covered by the city, so I was able to perform free of charge for schools, community centres, at carnivals and (when necessary) at demonstrations and rallies. I built my first small home studio there and began to record some of the local poets and singers and my friends' children. But my work extended far beyond that.

Maybe it was because I was an outsider that people would come to me and ask me for advice. I worked as a quasi-marriage counsellor. I helped people find somewhere to live. I gave drug counselling to people who needed it. I helped the prostitutes when they had no one else to confide in, and I was also there when people needed someone to talk to. At times it seemed that this type of work kept me more occupied than my poetry. If there were any political issues, I'd speak out. If gangs were at war with each other, I would be a mediator; if prostitutes were being blackmailed or hassled by the police or pimps, they knew they could come and speak to me in confidence. When I started the job, my contact person, Vivek Malhotra, told me it wouldn't be a

232

normal type of residency; the main point was that I would be there for people, whatever the people wanted of me.

Not long before I arrived they'd had all sorts of controversy with a Labour Party splinter group called Militant. I went to some of their meetings. I also went to Labour Party meetings, Communist Party meetings, Black Panther and other groups' meetings, and I can honestly say I had absolutely no problem with any of them; they all welcomed me. The fact that I had never joined any of them and was seen as an observer who would report on proceedings poetically meant they all hoped that some of what they stood for would rub off on me, or at least that I would find some inspiration from them. I never went to a meeting with the police; I didn't need to. They would come to me.

One night after leaving a meeting of political activists, I was followed home by helicopter. It was just before lam on a Sunday morning and I was about two kilometres from my home in Princess Avenue. I heard the helicopter but I'd heard it many times, so took no notice of it, until it put its light on me. This light was so bright and so accurate that the small area I moved in was suddenly like daylight; the police up above could see every move I made. I wasn't worried about it; I knew that you didn't have to do anything to get arrested, but I also knew this was happening to other people all the time without any major outcry. If they came near me there would be an outcry, and I would be crying out the loudest. They followed me home. I went in, and they hovered over my house for five minutes and twenty-four seconds. I counted. Then they went to shine their light on someone else.

But the strangest stop I ever had happened while I was jogging. It was pouring with rain, and I hate jogging when it's pouring with rain, but I was persevering. I was about halfway through my run when a male police officer stood in front of me with his arms spread open. He more or less blocked the pavement, but I genuinely thought he was joking. People do those kinds of things when you're jogging. But he wasn't joking. When he saw that I didn't intend to slow down, he shouted, 'Stop!' at me. I stopped. Remember, it's pouring with rain, and I'm not in the mood for any chit-chat.

'Where are you coming from?' he asked.

'Home,' I said.

'Where are you going?'

'Home,' I said.

'What do you have on you?'

'Keys,' I said.

He was getting as wet as me, so I thought he would think it was time to go, but no, he wanted more.

'I need to search you,' he said.

'Come off it,' I said, laughing at him. 'I'm jogging. I've come from home, and I'm going home, and all I have is a key, because when I get home I need to open the door. Does that make sense to you?'

'I'm not sure what you're finding so funny, young man,' he said, seemingly unaware that I was much older than him. 'But you fit the description of a wanted burglar and I would be neglecting my duties if failed to question you.'

There were so many times in my life when I fitted the description of a burglar, and I had been stopped and questioned many times, but this was one of the strangest. He searched me, and all he found was a key, but even as I jogged away I was looking for the TV cameras. I was so sure this was a prank. It wasn't. It was Liverpool.

36

Workers' Playtime

In 1988 I won the BBC Young Playwright of the Year Award. One year later I would have been too old, but what I had written was finished when I was still under thirty. I had been writing plays for a couple of years by then, although it wasn't something I'd actively set out to achieve; it had happened organically, like many of the best things. A guy called Derek Brown, who was active in youth and street theatre in east London, had seen me perform many times and approached me in 1985, suggesting I bring all my skills together to write a play.

As a kid I'd seen *Armchair Theatre* on TV and I remember thinking, *Why don't they just make a film?* I didn't understand why the sets were so minimal. Mum told me stories about message plays touring in Jamaica when she was young, as part of a government promotion advertising the fact that education had become free and that children should 'Go to school, learn the golden rule' and all that, but to our minds, theatre in the UK was for white middle-class audiences.

I never set foot in a theatre until I came to London, but when I saw *Welcome Home Jacko* at the Theatre Royal Stratford East in 1979 my mind was changed about it being the preserve of the middle classes. It was written by Trinidadian playwright Mustapha Matura, with whom I would later become friends, and was directed by Charlie Hanson. The story was about young people like me, growing up in Britain and wanting to be different from our parents but struggling to express ourselves. To see a play with young black people in it was inspiring, and I realised theatre could be about raising consciousness and bringing a message to people.

By the mid-1980s my obsession was getting Nelson Mandela out of prison and the liberation from apartheid of the South African people. I blended these themes together and wrote *Playing the Right Tune*, which is about a group of young musicians who are making meaningful music that reflects their lives. The problem is they don't have money. Their manager applies for a grant, which is approved on the grounds that the band helps promote the organisation that gives them the money. This begins to tear the band apart.

The cast was all very young, I was quite young and the audience was young, but it set me on my way. It was put on at the Theatre Royal and then went to the Riverside, Hammersmith. I didn't realise the significance at the time, but people would come to me later and say it got them into theatre and writing. At the time I thought it was just another gig.

My next play took me to another level. This time I was approached by Charlie Hanson, who had directed *Welcome Home Jacko* and was now achieving great things in TV and theatre, most notably producing the TV sitcom *No Problem*.

Once again I was given the freedom to write on a subject of my choosing. It was 1987, unemployment was high, yet I noticed even the unemployed were being exploited, so I wrote *Job Rocking*, set in a job centre of the future.

We called it a 'dub opera'. The story tells of a new manager at the job centre who has previously run a well-known burger joint and has made the business a success. Now his plan is to run the job centre the way he ran the burger shop. It was an obvious dig at Thatcherite working practices, yet so much of what I put into that play became a reality for job centres and other government or council offices that should be run for the benefit of the people but which have become profit-driven: computerisation, monetisation, absurd targets and a management completely disconnected from their workers and clients.

In that same year I worked with the Union Dance Company on a piece called *Delirium*. Strictly speaking it was dance rather than a play, but it's probably the most 'arty' thing I've ever done. It was about how people all over the world decorate their faces — from those who still live tribal lives, and use face paint to distinguish themselves as being from a particular tribe, to people who put on make-up to go dancing in clubs, to attract sexual partners or to simply make themselves feel better. There were two versions of this show: one where the dancers performed to pre-recorded music and poetry, and another where I would stand in the middle of the stage and the dancers would dance around me.

In 1987 a hurricane caused devastation in southern England. It was bad, but I remember thinking at the time that it wasn't as bad as many of the hurricanes that hit the Caribbean every year. There was a lot of talk about how Mr Fish the weatherman had got it wrong, but what struck me was the many stories told of that night: of how people had checked on their neighbours, rescued each other and found themselves in unusual situations.

So when I was approached by Radio 4 to write a radio play, I wanted to explore how a couple who had grown apart become close once more as they lie in bed listening to the hurricane outside. When pitching the idea to radio producer Jeremy Mortimer — the son of barrister and writer John Mortimer — I knew I needed to use an original approach. I went to his office and performed the sounds of the wind and the music and the voices all by myself. It was so important to me that he heard the rhythm of the piece, which could not be written down. As he sat listening, I could see that he completely got it. When I finished, he simply said, 'That was the most unusual pitch I've ever heard. We have a deal.'

After the play was broadcast in 1988 I went away, then, on my return, Jeremy told me *Hurricane Dub* had won a BBC Young Playwright of the Year Award. I didn't even know it had been entered or that it was part of a competition. There's nothing on my mantel-piece.

37

Dreadlock in Wedlock

When I had been in Liverpool, a young woman had introduced herself to me while I was doing a performance in a community centre. She'd been working for a radio show on a community radio station, and with a youth theatre group, and they were interested in putting on one of my plays. Her name was Amina. I'd actually met her a few years before, when I'd done a performance in Liverpool before I lived there. Then it was her sister, Ruckhsana, who I'd met, and as I spoke to Ruckhsana she introduced me to her little sister, Amina. I patted her on her head and said hello. Next time I met Amina, she had grown up and was keen to get into the world of theatre. I told her she should go right ahead, and that I would love to see their interpretation of my play. She had a genuine enthusiasm, which impressed me. As time ticked on we struck up a rapport, and agreed to meet again so I could listen to her ideas.

The next time we met the atmosphere was very businesslike. We discussed the theatre group and our conversation turned to the arts. We started talking about a film that was showing in the city. Amina said she and her sister, Hamida, were going to see it. I sort of invited myself along to watch it with them. Amina was about seventeen and we started to date. Our relationship blossomed and she moved in with me. She came from a poor family who were Pathans with roots on the Pakistan–Afghanistan border. Many people had expected that the family wouldn't accept me because of my race, but I got on so well with her mother that by the time we got serious she wasn't seeing my colour.

When my residency in Liverpool ended, I returned to London, but I kept the flat on in Liverpool so Amina could live there. My personal life had been complicated at the time because I'd also been seeing a girl I'd met at a university a couple of years before. This wasn't like it was in the old days; I wasn't collecting girlfriends or partaking in good old-fashioned two-timing. I was trying to decide if I should be leaving this girl or not. I liked her a lot, so much that I even took her over to Jamaica to meet my grandmother and the rest of my family, but in the end I couldn't forgive her for cheating on me. So I told her it was over.

I was thirty-something, Amina was eighteen, and her family wanted us to be a bit more serious about our relationship. I was at an age where I thought I ought to be growing up. I hated the idea of marriage, though. I had read, and was influenced by, Simone de Beauvoir, Andrea Dworkin and bell hooks, and after watching what my mother had gone through, I believed marriage was about ownership and control. But then it got personal, and there was a part of me that thought it would reassure

Amina's mother if I married her.

But when I told my mother I was marrying Amina and not the other girl she was not just a little disappointed, she went mad. Her actual words were, 'What! You're marrying a Pakistani?' She didn't even know Amina. She didn't have anything against people from Pakistan per se, it was that she was so fond of the other girl, who she thought was lovely and innocent and would make a good wife. I knew better, of course, but she had always wanted us to get married and settle down. My mother thought she was perfect, and refused to hear anything that wasn't praise for her, which meant she knew very little about her.

★　★　★

Amina and I were together for a year before we got married. If two years before you had asked me about marriage, I would have said something like, 'Me is a roots natty dreadlock, and natty dread nah check fi wedlock.' Although deep down I still felt marriage was a trap, I thought it would be great for Amina and both families to see I was serious, and it was a way of bringing both families together. I had to tell myself to forget all the stuff that church and state tell us about marriage, and that we should be able to marry for our own reasons and live in our own way. We had to know for ourselves why we were getting married and forget about what the priest or imam thought of the idea.

We married on Amina's birthday, which was

also St Patrick's Day, in 1990. I drove myself to the register office in my Peugeot 205 (good car!), and I parked illegally outside the office. The reception party afterwards was a very multicultural affair, with lots of drumming and people wearing their national costumes, but there wasn't a honeymoon. We talked about the idea of one but decided against it. I had some gigs to do, and neither of us were romantic types. We preferred to be practical. In fact, a couple of days after the wedding I went to the States on tour and had to leave Amina behind. Many of our friends thought this was a little cruel, but we just thought this was what life was going to be like. I'm a poet, I tour, and sometimes the show must go on. Amina moved down to my house in east London and I gave up the flat in Liverpool. It was sad leaving the city, but I consoled myself with the fact that I'd taken a bit of Liverpool with me. At first, life was pretty much the same as it had been before we'd got married. We didn't have kids, so there weren't little ones for us to look after. We did start to think about them, and some family members, especially on Amina's side, began to ask when the first baby would arrive, but I'd always suspected I was infertile, so I didn't hold out much hope.

Amina was a little more organised than me and she started to take care of some of my business affairs. After a while she actually worked for me and collected a wage. She loved theatre and wanted to be an actor but unfortunately she couldn't act. In fact, I thought she was a terrible actor. I told her as much, which was harsh but true. But because she loved the theatre so much she began to look for other roles available to her in the theatrical world. I spoke to my old colleagues at the Hackney Empire, and Amina found a job there for a while as an administrator.

Personally and professionally we got on extremely well and we made a great team. Although she was naive and inexperienced, her heart was in the right place politically. What was also great for me was that she loved literature and martial arts. She had done karate for a few years, and as I was still practising Chinese kung fu we were always sparring. Sometimes we would be sitting at our desks working and we would suddenly jump up and start play-fighting. Sometimes, as we passed each other in the living room, I would fire off a kick to test her reflexes. Her Japanese karate meant she was really strong, but stiff and straight, whereas my Chinese style was about being light-footed, flowing, with lots of circular movements. I would kick her very lightly on one shoulder and then move around to the other, whereas she would kick and punch me as if she were breaking bricks.

We also had our differences in working styles. She was an organiser, and very efficient around the office. I had always been very tidy, my office was orderly and I knew where everything was, but she knew how to file and she was good with figures. That was helpful, but her urge to make the figures add up sometimes proved embarrassing. I have always kept an extensive collection of books and DVDs, and when friends came to the house they would often ask to borrow some. Amina would write down the time and date of the loan in her own little book and, if the item wasn't returned on time, she would tell me or phone the person who'd borrowed it, quoting the time they borrowed it and demanding the items be returned — even the local library didn't do that! Sometimes I would tell her not to worry and to calm down, but usually I'd leave her to it. Sometimes it was useful, because if I'd lost something she'd know where it was, but on other occasions it would annoy people and I would find myself having to apologise to them.

Generally I was adjusting to married life quite well, though. I now had to think about someone else when I travelled, and I consulted Amina when important decisions had to be made, but that was good — I needed that. I liked having someone else to think about, and having someone else to think about me.

38

Nelson Mandela

On 11 February 1990 Nelson Mandela was released from prison. After twenty-seven years, the boxer, lawyer, freedom fighter and the figurehead of our struggle against apartheid and racism worldwide walked free, with Winnie Mandela at his side. I, like many others, watched his walk to freedom on television, and I remember wondering what the future held for South Africa. Nelson Mandela was a revolutionary when he was arrested on 5 August 1962 — how much would he compromise, and how much compromise would his people tolerate? I was pretty sure he wasn't going to promote revenge, but I could see him promoting a peaceful revolution. The question was, would his people go with him?

While in prison, Nelson Mandela had a government in exile. Some years later I'd go to Robben Island and meet an old prison guard who told me Mandela and his comrades were all incredibly well behaved. They knew they were political prisoners and not criminals, and that one day they would be guiding the nation, so they wanted to set an example. The way they behaved in prison was the way they wanted other people to behave. The guard told me the only thing they would take was newspapers because they wanted knowledge; they needed to keep up as much as they could with world affairs.

On 16 April 1990, a couple of months after his release, Mandela came to England. He came for a variety of reasons, but there happened to be a big concert being held in his honour. It was a concert that we activists didn't care much for. Most of us were simply not invited and, like the big concerts that had been held before, the organisers preferred to book big-name artists and pop stars rather than grassroots activist musicians. They also somehow managed to do concerts with Mandela in mind and not allow any politics on stage, which I think was an amazing feat in itself. One could say they had to do both those things in order to reach as many people around the world as they could, but I remember lots of people who had worked hard over the years feeling completely left out.

While Mandela was in London I got a message saying he would like to meet me, but he requested that the meeting take place at a ridiculously early time in the morning. He had a press conference booked, and a meeting with Margaret Thatcher, but he wanted to see me first. I made the effort and got up early, then drove into central London to meet him. We spent the first few minutes thanking each other for our works against racism and for human rights. I couldn't believe how much praise he was heaping upon me; it was almost embarrassing — so much that I had to get a little firm with him and say, 'Now, Madiba, it doesn't matter what you say about me, what I've done is nothing compared to twenty-seven years in prison and everything else you've had to endure.'

I found him to be a very rational person, and very warm; he never got overemotional or carried away. I didn't feel in awe of him, I didn't feel any special dust sprinkling from him, I just saw him as a human being. In fact I felt guilty because I didn't see the aura around him that some people talked about, and I didn't feel like I was in the presence of a saint. I saw a normal, ordinary man who had done extraordinarily great things.

We talked a lot about Mrs Thatcher and how strange it was that she now wanted to see him even though she hadn't supported the boycott and said the blacks of South Africa were all right under apartheid. We talked about the way in which so many people had jumped on the bandwagon in the years leading up to his release, and he really appreciated those of us who had been there in the very early days. He knew all about people like me and Tony Benn, doing benefits and giving talks, and in so doing had been branded 'terrorist sympathisers'. The thing I was most proud of was that he confirmed he had read my poetry in prison.

I spent a good half hour with him discussing his life and struggle, and the way people in the West had tried to highlight his plight. We even joked about the way some others had been against the boycott, even pro-apartheid, until they realised his release was inevitable and then were suddenly keen to be seen singing 'Free

Nelson Mandela' in nightclubs. It was this conversation that inspired me to write the poem 'Who Dun It', with the refrain: 'Nobody dun apartheid, they were all revolutionaries.' We left the room and were met by an army of photographers; he went off to do his diplomacy, and I went home to catch up on my sleep.

39

Us and Dem

One morning in 1990, after my morning run, the phone rang. The voice said, 'Hello, is that Benjamin Zephaniah?' I confessed to being me, and the voice said, 'My name is Chris Blackwell. I'd really like to talk to you. I'm in the air at the moment, flying into London. Can we meet tomorrow?'

Chris Blackwell was probably the most important man in the music business at that time. He started Island Records and was famous for introducing the world to Bob Marley, Robert Palmer, Millie Small, Traffic and U2, to name a few, and he was the person most musicians would like a meeting with. But I was no young kid looking for a record deal, so while I was surprised by the call, I wasn't running up and down filled with joy, thinking this was my big moment.

The next day we met in an apartment he owned in a posh part of London. He told me he had been reading some of my work and people had been talking to him about me, and he couldn't understand why we hadn't worked together. In fact, I was already having low-profile talks with a well-known Island Records man called Jumbo, but it was all a bit slow. Once I said that I would be willing to do an album on the Mango label, a subdivision of Island, things started to move quickly.

It didn't take long for us to sign a deal, and the idea was that I would find a couple of producers, work on a track with them in order to try them out and then pick one. Jumbo suggested that I work with Paul Smykle, known to us all as 'Groucho' — a name he was given simply because although he was black he looked like Groucho Marx of the Marx Brothers. He had done some great work in the past, most notably with Black Uhuru, and was well respected in the music-making world. We got on extremely well, and so we got down to work. His style was futurist; he hated drum rolls, and was very much into the emerging digital technology. I liked his style, I thought he would produce a great remix, a great single, or even an album in the future, but I wanted this album to be a lot more rootsy.

As I was coming to this conclusion, Chris Blackwell suddenly sold Island records to Polygram. The world was told that things within Island would carry on as normal, but I was informed there had to be cuts, and although my album could go ahead I had to stay with Groucho. As it turned out, Groucho and I had some great times together. As with many of my recording sessions, they would be part recording session, part political and philosophical debate, and Groucho loved that.

We produced the album *Us An Dem*, which was released in 1990. To this day I think it's a great album, but it was a flop commercially. Well, that may be a little harsh; after all, it sold a fair number and was deemed worthy of rerelease by Cherry Red Records in 2009. It was also popular in the USA. One track, 'Everybody Hav a Gun', was a big hit in Jamaica, but most of my hardcore followers thought it was a bit too funky and overproduced.

If you think outside of categories and labels such as reggae or soul or house, you can really appreciate the album; it stands alone. But when you start to think commercially, and wonder where to place it and how to market it, then you run into trouble. I was told that over £25,000 was spent on the recording of it, the most I had ever spent on the recording of an album, but yet in purely commercial terms it was my biggest flop.

By the early 1990s, dance music was firmly established as the dominant sound. Rave culture had happened at the end of the 1980s, turning a huge section of UK kids into a loved-up nation who would spend hours dancing in fields and warehouses. It wasn't really my scene — I didn't want to take ecstasy or drugs of any kind — but I was impressed by the way this music achieved something almost magical. For decades soul singers and ballad singers had been writing lyrics about people coming together to love one another: men and women, obviously, but also young and old, black and white. Now you had this minimal dance music — some of it with no lyrics at all, or just someone repeating 'Aciid! Aciid!' — and it achieved that very thing without saying it. It simply did it. I also liked the fact that the people involved with the scene didn't give a damn about how you dressed or what age or heritage you were.

I preferred the heavier drum and bass sound that emerged in the mid-1990s. I'd go to nights at clubs like Fabric and Heaven, which always had a great atmosphere, and I got into the stuff put out on the Metalheadz label, formed by Goldie. I was receptive to the new sound, but I knew a lot of established musicians at that time who were really frustrated by it. They'd practised their instruments for years and then, suddenly, it was all about computers.

★   ★   ★

I think some of my best musical adventures are my collaborations. By definition these are projects that take me away from reggae and into different directions. I like taking my reggae attitude and mixing it with people who might be more into dance music, or rock, or even folk. To date I have done some great collaborations including with the Wailers, Kinobe, Swayzak, Amira Saqati, Back to Base, Toddla T, Mieko Shimizu, David Lowe and Sinéad O'Connor.

Sinéad was somebody I'd always respected and wanted to meet, so when I was asked to work with her I jumped to it. Usually when I collaborate I'm the one with the heavy message and the others have to put it into context, but it was different with Sinéad. She put down some lyrics about a vampire sucking the blood of the people. Nothing new there, as this metaphor appears a lot in reggae, but then she says loud and clear, 'From now on, I'll call you England.' I thought, *Well, that's heavy!*

I came with lyrics about the evils of empire and it worked well. It was one of my favourite collaborations and, after we recorded the track, we became good friends. We used to talk a lot about what reggae was trying to do and what she wanted to do, and before long she flew to Jamaica to record a brilliant roots reggae album called *Throw Down Your Arms.* I loved it because it didn't sound like white reggae. She'd gone to Jamaica and worked with real reggae musicians, and she wasn't trying to sound black. Her voice simply blends well with that music.

★   ★   ★

I feel really privileged to have been the first person to have collaborated with the Wailers after the death of Bob Marley, but my dream collaboration would have been with Bob himself. He was a poet who sang his words — words full of social commentary, prophecy and wisdom. I am an angry ranter of verse. I think my lyrical chatting combined with Bob's angelic voice would have worked really well. Actually I know it would. Well, it works when I'm in the shower.

40

City Psalms

After a tour during which I performed all over the world, in countries including Argentina, Colombia, Kenya, South Korea and Australia, I embarked on a British tour. After one of my last performances of that tour, I came off stage in Newcastle and a strange-looking guy approached me. He had a round, chubby face with windswept hair (well, it had been a wild gig) and he looked a little out of place. I was convinced he was going to ask me for a lift home or for spare change — after all, by now my audiences were dressing up to come to my gigs.

He introduced himself as Neil Astley of Bloodaxe Books, and he said he would be interested in publishing me. He was really honest with me, saying he'd been aware of my name for a long time but hadn't really been that interested in performance poetry. He didn't think performance poets were able to get their words to work on a page, but he said he had listened to me and thought I could deliver material worthy of publication. And I was really honest with him too. I told him I'd got away with *Pen Rhythm* because it was released at the right time, when I was young and new, but I wasn't happy with *The Dread Affair*. I also told him being published was not a major priority for me.

I was already reaching millions of people with my performances on stage, on radio and on TV, so I was happy to carry on doing what I was doing. My mission was to take poetry to people who didn't read books. But I also told him I was ready to do another book if we could work together to bridge the gap, or make the connection, between the page and the stage. Neil was pleased, and said he knew exactly where I was coming from. So that was it. We parted and I started work on *City Psalms*, which was published in 1992.

Once again, many of the poems and even the title came from one of the prototype books I'd made years earlier. Since then I'd met hundreds of people but one significant contact was a guy called Bob Mole. I'd met this fellow lover of poetry a few years earlier. Not only was he a lover of the arts, he was also a cricket enthusiast and a great gardener. It was he who first turned me on to Shakespeare by sitting me down to watch a filmed version of *Macbeth*, and putting it all in context for me. He loved reading great poetry but he also had a good understanding of performance poetry, so I asked him to write an introduction to the book.

For the cover I used a colourful piece by an artist I had always admired called Michael Hawthorne. He created really powerful images of people exploding or experiencing pain. He was a white man who seemed able to capture perfectly the pain of the black man. His work exploded and danced and cried. Although on the surface the piece I chose for my book simply depicts a man and a woman walking down the street, the artist's graphic style and the sense of place he captures speaks volumes about the urban experience.

41

Cool Down, Rasta

In February 1993 my father died in Barbados. I didn't attend the funeral but relatives took care of things and a couple of my sisters went over. I wouldn't say I'd made my peace with him exactly by the time he died, but I was glad he spent his final years enjoying himself. Apparently he was the first person on Barbados to have a satellite dish. As a final gesture of respect, and because he'd loved his old job so much, he was buried in his GPO uniform. Apparently, in the days leading up to his death, he would sit and look at a photograph of me and Mum. I think there was something deep there, but those men of that generation really didn't know what to do with their feelings.

Back in Birmingham, love was blossoming in Mum's life. I first heard about it when she called to tell me she had 'found Mr Right'. He was in fact known as Brother Robin Wright, and she'd met him through her church. Brother Wright had been very dutiful and, after admiring my mum from afar, he'd gone to their pastor to talk about his feelings for her. Their church didn't allow for relationships outside of marriage, so once he had the pastor's blessing he proposed and Mum accepted. After a bit of playing with his name I

258

told her I had to meet him; I felt like someone had started dating my little sister and I had to check him out.

I made the trip to Birmingham and I immediately got on with Brother Wright. He was a retired reggae DJ but he still had his sound system with its massive speakers, and played heavy bass music, except instead of playing rude boy reggae he was now playing Christian reggae. The other thing was, like me, he was a lover of old Triumph cars. I'd been through a series of Triumphs by now — there was that GT6, of course, that the police had impounded back in 1977, but I'd also had a TR2, a TR4 and a TR6. I'd always loved the TR models, but Brother Wright had two classic Triumph 2.5 PIs, with two spare engines. He was also very interested in world affairs and loved listening to Radio 4, so we had a lot to talk about.

On 1 July 1993 they were married, and me and all my brothers and sisters attended the wedding. Brother Wright had his own kids, who would visit from time to time, but he didn't talk about them very often. Everyone got on with Brother Wright, and we also got on well with all of his kids, but it felt very much like he was 'ours'; he treated us like his kids, although we were all fully grown.

★ ★ ★

When I was in Britain all I did was work, and when I had time off I did more work, and when I travelled to get away from work I always ended up doing yet more work. I couldn't stop. It wasn't because I was ambitious, and I certainly wasn't seeking fame — I hated being called a celebrity — I just wanted as many people as possible to hear what I had to say about the world. If I was asked to appear at a political event or something I was passionate about, I couldn't say no.

My political campaigning was as important to me as my creative life, and in the mid-1990s it probably took over from my creative life. But it was unsustainable, and things came to a head when I came offstage one night during a tour in the USA, having just performed, and collapsed in the wings. Fortunately the audience didn't see me. When the hotel doctor came, he asked to see my itinerary. I was absurdly busy, with something like forty-six gigs in as many days.

The doctor told me to rest, so I did, and the next day I felt fine. I went back on stage the next night but the same thing happened — I collapsed as soon as I walked off. The doctor came out again and this time he shouted at me, reminding me that he'd told me to take a rest the night before.

'I did take a rest,' I said. 'I slept all night.'

He said that wasn't good enough. He meant a rest from performing. He told me I was suffering from exhaustion and I had to take a proper break from all the travelling and touring. I had burned myself out.

I had heard about artists being burned out, but now I was experiencing it for real, and it wasn't good. It was as if the electrical circuits in my body were shutting down, and fuses were blowing.

The doctor said I had to take a complete break. He didn't mean a few days or a few weeks; he said I should have at least six months off from touring solo and playing live with my band, and if I wanted to be active I should take up a hobby. But I had made commitments I didn't want to break, so I struggled on with the rest of the tour then, when I returned to England, I decided to make some big changes.

I was going to take it easy. I decided I'd take up a hobby to distract myself from work, because I'd stopped doing anything other than writing and touring. I bought a little sports car — a Triumph, of course. I got me a TR7. I'd originally got it for Amina, but she didn't like it, so I began working on it. That particular car wasn't great, but it had rekindled my interest in working on motors, so I got rid of that one and, with the help of some friends, started to rebuild another old one from the bottom up. When we'd done the job, I drove it for a while and then completely rebuilt it again, this time on my own.

I also started collecting banknotes — a strange hobby, but it happened by accident. I was on a TV programme and when I was asked what I did in my spare time, I said I collected money. I don't know why I said it, I think it was just to get a laugh, but then people started sending me banknotes from all over the world.

This might strike you as a low-key or even boring hobby, but banknotes can tell a lot as to what a country cares about, or what the rulers of that country care about. And there are some very interesting stories behind the designs of notes: some are about revolution, some about work and industry, and some are designed by the greatest artists of their day. I enjoyed looking at the detailed artwork and also getting hold of rare ones. I liked it when people laughed at my hobby, then I would pass them an album of notes and that would be it — they would be engrossed for the next two hours.

So this, and the rebuilding of old cars, took me far away from the world that had consumed me for the previous couple of decades. I'd switched my focus from anything else I was doing or had done and I started to feel better for it. A change is as good as a rest, after all. On top of all this, I began to take my martial arts more seriously and made sure I was super-fit. But it wasn't only about being physically fit; I started to really get into the mental and spiritual side of it. I went from concentrating on the external to the internal, and I started to meditate, and spent time forgetting time.

★　★　★

We were still living in a housing co-operative place, and I was still paying £5 a week rent, but a rumour had started that the housing co-op was going to fold. I didn't like the idea of renting commercially, and had always hated the concept of being tied to a mortgage, but we had to do something. Not far from where we were living, in Lonsdale Avenue, East Ham, a house was for sale, but it had no 'for sale' sign up and I'd heard the estate agent was finding it hard to sell. So I formed a plan. I found the owner of the house and made him an offer he couldn't refuse. It was cash, it was quick, and it was done. It was on Roman Road, East Ham, and it didn't take long for Amina and me to make it our first real home together.

42

Talking Turkeys

In the busy year that was 1993 I was approached by the children's publisher Puffin Books. They asked if I was interested in writing a book of poems for children. I wasn't. I was performing in schools, and some of my poems could have been called children's poems, but I didn't want to separate them into categories based on age.

Although I resisted at first, the scout from Puffin kept on at me. I started thinking about it. Lots of children were telling me they really liked seeing their own books, on their own book-shelves, and that having a few poems of their own in books for adults wasn't good enough. Secondly, there was an absence of black writers on those bookshelves, and I was in a position to change this. So I stopped resisting and started working on my first children's book.

I already had a handful of poems, but there was one in particular that would go on to have a life of its own. The previous year I'd been working on a TV programme with Gaby Roslin and Craig Charles. We were filming on a city farm, where I had to write and perform three poems. I had written two but was struggling with the third, and inspiration wasn't coming. The night before the last day of filming I called Craig and asked if he would write it, but he insisted that I do it. He said I was thinking about it too much, and I should just relax and write whatever came into my mind.

When we'd finished the call, I then imagined myself on the farm surrounded by turkeys, and I asked myself what I would want to say to the world. Then it flowed.

Be nice to yu turkeys dis Christmas,
'cos turkeys just wanna hav fun.
Turkeys are cool, turkeys are wicked,
an every turkey has a mum.

And so 'Talking Turkeys' was born. And it became the title of the book, which was published in 1994. I've no idea how many books were printed in the first run, but I was told they had to reprint very quickly because it had sold so well.

It has since become trendy for comedians and celebrities to write children's books, but when I wrote *Talking Turkeys* it wasn't seen as cool at all. In some circles I was even mocked for it. Twenty-five years ago, children's books that included animal characters tended to be about clever, fluffy creatures and their adventures, whereas the animals in my book mainly feared being eaten. Children in my book were being bullied, and the earth was being abused and polluted, just like the real world.

★　★　★

For many years I never considered performing 'Talking Turkeys' live, but one night I decided to end my gig with it. I thought it would be a nice change from all the heavy stuff I was doing, and I was absolutely astonished by the reaction of the audience. All I did was open with the first line, 'Be nice to yu turkeys dis Christmas', and the crowd went wild. I was shocked. And then I noticed, as I went through the lines, other people were going through them with me. When I said the last line, the roar from the audience reminded me of a football crowd. I hadn't realised what that poem meant to people, or how many people were coming to my performances waiting for me to perform it and going home disappointed.

I've turned down five requests for the poem to be used in advertising, most notably and bizarrely by Bernard Matthews meat products, which was probably the most surprising and made me the most angry. Some of my hardcore followers really don't like the fact that it's the poem the establishment goes to when they speak of me, rather than my more revolutionary poems, but there's nothing I can do about that.

It has captured the imagination of so many children and young people, and I've even known situations where teachers have got competitive about whose class or school has a child that can perform the best recitation of the poem.

What has given me most joy over the years is when new generations of children discover the poem, and the number of children who have performed it, many of them posting their performances online. This happens all year round, all over the world, but there's always a noticeable spike around Christmas.

The poem lives through them for sure.

43

Maybe Baby

Amina and I started to discuss children, but as far back as my rude boy days I'd realised I wasn't making babies, so I told her I was pretty sure I couldn't have any. Back in Birmingham there were times when me and my friends seemed to exchange girlfriends, or looking at it from the other side, our girlfriends were exchanging us, and many of them were getting pregnant, but none of them were getting pregnant by me. I told Amina all this and we decided I should go and get tested.

Over the course of a couple of months I went through many tests and, sadly, all the results came back negative. I knew of men who had a low sperm count, but I had a no sperm count. Even though I was expecting it, it was still an emotionally difficult time. I was keener than Amina to have a child, I had always loved children, but now I suddenly felt a big-time urge to have my own. I would walk in the park and watch men playing with their kids and feel a kind of paternal jealousy. It wasn't rational; I knew I shouldn't be feeling jealous, but when I watched men passing on skills to their little ones I wanted someone to pass mine onto as well. I wanted to recite my poems to my babies.

I started visiting friends who had kids just so I could play with them; I even began to fantasise about Amina and me living in some kind of domestic bliss in a revolutionary household with a large family. I remembered people saying when I was small how special our family was because we had two sets of twins. I used to say then that I wanted nine kids, but with just three pregnancies; three sets of triplets would do it. I grew out of that idea when I learned now much childbearing takes out of women, but still, the need to be the daddy was urgent. Actually it was overwhelming and it dominated my thoughts. Amina wasn't feeling the same, but I warned her that her time would come.

We began looking into adopting, and when we first made enquires the agencies were over the moon that we'd approached them. It's always a struggle for them to find homes for kids; it's hard for white kids, hard for black kids, hard for kids who have dual black and white ancestry, but even harder for kids who are mixed black and Asian, so agencies welcomed us and at the same time wanted to use my public profile to publicise the need for people to come forward and adopt these kids.

In the end we went with an agency in north London. Our social worker, an Australian, was a great guy. He began to take us through the process, which is a long, difficult rigmarole that involves lots of probing questions and checks to make sure the couple are suitable to be parents. As part of the process the social workers had to look at our police records. I told them I had a long record — one that listed violence against police officers and other such serious offences, but he said because my years of offending were such a long time ago, the offences would be wiped.

He sent off my details to be checked, but when the results came back there was one conviction that meant I wouldn't be able to adopt. It all went back to that time when Trevor walked free from court and I teased the cop who'd had a grudge against me and who'd framed me using the sex worker. The one I'd called a dirty Babylon and a loser. Yes, that case had come back to haunt me.

The Home Office had wiped all my other offences, but the reason they couldn't wipe this charge was because they needed to prove that the girl I'd allegedly robbed was over eighteen. If she had been under eighteen at the time of the offence, it would be seen as a crime against a child. Of course, there was no record of her.

We tried to find her from the court records, but we couldn't find any record of anyone who had lived in Birmingham with her name, and the street where she was supposed to have lived did not and had never existed. I also found out that the two officers involved in my arrest were now in prison for importing marijuana.

I spoke for a long time to Lenny Henry and Dawn French, who around this time adopted their child, and they recommended a solicitor who they thought might be able to help me. He suggested I go back to court and challenge the original conviction, get the case reviewed and recorded as a miscarriage of justice. He warned me that it would be a long, hard process that could take a couple of years, and his charges were in the hundreds of pounds per hour ballpark. We thought about it and I decided not to pursue it. My social worker told me he had to drop the case; we could not be given approval, and that was the end of that.

Not long afterwards, at the end of 1995, Mark Fielder, a BBC producer, approached us asking if we would participate in a TV programme about couples that couldn't have children. I said yes. Amina hesitated — she was never keen on being on screen with me — but eventually she agreed and the BBC asked me what I'd like to do in the programme. My answer was immediate. I'd seen Professor Robert Winston on TV and had heard he was the best in the country when it came to reproductive medicine, so I said I wanted him to work with me. He came on board straight away and we started filming.

It was the kind of documentary that followed me as I went through the process of exploring why I was infertile. Camera crews followed Amina and me as I did my tests and interacted with Robert who, by the end of the programme, only confirmed what I already knew — I had what I called a 'no sperm count', or what he called *azoospermia*. I would never have children.

I'd been put through the emotional wringer again, this time in front of the entire nation. It caused me a lot of distress and ended our hopes of ever having children, but it got a lot of other infertile black men talking. Many of them wrote to me, many of them cried to me, and I realised I had touched on something the black community was unwilling to confront. Not only did I become a champion for that cause, I also started a campaign to encourage black men to donate sperm, something I had never dreamed I'd end up doing when I was performing poetry on the streets of Handsworth.

There was no change in my condition, but the documentary was very informative and did help a lot of people. But there was a rather sour ending. At the end of the programme, before the credits rolled, Robert Winston said he was doing research and that I should get all my notes sent to him because he thought he might be able to help me further along the line. This began to give me renewed hope. Straight away I got my doctor to send my notes over to him, but there was no reply. I tried to call him, but he didn't return my call. I got so desperate that the BBC producer wrote to him, reminding him that he'd made a promise to me that had broadcasted to millions of viewers, but still no reply.

I never heard from Robert Winston again. I was told by people who knew him (and an ex-member of his staff) that he was very good at getting publicity, and he probably made the promise to impress other people working in this field. I don't know, and I probably never will because he wouldn't let me get near him. At the Radio 4 *Woman's Hour* fiftieth birthday party in 1996, I made a point of finding him and standing next to him, but he took his champagne, and his meat on a stick, and slid away from me. The programme gave hope to others, but it ended up causing me more distress by offering me false hope.

★   ★   ★

Most of the letters I received after the broadcast started with the person begging me not to reveal their identity — such was the fear of them being 'found out' by people in their community. They would then go on to outline how they grew up thinking everything was okay, until they noticed they weren't fathering children when their friends were. Very few suffered silently; most took drastic measures or simply told lies to cover up their infertility.

I was horrified by what some of these men had done to appear 'normal', and I was surprised at the diversity of people contacting me. They ranged from gangsters to religious people, and from poets to well-known television personalities. Most thought that as black men who looked fit and healthy they had to live up to the image of the virile male. Although most of them functioned normally physically, they would still associate fertility with virility.

Men stopped me in the street and took me into shop doorways to talk. They waited for me at stage doors after concerts; they pretended they had poems they wanted me to see in order to get access to me, and one even flew from England to Finland to see me when he heard I was performing there. In terms of negative feedback from the community, there was but one. Shortly after the programme aired, a well-known black personality said I should be ashamed of myself; black men should not talk about these things in public.

44

A Novel Idea

Like most people in the English-speaking world (and probably beyond), I'd heard that everyone had a novel in them. I too may have had one, but I wasn't thinking of writing one. When I won the BBC Young Playwright of the Year Award in 1998, the producer Jeremy Mortimer kept telling me I must write a novel. I said yes to keep him happy, but didn't think seriously about it until Emma Matthewson came into my life.

Emma had been my editor at Puffin, and through her I learned how important editors are. She could read a poem with a child's mind, and she taught me how to use constructive criticism to my advantage, but she also taught me how to stand my ground when necessary. Emma was a rock. I had by now done three books with her at Puffin, then suddenly she went to Bloomsbury. She was going to a job she wanted, which was cool, but I was losing her, which was bad. After working with Emma I felt that my key relationship with a publisher was with the editor, rather than the contracts department. This was before I had an agent. So when my editor moved, I felt my partner in rhyme had deserted me.

But it wasn't long after Emma joined

Bloomsbury that she asked me if I would consider writing a novel for teenagers. She had spent many hours listening to me tell her stories about myself as a teenager, and she knew I had a strong empathy with young people, but I wasn't sure that meant I could write a novel for them. I told her I'd think about it.

A few weeks later I found myself in Ramallah, in Palestine, where I was touring with a great Palestinian poet called Mahmoud Darwish and other poets from the region. With us there was a British poet and translator called Sarah Maguire. Sarah had been a friend of mine for years, and over that time we had given each other advice on various matters, so I trusted her. She was one of a large group of poets who think we should stick to poetry, and that writing a novel is like selling out.

I told Sarah about Emma's offer and asked what she thought. She said: 'You go back there, Benjamin, and stand in front of her, stamp your feet and tell her you're a poet and not a novelist.'

So I did. I went back to see Emma, and although I didn't stamp my feet (I just placed them gently on the ground), I said, 'I'm a poet, not a novelist. I write poems, not novels.'

Emma heard me out and then smiled. She said: 'Okay, Benjamin, here's a cheque. Go away, write a couple of chapters, and if it doesn't work out, don't worry, keep the money and forget it. But if you like what you've done, then carry on.'

I'd often been told I had it in me to write a novel, and other people had watched me entertaining their children, but what really persuaded me wasn't the lack of black authors generally, but the lack of black authors writing for young people. I felt there was a need to write about issues concerning black youth, and more importantly that young people needed to see black writers on the bookshelves of their school libraries.

I had nothing to lose, so I decided to give it a try.

Word began to get round that I was doing this, and I became acutely aware that many people were expecting me to write a 'black novel' — one set in Brixton, Moss Side or Handsworth; one that would have obvious connections to my poetry and was at least a little autobiographical, but I wanted my first novel to take me into a different world. It didn't need to be immediately identifiable as having come from a black writer, and it didn't need to be set in the black underworld.

However, I did want to write about discrimination, so instead of writing about racial discrimination or sexual discrimination, as I had been doing for most of my life, I came up with the concept of facial discrimination, and the story slowly developed. The main character in the book, called *Face*, is Martin, a good-looking fourteen-year-old white boy who wants to be an actor and model, and seems to have everything going for him until he suffers severe injuries in a car crash and is terribly scarred. Then his life and outlook change forever. His face is no longer what the acting world needs; he isn't going to work as a model, for sure, and his friends change. Most importantly he learns not to judge people by their looks.

Normally the time spent writing a poem from beginning to end isn't too long, but I suddenly found that I was living with characters I'd invented. I might be standing at a bus stop and I'd start wondering what a character would be thinking. A woman might smile at me (that happens from time to time), and I would ask myself, would she have smiled if my face was disfigured? I would go into a shop and wonder what a particular character might buy. I began to inhabit the world I was creating.

Before I started writing *Face* I used to listen to white, middle-class writers on Radio 4 talking about how their characters would take over and walk into rooms and places without their permission. I would mock them and think them deluded, but then it started happening to me. I became my book, obsessed with everything from the way my characters thought to the way they breathed. It was a beautiful torment, a creative madness I would come to crave.

Officially my novels were for teenagers — well, that's how they were marketed — but deep down there was a lot in them that I also wanted to say to adults. Teenagers knew a lot about what I was writing about, so I wanted old adults to look into the world of young adults. I'm amazed at how quickly adults forget they were children. It's as if after they've outgrown their childhoods they get envious of the next generation and so blame them for all society's ills and curse and scorn them for having young fun.

In twenty-first-century Britain it's unacceptable to say, 'I hate black people' or 'I hate white people'; you cannot go around saying you hate someone because they are disabled, gay, straight, dyslexic or even eccentric, but somehow it's okay to say, 'I hate kids.' Posh people say it at dinner parties, sexy people say it to sound forever sexy and comedians say it to sound funny. We can't all be black, white, gay or straight; we can't all be posh, sexy, funny, dyslexic or eccentric, but we were all once kids. Can we really hate our young selves that much?

★   ★   ★

The response to *Face* exceeded expectations — well, they exceeded mine — and the publisher was pleased too. When I began to write it I thought it would be my one and only novel, and when it was done I thought, *Cool, I got away with it!* But an excited Emma came back to me with the sales figures, others began comparing me to all these big names in children's literature, and my readers started asking for more. Emma said I should get an agent, so I did, and then I got to work on my second novel, *Refugee* Boy.

Again, I wanted to tell the story from the perspective of a fifteen-year-old. This time I created the character of a young man who has just left a war situation in Ethiopia and moved to a strange country called England. It struck me that most people thought of refugees as adults, and I could understand why. In news reports the cameras usually focus on the grown-ups, and the big questions are always about whether they are 'real' or bogus, and what to do with them. But I would watch the children they had in tow, and I'd always wonder how they coped with what was happening to them.

I knew what it felt like to go from city to city, but what would it feel like to go from country to country? Kids need friends and family; they like to play, and they like stability, so what would it be like to have those things taken away, or to have seen war and brutality at such a young age? These were the questions I wanted to explore in *Refugee Boy*.

I didn't turn my back on poetry, as some people feared; I began to appreciate it even more. I read a lot more, and even found myself doing a residency. It started with a guy called Chris Mead, who was the director at The Poetry Society. He had the idea of placing me with the International Red Cross. I was asked to do an interview with them, which I did, but during the conversation I began to interview them. For me, the biggest issue was about neutrality. When I asked them how far they took this principle they told me it was absolute.

I understood how they needed to assure all parties they would stay neutral if they were to be allowed to work in war zones, but I told them that if I saw an atrocity being committed, or knew for sure who had committed any such act, I would have to speak out. I understood them as an institution but I also knew me as an individual, and so I said, 'This is not going to happen.'

Chris Mead wasn't put off by this; in fact it inspired him to think again. We talked about the possibility of me being a writer in residence in a police station, which I thought was a good idea, but we went with a residency at Tooks Chambers, a legal firm headed up by Michael Mansfield QC. Michael and his family was already like family to me. I can't remember how I first met them — I'm sure it had something to do with campaigning work, or trying to get someone out of jail — but I do know that we became very close over the years, and I have a special place in my heart for Freddy, Michael and Yvette's son. I watched him grow up to become a deeply caring and creative poet, rapper and teacher.

The placement at Tooks Chambers was just right. I already knew most of the team there, and I was familiar with the work they did, but being attached to them gave me a much deeper insight into legal processes. Having been in court myself a few times, it wasn't strange territory for me, but being in court as a creative person provides a unique opportunity to express the emotional aspects of what actually takes place.

I gave a poetry reading to mark the end of my residency. Michael Mansfield sat behind me, Doreen Lawrence stood at the side of me, and many barristers stood in front of me. Most people knew Doreen as the mother of a murdered young black man called Stephen Lawrence, but I knew her as a lover of art and poetry. That other stuff was put upon her by the evil that men do.

After the reading I noticed that more than half of the attendees were in tears. I spoke to many of them afterwards. I didn't just come out and ask, 'Why are you crying?' I asked in a general way how they felt the reading went, and they all said roughly the same thing — which was (to paraphrase) when they are in court they are so involved in the case and the need to deal with the facts that they detach themselves from what may be going on emotionally. And that's just what I didn't do. I had a minor interest in legal procedures, but I was more interested in using the power of poetry to capture what was happening to all those involved emotionally, and that included the judges.

For some reason unknown to me, the judge in the Ricky Reel inquest asked me to sit next to him. Every now and again he would ask me if I was comfortable, and then he would carry on regardless. The residency was the main inspiration for my 2001 collection of poems, *Too Black, Too Strong*.

45

Things Fall Apart

In my marriage, it was me who had felt the overwhelming need to have children. I was the driving force behind the hospital treatments, the adoption and the television programme, but when I got the results I gave up. Defeated, I had to come to terms with the fact that I would remain childless for the rest of my life. But then, a year or so later, Amina began mentioning various clinics and treatments she'd heard about. She would do in-depth research into the nature, science and law surrounding the treatments, and then pass her findings over to me at a carefully chosen time.

After all I'd been through I didn't want to hear any more suggestions from friends and family: the stories about old men in the hills of Jamaica who'd had no kids until they were sixty; the African man who could pray for me and make it all happen, and the woman who would take me into my past lives and clear blockages. I had had enough of the science, enough of the religion and enough of the mumbo jumbo. I was simply unwilling to go through it all again. Anyway, I was touring. Baby time was over. We didn't have any major arguments but I was beginning to feel some stress, and every now and again Amina made me feel as if I wasn't quite a whole man. I wasn't the daddy.

We always took holidays together, mainly to India and Pakistan, but to ease the stress I suggested she have a holiday alone or with a girlfriend, and she did. She went off with a friend to Tunisia, while I stayed at home. When she returned I felt something had changed, but it could have been me, and I didn't have time to think about such things — remember, the show must go on.

My next tour was to take me to Australia, New Zealand and Papua New Guinea. Amina wasn't coming; even though the option for her to travel was there, she didn't want to, so I went alone. I was in New Zealand, about to leave for Papua New Guinea, when I got an email from her. She had some information to give me about future gigs. These types of emails were quite normal, but there was something not quite right about the tone of her writing. It was businesslike, it dealt with the issue, but it was like an email from a stranger.

Amina was very professional, but normally when she had done with the business at hand she would end on something personal, but not this time. I called her and asked if she was okay, and she said she was fine, but she didn't sound fine. I came home a couple of days later, opened the front door, and immediately I could see she was gone. It was sudden; it was out of the blue, but there had been no bickering, and we'd had no arguments. After speaking to friends who had gone through divorces and separations, I thought it would have been easier if there had been arguments, or some obvious deterioration of the relationship; at least then I would have seen it coming, and maybe, just maybe, I could have done something about it.

★　★　★

This was one of the lowest points of my life, not because I'd been dumped, but because it came out of the blue, and at a time when I would have said that life was good.

I closed the curtains and locked myself in the house. I cut myself off from the outside world, only going out once to buy a large can of Guinness. I was never a drinker, so I knew that if I had only a few sips I would get drunk, and I thought that if I got drunk I would forget all my problems. I placed the can in the middle of my dining table but, instead of drinking it, it became the focus of my meditations.

I began thinking about all the people I knew in the world of showbusiness who had drink problems, and all those who hadn't returned from the dark place drink sends you. I also remembered the actor Timothy Spall telling me that you shouldn't start drinking if you are feeling down because you will always associate drinking with problems, and that's not a good way to start a relationship with drink. Fortunately I didn't drink it. I kept it, and even as I write these words that can of Guinness is in my cupboard with the breakfast cereals, by the bread bin. I guess it's now undrinkable. Either that or it's worth millions of pounds.

46

Divorced Absolute

Two weeks after Amina and I parted, and I was still locked inside the house feeling sorry for myself, I turned on the TV and, completely by chance, there was a programme announcing the nation's favourite children's poems of all time, as voted through the BBC. The very first words I heard were those of the presenter saying, 'And in fifth place it's Benjamin Zephaniah with 'Talking Turkeys'.' Quite taken aback, I sat down as they played a short piece with the children saying why they liked the poem so much and what it meant to them. The presenter then asked if they had a 'message for Benjamin', and all the kids turned, looked directly to camera, and said: 'Benjamin, we love you!'

Well, that went to the core of me. In fact, I was moved to tears. There I was sitting in a darkened room feeling like the most unloved, childless man in the world, and there were all these kids telling me that they loved me. That was the jump-start I needed to motivate me to get off *my* backside and do some work. There wasn't much I could do about Amina, but I thought of the kids on TV as being *my* kids, and told myself I had to pull myself together for the sake of my children. Those four words to camera, directed at me, gave me focus and spurred me on.

I didn't know how to tell my mum about our separation; I sensed she would have told me that she'd warned me. It took me about three weeks before I had the guts to say anything, but when I did she said, 'I knew something was wrong.'

I had no idea where Amina had gone. I tried tracing her by talking to her family, but they were being evasive. Eventually I found out she was at her sister's house, so I telephoned her to ask why she left. She told me she was fed up being married to somebody famous and fed up with all my travelling — either with or without her — at which point I told her that she knew who I was before we got married.

Whatever I said, I couldn't win. The only time I saw her after that was when I took some of the few things she had left behind to her sister's in Nottingham. I was quite emotional, but when I tried to talk to her she flippantly said, 'Get over it, people get divorced all the time'. I then realised how old and old-fashioned I was.

I'd had some big fallouts with girlfriends in the past but I'd stayed good friends with most of them, and I thought it would be so with Amina, especially because we had been together for so long — thirteen years. We had a couple of conversations, and in one of those conversations — when I realised we really were heading for divorce — I suggested possible terms for a financial split, in order to keep things simple and not involve lawyers and big costs.

A couple of days came and went, and then a

few more days came and went, and I heard nothing from her. So I called. Her younger sister answered and told me bluntly that Amina was not going to call me, and the only place I would see her was in court. And so divorce proceedings began. She had spoken to her family and I got the impression they had told her to 'take me to the cleaners', because the next time I spoke to Amina I was talking to an angry woman who I felt wanted to talk to me only about money and nothing else.

The divorce was getting messy, and after initially retaining a solicitor, I thought I could do it better and cheaper myself, so I bought a 'do your own divorce' book and began to take care of myself. The early stages were surprisingly easy — just a process of sending standard letters to her solicitor. I couldn't believe people paid so much for such paper shuffling. Using this book I saved thousands of pounds. I only engaged a new solicitor when we were ready to go to court, and that's when I really needed him.

Amina began to claim money I'd earned long before I knew her. She wanted my house, my mother's house, and she even wanted to claim on future earnings. I thought the claims were outrageous, but she kept on pushing for more, encouraged, I believed, by members of her family. In the end, the day before we were due in court, when I believe she must have felt that things would not go well for her, she capitulated and settled out of court.

It was a very sad way to end our relationship. We both lost out, in that we never spoke to each other again. Moreover she lost out financially because, in the final settlement, she had to pay all the court costs and ended up with less money than I had originally offered her. It's a nasty business.

I hated the whole divorce process and, since then, if I ever think of marriage, I think of divorce. My solicitor warned me that divorce is not like falling out with a girlfriend. He said, 'This is war.' Friends had told me that you never really know your husband or wife until you face them in a divorce court and, I have to say, I now agreed with them.

47

Justice for Us

On 7 September 2003 my cousin Michael Powell, or Mikey, as we used to call him, died while in police custody. Mikey was prone to very high highs and very low lows, and could be quite an unpredictable chap. But he was harmless and loved by all who knew him. He once climbed onto the roof of his mother's house — his mother being my Auntie Claris. Auntie Claris couldn't get him down, so she called the police. A policewoman turned up, smiled at Mikey, and promised to hang out with him for a while. Basically she chatted him up, and he came down. It was all very light-hearted, with the police-woman telling him to try and behave and be nice to his mum, before she went on her way.

So, a few months later, when Auntie Claris was having problems with Mikey again, she called the police once more, thinking that a nice officer would come round and sweet-talk him again. But this time it was different. This time it was 1am, and the police turned up in riot mode. They weren't in the mood to try to pacify him; they weren't interested in talking to him. A loud black man on the streets at that time of the morning could only mean trouble, so the first thing the police did when they saw him was run him over in their car. They did that, they said, because they couldn't see his hands, and because they couldn't see his hands they presumed he was armed. After they ran him over they took him away. When they took him away he was alive; two hours later he was dead.

I first heard about it on a radio news report that said a young black man had died in police custody in Birmingham in the middle of the night. Sadly the news of a black person dying in a police station wasn't news to me. I knew about the deaths of David Oluwale, Joy Gardner and Colin Roach, so I cursed Babylon and went to sleep. I woke up very early the next morning with my phone constantly ringing and various members of my family telling me Mikey was dead.

It was difficult for all of us, but at a time when a seasoned campaigner like me should have sprung into action there was little I could do or say. The police and their lawyers watched everything I did and listened to everything I said in the hope I would say something that would prejudice the case. With the case ongoing we were all subject to the law of subjudice, which meant we had to be very careful. Especially me.

For example, we couldn't say that Mikey was *killed* in custody; we could only say that he died in custody. We couldn't say we knew that something had happened, as that would imply we had evidence; we could only talk about wanting to get to the truth. The police carefully combed through anything I wrote in the press, and everything I said in public was monitored. I

291

suspect that much of what I said in private was also monitored.

We fought a long, hard campaign for justice, and in 2009 we finally heard what we'd known for a long time when we got the verdict from the inquest. It found that the way Mikey had been restrained had resulted in his death from positional asphyxia. Our family had always known how he died; it was very sad that it took us so long to get that official verdict. Mikey's sister, Sieta Lambrias, campaigned tirelessly for justice for Mikey. She was also pleased that the truth came out, even though it took six years.

The factors that led up to Mikey's death make for sickening reading: being in contact with a moving vehicle; being sprayed with CS gas; being struck by a baton and being restrained on the ground while suffering a psychosis.

If there was any good that came out of this it was that it united the black community in Birmingham (and other parts of the country) and it united my family too. Relatives who once thought I was too political were now getting political themselves. Their front rooms had become campaign headquarters or meeting rooms; they became activists and organisers; they were marching and lobbying MPs, and working with other activists around the country. They were standing in solidarity with other families that had lost loved ones in institutions around the country, and becoming aware of how the issues that affected them were connected to issues affecting other working-class people. They were awake, and I now took pride in the fact that people didn't only think of me as a campaigner, they thought of my family as campaigners.

★ ★ ★

Race relations have changed enormously during my lifetime. In 2015 I did a short film for BBC's *Newsnight* to mark the fiftieth anniversary of the Race Relations Act, which came into being in 1965 to outlaw discrimination on the grounds of colour, race or ethnic or national origins. The Act wasn't perfect. For instance, when it was brought into being it was all about outlawing racism in public places. That meant it was perfectly okay to be racist at home or at the local pub, as long as the landlord didn't mind.

I also thought the title was wrong. It should have been called the Anti-Racism Act rather than the Race Relations Act, which was a typically quaint British way of phrasing it. The Act was initially about stopping black people being beaten up after the Notting Hill Riots of 1958 and it's since been amended and amended and amended.

The Act was worthwhile, but while you can control people's actions you can't control their thoughts. We had come a long way and it would have been wrong to say that things were the same as they'd been when I was a boy. Racism in the first decade of the new century was not as bad as it had been in the 1960s, '70s or '80s, but that's not to say things were great. The new racists had learned to be subtler than they used to be. There were plenty of them out there, but their brand of racism was more insidious, more sophisticated, more institutional. It had to be.

The old racists didn't all die off; they got jobs, and many of them got jobs in our institutions. So we couldn't let our guard down. We still had work to do. Most gangs of young black kids weren't scared of young white kids any more. There weren't gangs of skinheads going out and beating people up as they used to — well, not as often as they used to — but black kids were rightly scared of the police. They were stopped and searched a lot more often than white kids because they had a different colour skin. If you're a black kid walking home at 1am or 2am, the last thing you want to see is the police. If you're stopped and searched, it's frightening. If you're seventeen or eighteen and don't know the law, you might not know what could happen. But these kids now knew they could end up like my cousin Mikey Powell.

The racists had grown up; they had put on suits and ties and formed political parties. They were working in the local council, in marketing, banking and in furniture upholstery. They were building websites. They were blending in.

★ ★ ★

A couple of friends from Peterborough called me one day and asked me to do them a favour. They had put their house on the market and were going to have an open day. They had a young child called Glory, who I know really well, and they asked me if I would look after her while they cleaned the house to make it presentable.

So I went over and took Glory to the park so they could get on with the job and welcome their potential buyers. It was a warm spring day and I was probably enjoying the park rides in the play area more than Glory was. At one point I was pushing Glory on a swing when a woman came to admire her, as ladies sometimes do with children in parks. She asked me the age of the baby and I said she was almost two. She waved to Glory, who paid no attention to her, and then walked away. Ten minutes later the police turned up — one male and one female — and asked if the baby was mine.

'No,' I said. 'She's my friend's baby.'

'What are you doing with her?' asked the male officer.

'Playing. Just like all the other parents, grandparents, uncles and child minders you see around you. Is there something wrong with that?'

A crowd was gathering and it was obvious to everyone present that I was getting hassled because I was a black guy with a white kid, but the police refused to say why they were quizzing me.

'Can you call the parents?' asked the male officer.

'I can but I won't,' I replied. 'That would only upset them and make them worried.'

'Why don't you know the age of the little girl?' asked the female officer.

'I don't remember her birthday, but I know she's about two.'

I was now holding Glory in my arms, when the female officer reached out and asked if she could hold her. Glory was horrified by this. She turned back to me, putting her arms around my shoulders as she clung onto me for dear life. The crowd was getting bigger. They saw this and began to let the officers know via a series of one-liners and groans, that if the baby feared me she wouldn't be clinging onto me, she would want to get away.

We were having a standoff. The crowd was getting more vocal, some telling the police directly that they were reacting to a racist call and were being racist. I could have stayed there much longer, but to make peace and defuse the situation I called Glory's mother and put the phone on speaker. The first thing she said was. 'Are you two having fun?'

The police realised there was nothing wrong and said we were free to go, but it was 2014 and I found it hard to come to terms with the fact that if I, a black man, am in the company of a white child, I am suspicious. Glory could have been my adopted daughter — my baby. After this event I asked some white people who had adopted black children if they had ever experienced anything like this, and they all said, 'No.'

48

The Blair Affair

When Mikey was murdered Tony Blair was prime minister. I didn't know him well, but I had met him a couple of times; the first not long after he became prime minister. Black people all over the country were celebrating fifty years since the arrival of the *Empire Windrush* — the ship that landed at Tilbury Docks in 1948 carrying the first big group of Caribbean immigrants.

Robin Cook, who was Foreign Secretary at the time of the fifty-year celebrations, had recently told the country that he wanted to bring a bit of colour to the Foreign Office, so as a way of getting the government in on the celebrations he employed a black-run PR company to hold an event at the Foreign Office. That PR company then asked me to perform, and for some strange reason I said yes.

It didn't happen to me very often, but this was one of those times when I wondered why I'd agreed. First of all I wondered if, in an indirect way, I was working for the government, and secondly the room was full of people who in other circumstances would order that I be removed from the premises. But I had said yes, I was there, and I only had to perform one poem, and that was a piece I'd written about the voyage, called 'The

297

Men from Jamaica Are Settling Down'.

Robin Cook went on stage after me. I knew him quite well from TV programmes like *Question Time*. He thanked all the black people in the country for coming over and teaching him how to dance, and bringing curries and culture, and then he told everyone that when he'd become Foreign Secretary he'd promised to bring a little colour into the place, but he didn't think that would involve performing after Benjamin Zephaniah. He said he thought we'd make a good double act and we should go on tour together. Now none of that is particularly funny, but these government types really laugh at these kinds of things, and laugh they did. 'Ho, ho, ho, jolly good, Robin, old chap.'

When he left the stage he came over to me. He was one of those people who were constantly looking over the shoulders of the person in front of him to see if there was someone more important to work his way up to. Then he saw Tony Blair, who'd just arrived.

Blair was too late to hear Robin Cook or myself, but Robin's eyes lit up. 'We must say hello to Tony,' he said.

'Must we?' I asked.

'Of course,' he said. 'He'll be so pleased to see you.'

Everyone knew about Tony Blair's plastic smile. Well, I got it full on.

'I've been watching you on television,' he beamed. 'My kids love your books, and I can play a bit of reggae on my guitar. We should get together and share some ideas.'

Robin repeated his joke, about the two of us performing as a double act and going on tour, probably thinking that Tony would react like the assembled ladies and gentlemen, but he didn't. Tony flipped. His plastic smile disappeared; he wagged his finger at Robin and said, angrily, 'You'll do no such thing. That's a ridiculous idea. I need to speak to you. See me in my office in the morning.'

Robin stood as if in shock, and quite a few people heard it. For a moment I wondered if this was some kind of act they were putting on, but when I realised it wasn't, I actually felt sorry for Robin as he walked away, head hanging down like a naughty schoolboy.

For a while I was really puzzled by this outburst, until a year or so later, when I was in the Seychelles. I had done a couple of performances and was hanging out with the British ambassador (as you do) and I told him the story. 'I heard about that,' he said. And he proceeded to explain that it was all to do with Robin Cook being found out for having an affair with his secretary.

The previous Conservative government became known for what some called sleaze, and others called corruption, so when the Labour Party (or New Labour, as it liked to be called then) had got into power they had pledged to get rid of all that sleaze. And they did — for about a week. There was probably lots of bed-jumping going on, but Robin was seen as the first person to bring the party into disrepute. So Tony didn't want any playing around from his Foreign Secretary. I tried to imagine going on tour with

Robin Cook, and it wasn't happening, but neither was bringing Tony Blair into my band as my guitarist.

49

Benjamin Zephaniah No B E

Call me naive but I thought I should follow up Tony Blair's invitation to share some ideas with him, so I wrote to him. I wanted to talk to him about the death of my cousin Mikey Powell. I wanted to share the idea of peace-talking as opposed to war-mongering. I wanted to share the idea of a police service as opposed to a police force. I wanted to remind him of what the Labour Party used to stand for, and give him the word on the street. I wrote to him a few times, but I got no reply. I had a lot to say to him. I knew stuff. I was involved in many demonstrations, so I could tell him how a lot of people were feeling.

Every year there's a march for the families of people who have died in custody, and I regularly attend. There were also many protests about animal rights issues at this time, which I was also involved in. Our country was involved in two illegal wars, one of which brought over a million people onto the streets, and most of them would have heard of me. So I thought I could really help Tony out.

At one of these marches I was at the head of a delegation concerned with deaths in custody and it was my job to hand over a petition. A man who thought he was important stopped me outside Number 10 Downing Street, telling me I couldn't go any further. So I said, 'Look, Tony said I could pop in and see him, share some ideas and stuff, so tell him I'm here.' He went away but Tony didn't come. So when, out of the blue, I got a letter from Mr Blair, I was perplexed. This time it was he who'd had an idea. He wanted to offer me up to the Queen of England; he wanted me to bow before her and receive an OBE. *What was Tony thinking?* I thought. *Did he really know who I was?*

That week George W. Bush was in town, and I already had a small article printed in the *Guardian* called 'Dear George'. I was among a group of people who'd written letters about the things we'd like to say to George Bush. I knew I couldn't accept the OBE — it was against everything I stood for — but I didn't want to go public on that for a week or two. So I wrote an article explaining why I had decided to reject it, and I sat on it for a couple of weeks.

The only person to see the article in those weeks was the poet Michael Rosen. I was never confident when it came to writing newspaper articles, and Michael was someone I could trust to keep it quiet and to give me honest feedback. After reading it he pointed out some misspelt words and said, 'Benjamin, you really have something here.'

Tony Blair's office rang my agent to ask what was going on, but she really didn't know. She had to call me to ask if it was true that I was being offered an OBE, and I said, 'Yes, but I

302

don't want it.' So we left it and did nothing. Then I heard that Tony Blair himself had started ringing around for me, but I told everybody not to say anything. I wanted my rejection to be completely public. I had nothing to hide and I wasn't going to respect his request for secrecy. Too much secrecy had been the problem with his administration; I wasn't going to play that game. I wanted everyone to know my decision and why I'd made it.

When George Bush had gone home, and I felt the time was right, I handed the article over to the *Guardian*. They published it, for all the world to see, in November 2003. Tony read it when everyone else did, I guess. I wouldn't know, as we haven't spoken since.

$\star$ $\star$ $\star$

I was absolutely sick of hearing people say how much the OBE and other government honours didn't mean anything to them, and that they would never bow down before the Queen, but then, as soon as they were offered one, they found all kinds of excuses for their sudden change of mind. Most claim they did it for the kids, or for their parents or, the saddest one of all, for the community.

I say to anyone who accepts an award from the Queen and says it is 'for their community' — don't keep the award, give it to the community. I knew what I did for my community, and I didn't need a medal from the Queen to remind me. I hated the word 'empire', I hated the idea of empire, whether it was the Romans or the British or Christians or Muslims. In my little mind, anybody ruling over anybody else was wrong. And for those who would say that the Order of the British Empire doesn't really have anything to do with the empire — and that it's simply a word that's been left attached to the award — I say, if it's just a word and not that important, then they can remove the word. But I still wouldn't take it.

The right-wing press used Trevor Phillips, who was then the head of the Commission for Racial Equality, to attack me. The commission, which was set up to support black people, was becoming an embarrassment to many in the community and Trevor was beginning to be seen as a stooge, which was rather sad because he was once seen as a progressive community activist. His attack on me might have been an attempt to help his friends in the media, or to get involved in the debate, but it backfired badly on him. The tabloids love it when one black person attacks another, but I was a bit bemused by his criticism because he had my number and could have called me if he had something to say to me.

The black community, and the wider community, really rallied behind me over the refusal. A week after my letter to the *Guardian* I counted over 3,000 letters, and then there was a short delay until the second wave arrived. These were from people based abroad, and in came another 3,500 letters. So I'd written one article and received over 6,500 letters, with only three being negative. Compare that to the government who invited letters from the public when it held an inquiry into the honours system, and they received 100 letters. I even had letters from people who said they'd accepted honours because they didn't know how to refuse them.

Channel 4 asked me to go into their studio to talk about my rejection of the OBE on the day I should have been picking it up. I said I would do the interview but the TV crew would have to come to where I was, and I was spending the day with a group of children and supporters in a bookshop in the East End.

The interview was with Jon Snow. Coincidentally, Jon had also refused an OBE, but not a lot of people knew that. In the studio with him was my good friend, the journalist Yasmin Alibhai-Brown. Yasmin, to my surprise, had received an MBE some years before, and she was now challenging me about my position, saying that she accepted her award because it was an honour from her adopted country, and that she thought it was recognition and young Asian women would look towards her for inspiration.

But I told her young Asian women were already inspired by her — many had told me so — so she didn't need some sort of royal or government approval. The programme was live, and it was a lively debate. Then, at one point, as I was mid-sentence, she interrupted and said: 'Benjamin, Benjamin, stop, stop. You've convinced me. You're right. I'm giving my MBE back.'

A few journalists and others said afterwards that they'd never seen anything like it. When live on air people tended to hold their ground and, even if they change their mind, they don't admit they're wrong until after the programme. I really respect Yasmin for having the guts to be so honest live on air.

The next day she wrote an amazing article about how she felt. It posed the question, 'What do you do when you want to give your OBE back? Do you knock on the door of Buckingham Palace and say, 'Hello, here's your OBE, Your Majesty. I no longer want it'?' It was a great, humorous article. She did get some criticism for giving it back, mostly from people who said she shouldn't have taken it in the first place, rather than waiting for inspiration from me. Some suggested there was a whiff of hypocrisy in taking it and then returning it, but I thought she showed real courage.

★   ★   ★

I was also spoken about many times as a possible Poet Laureate — both before and after the OBE episode — but I've always made it clear I wouldn't accept it. I had some sympathisers who thought that being Poet Laureate would be a good thing because I'd represent them really well, but I still say no. It's a job where officially the Queen, or whoever sits on the throne, is your boss. You have to write poems for the Royal Family and their royal events, and yet you're not expected to criticise them. It is this being unable to criticise them element that I can't stand. The poet should always be critical. As well as all the praising a poet can do, the poet should also criticise the country, criticise the weather; poets should even criticise themselves.

As I've previously stated, I've worked with the British Council, which some may call part of the establishment, but in reality most people don't know the ins and outs of the organisation. The so-called 'Head of State' is the patron of that organisation, so when I turned down the OBE I made it clear I had nothing against the Queen personally. I've met her; she came to one of my poetry readings at the Royal Albert Hall, and I remember thinking that she couldn't help being born into that family. It must a burden for her. She was stiff and false, though, unlike Nelson Mandela, who was also present. He was open, smiling, huggable. He danced as he walked towards me, whereas the Queen marched.

Wealth is one thing, and most people want wealth (usually for all the wrong reasons), but who wants to live a life unable to walk down the street or to simply get lost without a load of minders knowing where you are? I've always considered this a rather sad existence, but I don't feel sorry for the institution of monarchy. I find it difficult to respect an institution that has its roots in class division, robbing people of their lands, subjecting people to slavery and claiming a divine right to rule. Then there's the fact of their privileges, their undemocratic positioning, their arrogance, their love of hunting, their support of evil wars, their ill-gotten fortune and their lack of accountability. Not much really! So why would I want to be their personal poet?

Hereditary privilege does not a meritocracy make, and I've always thought we are being hypocritical if we criticise countries that don't allow people to vote for their head of state when we can't vote for ours. My family is royal, and my mother is my queen. There are thousands of royal families around the world, and many live modest and humble lives with no wish to rule over anyone. So never mind the family, but damn the monarchy.

As every new laureate turns up, they say they want to change the role a little bit, but the bottom line is that it's an antiquated role that compromises you. If you don't mind being compromised that's fine, but when the caged bird sings of freedom, it doesn't mean it's free. Every laureate claims he or she wants to bring something fresh to the job, and wants to connect to the grass roots, but they never do. I have no wish to leave the grass roots, work for the establishment, and then try to reconnect with the grass roots. It's back to front, the wrong way round. The grass roots is where my heart is. Nuff said, so here's a full stop.

50

Going Country

Since my break-up with Amina, I'd been slowly renovating my house with the help of friends. We'd put up new wallpaper, put down new floors, painted the woodwork and spruced up the garden. I think deep down I had to do this to make the house more 'mine' than what had been 'ours'. We did a grand job, but when it was all finished I sat back and thought it was nice but something was nagging at me.

It wasn't the house, it was the area; I wanted a real change. I knew in my heart of hearts that what I really wanted was to live in the country-side — in one of those villages you see on postcards where there's a pub, a church and a post office, and people say good morning or good afternoon to you before they get into a deep analysis of the weather.

When I was a kid we couldn't afford holidays, so we went for days out in the Malvern Hills with Pastor Burris. I was the kid with his face at the car window. As soon as the doors were open I'd be off, marvelling at everything around me — the animals, the trees, the sky. I'd always longed to live away from the city. I now had freedom. I didn't have to ask anyone what to do. I wanted to live in the countryside and now I could just do it.

At the end of 2006 I very quickly found a place in a small village in Lincolnshire. It was the kind of village I had been dreaming of, and it worked out perfectly. Angela, the woman who was selling the house, wanted to move out really quickly and get off to Australia. I was about to start touring in South Africa, so I needed to get in quickly. So together we moved much faster than the estate agents could get their act together. Within a month I was in.

Being in a village gave me everything I'd always wanted. I still had time to spend in London and, if anything, I probably appreciated London better. I could enjoy going to community centres, concerts and theatres there but, at the end of the night, or come the weekend, I could drive away from it. I started noticing the difference in the air, as I'm very mindful of pollution levels. If I go jogging in London I can taste the pollution at once. My life was rooted in the city, and my political perspective came from the inner city, but when I moved to this beautiful little village I began to understand rural issues. I learned about communication, the transport issues that cut people off in the countryside and rural poverty.

As if to help me on my way, the BBC asked me to present a couple of TV programmes about life in the countryside. With the help of their researchers, coupled with what I was hearing from people around me, I began to see a community in crisis. This wasn't about millionaire farmers complaining about the European Union, or the lack of help they got from the government; this was about young white people who felt hopeless and saw no future if they were to stay in their villages.

When people are poor in the city, there are still things for them to do; there are usually services and amenities, and if they don't want them they can hang out on the streets with their friends. But in rural areas there is nothing. There may be a village hall, but they would have to share it with their grandparents, and it doesn't matter how good your grandparents are, that's not cool. In small villages kids can't even hang out on the streets because when it goes dark, it goes really dark, and they need to see who they're snogging.

If they want to head out to nearby towns or cities, well, the bus only goes through the village a couple of times during the day, and at night there are no buses. Young and old can be really isolated, and that isolation can lead to desperation. The week I arrived in the village there were two suicides and one death by accident with farming machinery, which was the major cause of fatalities in the area.

★ ★ ★

Despite those issues, I'm very glad I made this one big change in my life, even though it was a risk, and plenty of friends and family thought I was crazy. A few black friends thought it was great, but some people, like my mum, couldn't understand it. She thought it was going backwards.

'What you going there for?' she asked,

astonished. 'You don't know anyone. What if there's an emergency? There's no Co-op!' But other people I knew, white people, were also shocked, their disbelief somehow implying that it wasn't my place — that I should be in a city.

There's something a lot of people overlook, and that is the majority of people who are immigrants of African, Caribbean and Asian descent are not from cities. We're stereotyped as city people when in fact most of us originated from rural places. Most Indians are not from Delhi; they're from villages. If you look at the Punjab, it's all farming land. Most Jamaicans who originally settled in the UK were not Kingstonians — they were from St Elizabeth, St Ann, St Catherine. It's only in England that we've been put into cities because it's where we could find work. When most of us go to the countries of our heritage, we go to a rural place.

Gardening — especially growing my own food — is now one of my greatest passions. I didn't know a thing to start with, and at first I had to get someone to show me how to mow the lawn! But because I'm vegan I'm tapped into a network of vegan organic gardeners. Not long after moving to the countryside I was approached and asked to write a foreword for a book called *The Vegan Book of Permaculture*, published by Permanent Publications. And, in a nice bit of synchronicity, when I looked at the book I realised it was the one I needed to read.

A friend put me onto an organic gardener, who came and spent a day with me, and I learned a lot in a short space of time. He told me to order some 'green manure'. Putting energy into your soil has to be your obsession if you are an organic gardener. The green manure plant takes energy from the sun and puts it back into the earth rather than using it to grow itself. It's a way of giving the land a rest and rejuvenating it.

A lot of organic gardening is trial and error but I love it, even though it takes time. A neighbour who comes from a farming family gives me tips — and the county I live in is the biggest area in the UK for growing veg. So far I've successfully grown sweet potatoes, courgettes, cucumbers, garlic, onions, marrows, peppers, pumpkins and loads of tomatoes. I've even grown grapes. I like to make dishes like curries and stews, blending my homegrown veg with kidney beans, chickpeas or butter beans. I hardly ever have to go to a supermarket. And I listen to *Gardeners' Question Time* more than you might imagine.

I remember the first meal I ate which I'd grown myself. I looked at my plate and was amazed. I got so emotional I had to call somebody. I got on Skype as I was eating. I was exclaiming: 'See this potato, it was just a seed!' I picked up something else: 'I knew this when it was a clipping!' It was the realisation that I was connecting with the land and nature in the most basic but rewarding way.

I think the way I live now is like a mixture of England and Jamaica, but mostly England. I love where I am. Sometimes I've closed the gate and not gone anywhere for two weeks. Normally that would mean a lack of exercise, but not for me.

I've got a gym, a lawn, a sauna. I can communicate. If I want to be creative, I can go into my recording studio or my library. If I decide I don't want to go out for three weeks, I can be completely self-sufficient. I've even dreamt of going off-grid and having solar panels. When I first moved to Lincolnshire there used to be power cuts, and that's what gave me the idea. Maybe that'll be my next step in self-sufficiency.

51

De Botty Business

Of all my plays, the one I'm most proud of is *De Botty Business*, which toured in 2008. Most people wouldn't think it possible to write a comedy about cancer, but when you're using actors whose characters are speaking in Caribbean dialects, and being very physical and vocal, you cannot help but raise laughs with the target audience — in this case, black men of a certain age.

The play was commissioned by Prostate Cancer UK, a charity rather than a theatre company, and the aim was to get the message out there that middle-aged African-Caribbean men are three times more likely to suffer with prostate cancer than their white counterparts. This demographic is also often unwilling to get themselves checked out, as they fear the medical procedure for testing for the cancer involves digital anal penetration. In fact, a rectal inspection is often way down the line in the list of tests a doctor will do. Before that, there would be blood and urine tests. Research has found that men are more positive about getting checked out once they know this.

Our aim was to tour it in places where people who aren't theatre-goers would see it — community centres, domino halls and barber shops — although it also played in Birmingham Rep and at the good old Hackney Empire. I wanted to make the central character a Rasta who inherits a barber shop. Now, a barber shop isn't much use to a Rasta, who doesn't believe in cutting hair, but the location is a recognised focal point of social exchange and gossip for black men the world over. So it was the ideal location in which to explore the issue. It was set in a barber shop, and would be performed in barber shops.

And it worked. The comedic element comes from the way that one character would repeat a myth about the issue, and then another character would dismiss that myth in true Caribbean style.

I wanted to tackle the issue of machismo. One Trinidadian character thinks having a finger up the bottom is a plot by the white man: 'Nah man come put him finger up mi botty, choh! You know all dem white men are gay!'

I didn't want the play to be dry with statistics, so issues and anxieties are thrashed out in a way that's entertaining to an audience. And of course the play shows what happens if you ignore the warning signs by trying to preserve your masculine dignity. There are statistics, but the delivery is how real people in the community talk about things. So instead of a load of numbers, a guy might say, 'A whole heap of people get dis.' I didn't want it to be worthy; I wanted the characters to be like real people I've known, speaking in no-holds-barred language. I wanted people laughing their heads off rather than being blinded with science.

Once I'd written the play, the charity arranged for the first audience to be prostate cancer doctors and researchers. Most were white European, a couple were Asian, all in suits. I watched as they started tuning into the dialect, and soon they were laughing. When it was done, I was told it was perfect. One doctor said, 'This is exactly what you should be doing.'

I was really pleased. I really didn't want the message to get bogged down with doom and doom. And as I'd had it vetted by the doctors and researchers, I was also able to put in the latest findings that certain foods, such as cooked tomatoes, pomegranate and cranberry juice, has been found by some researchers to reduce the risk of getting the disease.

When it performed at the Hackney Empire, the audience included the great and the good of the entertainment industry, who filled the first few rows of the auditorium. At first I was nervous, seeing all those faces from TV, but when I saw them laughing I was so relieved. I wanted to put on a play that wasn't arty, and in a way it was my most satisfying play. There was hardly any money in it, but I did it at a time in my career when I wasn't writing very much because I was concentrating on touring and radio broadcasting. I'm very proud of it and I know it made a difference to exactly the people it was aimed at.

I later heard about a guy who said he'd started going to the toilet a few times every night and then he 'remembered seeing Benjamin Zephaniah's play', and so went and got checked out and they caught his prostate cancer early enough to treat it.

I've come to realise that when you put your message out there as a poet or a playwright you won't necessarily see first-hand the good you're doing; your play performs somewhere and the audience sees it and disperses, but people out there can be changed by your work, and in the case of *De Botty Business*, there might have even been lives saved. You can't do better than that.

52

Farewell, My Friends

On the morning of 25 June 2009 I was performing in schools around the Portsmouth area. I went back to my hotel at lunch-time to download the vegan chocolate cake that I'd hidden in a cool place. As I put the key card in the wall the room woke up and the voice in the TV set said, 'Farah Fawcett, seventies pin-up girl and star of *Charlie's Angels*, has died.'

I jumped in front of the television, where they were showing the famous poster of her smiling happily and dressed, or undressed, in a red swimsuit. I was never a fan of the programme, or her, but the music and the whole atmosphere of it brought those times back to me. I said something like 'poor thing', and then went out to meet up with a friend.

When I got back I put the rest of the cake into myself and lay in bed rubbing my bloated stomach and watching *Question Time*. That week, Nicolas Sarkozy, the then president of France, announced he was setting up a commission to look at ways of restricting Muslim women wearing the burkha in public. For some very French reason he thought wearing such things shouldn't be done in secular France.

On the show was the Tory Pauline Neville-Jones,

who thought that in a democracy like ours the burkha should be banned. She was worried about teachers teaching children who could not see their faces. The other guests were Esther Rantzen, the Liberal Democrat Julia Goldsworthy and Kelvin MacKenzie of the *Sun* newspaper. They were all getting worked up about politicians over-claiming expenses. After a bit of ranting and raving the audience in Newquay clapped and went home. I was about to turn the TV off when a newsreader made an unscheduled appearance, saying he had breaking news. He said Michael Jackson had died. I turned the television off and stared at the blank screen for a while. Then I turned it back on to check, and another reporter was saying Michael Jackson was dead.

I flopped back onto my bed and looked at my ceiling for a while. The first record I ever bought when I was a small kid was 'Rockin' Robin' by the Jackson Five, with Michael taking the lead. For years Michael Jackson was a dependable voice, a solid black image on posters and TV screens, and although he wasn't political there was something very inspiring about having a family that sang and lived (we thought) in such harmony; a family led by a small boy with a great voice.

I loved Michael Jackson, but I have to say I loved him when he was black. When he started all that monkeying around, having all those operations and strange relationships with women and children, I went off him. And I'm not forming my opinions by things I've seen in the media; my knowledge comes from elsewhere.

Three months before he died something came over me. I suddenly had an urge to get some of him, so I bought most of his CDs. I told myself to forget about all the weirdness and just check out his music — most of which was produced by Quincy Jones, and I loved Quincy Jones. I had recently purchased a wicked pair of powered speakers, which greatly enhanced my listening experience, and I was listening to lots of music I had liked in my past. Through these speakers I could hear things I had never heard before.

I didn't want Jackson's problems to come between me and the music, and I wasn't let down. Suddenly I was singing 'Thriller' and 'Billy Jean' wherever I went, but still, every time I saw Michael I saw a confused drug addict who needed help. I used to feel so sorry for him, but I was angry with those around him that let him slip, slip — so much that he just slipped away.

As I lay in bed with the lights off, a text arrived. It was from a friend in Edinburgh telling me that the poet Swells had passed away. In the mid-1980s I did many gigs and a few tours with Swells, but over the years we had lost touch. From being a radical, angry and funny ranting poet, he had turned into a sports writer, in the US of A of all places — a change in direction that nobody saw coming.

I did a lot of thinking that night. Farah Fawcett, Michael Jackson and Swells all seemed (in their very different ways) to represent my generation, and they all went within twenty-four hours of each other. Swells died of enteropathy-associated T-cell lymphoma, and the day before he left us he wrote an online blog where he compared the important differences between getting worked up about world poverty and getting angry because you've lost pieces of your jigsaw.

He wrote: 'I speak as someone whose greatest craving at this exact moment is not world peace and universal democracy or a rational and global redistribution of wealth, but a can of ice-cold ginger ale.' Swells had been ill for some time, and he saw his end coming, but we're pretty sure he didn't see the death of Michael Jackson coming. There was no way he could have known that MJ died a few hours before he did. Everyone knows the lyrics to 'Blame It on the Boogie'. So it was quite spooky to read that Swells had finished his blog by saying: 'When it comes to poor education, cultural deterioration and moral decline, me . . . I blame it on the sunshine. I blame it on the moonlight. I blame it on the boogie.'

★ ★ ★

I grew up around a lot of death. When I was twelve years old a friend called Stephen Riley took a heroin overdose and killed himself. One of my friends stabbed another friend with a knife and killed him right in front of me outside a club. On 21 November 1974, two of my closest friends, Neil Marsh and Paul Davis, were killed when the IRA bombed the Tavern in the Town pub in Birmingham. I had lost other friends because of gang fights and tribal wars. So death was never far from me but, as I was getting older, I began to notice that many of my friends were dying of natural causes.

Musarat Ahmed, a close friend who I had mentored and counselled after a terrible childhood with an abusive father — and who had then been forced to marry her cousin, who had no love for her — was hit by cancer of the throat, then cancer of the tongue, and from the tongue it spread to other organs. She was a lover and writer of poetry, and tried to educate herself even though she was surrounded by people who expected her to be a passive, obedient housewife. She died a slow, painful death, but she told me that her dying was better than the life she had lived because no one was expecting anything of her, no one wanted her to work, and no one wanted sex with her. Most of all she was convinced she was going to a place of peace.

Terisa Meyer was someone I called my sauna partner. We were both addicted to saunas and, because I had one, she would often come round to my place so we could sit in the heat and just talk. Some of my friends were horrified and some were amazed that two grown people could sit in a sauna and chat about food and politics, but that's all we did. Then one day she told me she had breast cancer. She put up a great fight but in the end the cancer took her.

* * *

When it came to British politicians, there was only one person I could truly trust and confide in, and that was Tony Benn. We had known each other since the days of Rock Against Racism; we campaigned together against apartheid, wars and unfair taxes. He was a man of true conviction, a great public speaker, and he became president of the Stop the War coalition from the year 2000, when he was already retired, characteristically saying he was leaving Parliament in order to spend more time on politics.

At first it was an inspiration simply to be on the same platform as him, but he eventually became a great personal friend and mentor. He was always happy for me to talk things through with him, and it was inspiring to be sitting in the same room as him when he was working. For a sense of the kind of man he was, if you think about the lengths people go to, to get gongs and OBEs, well, Tony went to court to get rid of his hereditary peerage.

He was passionate about keeping alive the roots and history of the labour movement and was hailed by all political parties as a great parliamentarian. He never forgot the achievements made for the benefit of the masses by those such as Clement Attlee, when the Tory way would have been to keep them down at heel, begging their masters for handouts.

Last time I saw Tony Benn he was doing a 'desert island poems' slot at the Ledbury Poetry Festival in July 2013. He'd chosen one of my poems as one of his 'discs'. The organisers wanted him to read it on stage and, at that point, unbeknownst to Tony, I would appear. So it was all arranged. He started reading the poem and then I walked on, to the delight of the crowd and all concerned. When I came off stage I kissed him. He was very frail, and I knew it would be the last time I'd see him. He died on 14 March 2014, and when I heard the news I thought, *Oh, there's nobody like him there now*, but then Corbyn came along, so there might be a fraction of hope for a non-Blairite future for the party. But there'll never be another Tony Benn.

53

Kung Fu and Meditations
on Funky China

Back in the year 2000 I did a tour of clubs and
schools in Hong Kong as part of my work with
the British Council. When the performances
were over I was asked if I wanted to go for a day
trip into what people called mainland China.
How I hate that term. I won't go on about how
the British stole Hong Kong (along with lots of
other stuff) and then did a ninety-nine-year deal
that was completely unfair to the Chinese. Or
how hypocritical the British were in criticising
'undemocratic' China while at the same time
denying citizens of Chinese origin the right to
vote in the British bit of China.

But the reality was there were now two
different systems and, whatever you thought of
the politics, Hong Kong was more like London
than China, so I wanted to go to China. All you
had to do was join an organised coach party,
leave your passport at the border and pick it up
on the way back. I had never travelled with a
tourist group in my life — to be honest, I hated
the idea — but it was only for one day.

China has fascinated me my whole life: the
sound of the language, the history, the size of the
place and, of course, the kung fu. As a child I'd

sat enthralled by the films of Bruce Lee. I first started training at the age of ten, simply copying the moves from a book. I went to various martial arts schools as a teenager, but this was all very on and off; I never stayed at a school long enough to get into a particular style. But I listened to my various tutors going on about the old masters back in China, and I wanted to find the old masters. This trip wasn't going to put me in touch with any of them, but at least I would be in the same country, and maybe I'd see one walking down the street, all monk-like.

After a two-hour coach ride from the border, we arrived at a city called Guangzhou and were let out to walk the streets. We went to a museum and then stopped at a restaurant which, from the outside, looked like a pet shop. The front window had live cats in cages that were there to be chosen by customers who would be eating them twenty minutes later.

I never normally go into a restaurant that sells meat, but this time I followed the crowd, partly because it was important that we stick together, but mainly because I wanted to listen to their conversations about how cruel it was to eat cats. To me, eating meat is eating meat, no matter what the species, so every conversation I hear about 'strange' people eating exotic animals sounds to me like racism, plus ignorance. Being with a group of tourists from all over the world arguing about what you should or should not eat is interesting. It reminded me of all the reasons I opted out of meat consumption altogether.

We didn't see any monks, and the trip wasn't

that interesting, but it gave me a taste for the place, so not long afterwards I organised my own trip. I didn't want it to be a normal holiday, and I certainly didn't want to be a typical tourist, so with the help of some friends I planned to visit Beijing, and from there I would travel to Henan, in the Northern Central Region, to the Shaolin Temple, to train with the real kung fu masters.

On my return, I quickly realised I loved the place. This was the time when everyone started talking about China's rapid growth, and I saw it happening right in front of me. The whole city was like a building site. I've never seen a country growing so quickly. Before I went to sleep at night I would take a look out of the window because I knew that when I woke up the next day the view would be different.

I met people who by Western standards were middle class, but one generation ago their families were slum dwellers. Everything on the east coast is so new that it's difficult to find vestiges of the old way of life. But the Chinese are very unromantic about history. They don't seem to have the same nostalgia as the West. For instance, when they were preparing for the Olympics in 2008, they didn't think twice about knocking down a temple that was 3,000 years old. The typical Chinese attitude is to say, 'What's the problem? We'll build a new one down the road.'

After partying in the city for a few days, I headed for Henan. Henan Province is regarded as the cradle of Chinese civilisation, and it's where a lot of martial arts originated, but it also has a reputation as being like the Wild West. If there's a theft, people in cities outside the province say, 'Oh, it must be someone from Henan', similar to how people in the UK used to talk about Liverpudlians as being scallywags.

Although much of what now surrounds the temple was created for tourists, I found a great teacher there who organised something I had always wanted to do — something I had seen only in films. He fixed it so that I spent some time training in the heart of the temple itself. Very few people are privileged to experience this. I documented much of this experience in my book *Kung Fu Trip*, which Bloomsbury published under the Quick Reads initiative in 2011.

★   ★   ★

After that first independent visit, I would return to China many times. I was unknown there, and I found it a great place to be creative. I wrote much of my books *Gangsta Rap*, *Teacher's Dead* and *Terror Kid* there because I was left untroubled. Every day I learned something new about the place. I would go to one area where they ate cats and snakes, then I would go to another part where they were all vegan. One city would look like something from a science fiction film, and a few miles away they would be living as they had for the past hundred years or more.

I love villages the world over. I love walking through them, meeting local people and listening to elders. I love the oral traditions you hear from people in their seventies, eighties and older, who have seen unprecedented changes take place during their lifetime. In these villages I made a point of riding around on a bicycle, so I was pretty easy to spot and was made very welcome. People wanted to sit down with the black man and talk and share food. Some were surprised when I told them I was vegan; then it was my turn to be shocked (and saddened) when I heard accounts of how rural skies, once blue and full of birds, were now polluted and empty. I also started to learn Chinese, because very few people in these villages spoke English and I needed to have conversations with them as well as with funky Beijingers.

In 2008 I discovered a small village in Henan called Chen Jia Gou, where the Chen style of t'ai chi originated. I had begun learning Chen style in Shaolin, but I knew the 'external' style of Shaolin kung fu had its limits, so I started to visit Chen Jia Gou, where I found a great teacher, the Grand Master, Chen Zhaosen. The place he taught from was typical of martial arts schools around the country — simple buildings where students could train, with a dining room and upstairs quarters for sleeping. The first thing the master said was 'Show me your t'ai chi.' I did about three minutes and then he stopped me and gave me the best lesson ever, explaining what I was doing wrong. I've now been visiting Chen Zhaosen for the past seventeen years.

Instead of focusing on external fighting styles, I concentrated on the internal aspects of the practice, learning how to generate power from breathing, balance, meditation and relaxation. With wing chun, instead of blocking punches, you learn to use an opponent's force by 'completing the circle' and never blocking their energy but instead using it against them. Even if it looks peaceful, every movement has a fighting application.

Along with poetry, the discipline of martial arts has been instrumental in turning my life around. It is a fantastic way of teaching you how to control anger and convert that energy into something positive. Some people recommend boxing as a way of keeping young men out of trouble, but I'd always say martial arts is the better way. You have to learn self-control and how to be humble; you can't just pile in and start throwing punches. It has helped me to stay focused and grounded when the annoyances of the world make themselves apparent.

54

Wot's Rong wid North Korea?

I've spent so much of my life travelling the planet that writing about all the countries I've visited would take up far too much room, but I have to say a little about one of the strangest places I've been to: North Korea. People think it's really difficult to get there, but it's not. Well, it wasn't when I visited in May 2012. There's an agency in Beijing that specialises in sending Westerners there, and they quite quickly fixed my trip. There's no visa needed, there were no long forms to fill in, you just go.

On arrival I was met by a person who would be my minder for the whole time I was there. Of course I was shown only the best bits, and a lot of the time it was like walking around a film set, but it was eye-opening to see a totalitarian state first-hand. Everybody talked about the Great Leader. I asked them who was the first man on the moon and they said King Jong-un. When I asked who invented the typewriter they said King Jong-il. I enquired who were the happiest people in the world, and they answered, 'North Koreans'. It was incredible. I asked people whether they really believed the things they were saying and they said they did. I couldn't tell if they were acting or if they did really believe it, but I didn't push them on things. What might have been a little push for knowledge from me could mean death for them.

After one girl showed me around an arts complex, I shook her hand and, as I did so, I discreetly palmed some money to her and she almost screamed. She thought I was handing her something illegal, and she feared the state so much that she nearly freaked out. I was only giving her a tip. But I must say that visiting North Korea helped me to understand it better than I had before.

I look at North Korea as an entity that has been abused and is now very paranoid. The country was occupied by the Japanese for thirty-five years, and it was a brutal occupation. And then other people, including the Soviet Union, came in until they felt as though they'd been brutalised and hated by everyone, so they wanted to be on their own. Visiting was important for me because I got to understand the way they thought about the world. That doesn't mean I agree with them. If an abused child goes on to be an abuser, or has bad behaviour, you don't condone it or agree with it but you can understand how it happened.

I was really lucky in that my guide was the daughter of the head of the nuclear programme. She'd been well educated in Austria and had also been to England. She said she knew my point of view, but she wanted me to understand her point of view as well. She knew how worried people were about North Korea having a bomb, but then she went off the tourist route and took me to a place where, using fancy vision equipment, you could see bomb launch sites in South Korea that were owned by the Americans and were pointing towards North Korea. She knew exactly how many bombs there were, and in Japan.

She said: 'If they fire at us, we want at least one to fire back. We're not very advanced, I know, but there are so many pointing towards us that we want to have some kind of reply.'

I couldn't agree with everything she said, but I did understand. My empathy is with the people who, like most people in the world, aren't thinking about history or philosophising about the merits or the ethics of a nuclear-free state. They just want food on the table.

★   ★   ★

After visiting North Korea I genuinely felt like kissing the ground when I arrived back in China. It's strange that in China I have never felt I couldn't go anywhere that any other Chinese citizen could go. Yes, there are restrictions on what you can read online, and the news you get, wherever it comes from, is government-approved, but the only time I was ever stopped and questioned was at the airport when I was leaving for Tibet, somewhere I'd always wanted to visit.

I was getting ready to board the plane when the police pulled me to one side. They told me they knew who I was and asked if I was going to write something while I was there. I told them I wasn't, that I just wanted a holiday. I kept saying

I wanted to see all of China. I told them I loved China. Once I'd used the word China, rather than Tibet, they decided I was okay. I'd stuck to the script and was allowed to board the plane.

My guide was Tibetan and very anti-Chinese. He refused to speak to me in Chinese, so we spoke in English and Urdu. He really told it as it was, insisting it was a real occupation. The Chinese there are much more privileged than the locals; they get all the top jobs and drive around in Range Rovers while the locals have very little and are poor.

The people are very religious. They pray on the streets, and in town squares, and walk endlessly around, seemingly going nowhere. If I left my hotel and turned right there was a vegan restaurant, but outside this restaurant there was always an old lady standing, massaging her prayer beads. One day as I was leaving the restaurant I offered her some food, which she refused.

'I'm not hungry,' she said.

'What are you doing here?' I asked.

She looked directly into my eyes, and said with a hint of a smile. 'I'm waiting for the Dalai Lama to come back. I was standing right here the last time I saw him. It was very different then.'

★ ★ ★

I later took an internal flight in China, sitting in what was business class. It was a small plane, so business class was just the first three rows of seats, but I guess it must have made me look important. People were still getting on the plane when a man in his mid-thirties came up to me brimming with excitement, holding a pen and notebook.

'Autograph,' he said in broken English.

'No problem,' I replied. One of the reasons I took to China was that no one knew me there, so I was pretty surprised by this. I didn't really want it to happen again, and I didn't want to encourage others. I signed it and sat down. But the man didn't go away. At first he stared at me, and then he shouted.

'Give me your real autograph. This is not real.'

'It is,' I said. 'That's my autograph.'

'No,' he shouted, 'you must write 'Bob Marley'!'

I burst into laughter. 'I am not Bob Marley,' I said.

'You are Bob Marley. You cannot trick me. So now, Bob Marley, give me your autograph,' he demanded.

I really didn't know what to say or do. Then another man, slightly older, came to my rescue.

'Hey,' he said, in a deep, reassuring voice. 'Don't be silly. This is not Bob Marley. Bob Marley is no longer with us. I know exactly who this is,' he said confidently. 'This is Kofi Annan.'

I looked around in despair to see if there was anyone else who could help me, but alas there wasn't. I signed one autograph as Bob Marley, another as Kofi Annan, and then I sat down to ponder the meaning of me.

55

Professor Zephaniah — aka Jeremiah Jesus

I was happy living in my Lincolnshire village. I had made, converted or constructed everything I wanted at my house: a small gym, a large gym, a library, a recording studio, a sauna, an artificial football-basketball-tennis court and my small plot of land that allows me to be self-sufficient in organic vegetables.

I don't believe a poet should ever think of retirement — we should stay creative forever — but I had reached the stage where I was only taking work that was important to me, or of political importance. When I wasn't working I was spending time in China, or to put it another way, I was spending most of my time in China but sometimes I was coming home to do some work.

So I was happy with my work/life balance, and I could have carried on like this for years, but then, in March 2011, I received a rather strange email from Professor Wendy Knepper of Brunel University. At the time I had fifteen honorary doctorates and at first I thought this was the offer of another one, but then I read the email and realised they were offering me a job, a professorship, a salary and students.

For months I thought about taking up the post. I needed to, because for the first time in my life I was going to join an institution, and I had spent my life trying not to be institutionalised. I needed to find out as much as I could about the university. Would it oppress me? Would I become an oppressor? I only really came into contact with universities when I performed at them, and I had performed at Brunel University in the mid-1980s. My support act back then was Julian Clary, before he used that name. Back then he was The Joan Collins Fan Club, featuring Fanny the Wonder Dog. Very weird, very camp, and I knew he was going places.

It was very important that I make the right decision, so I visited the campus on a number of occasions to see what it was like from the staff's point of view, and sometimes I went and hung out with the students to see it from their side. Sometimes I went there and didn't meet anyone at all; I'd walk around to see the lie of the land. After giving it much thought, I decided that my work in the university would be a continuation of what I was doing anyway: mentoring people and helping up-and-coming poets. It would be a formalisation of my creative life, so I took the job.

It was around this time that tuition fees were raised to £9,000 per year, so I felt it was important to be the best professor I could be. I knew from talking to students that it wasn't only about teaching; it was also about being positive, making sure students knew you cared about their education and giving them a good all-round experience. They had to leave university feeling ready to take on the world, and brimful of hope.

Many universities were trying to make their student populations more mixed, but Brunel never had that problem. It was one of the most multicultural institutions in the country. Like a lot of centres of higher education, there were students from all over the world. The Middle East, Africa and Eastern Europe were well represented, but by far the most foreign students came from China. But it was the make-up of the homegrown students that was most important, and this group was so mixed that ethnicity was not an issue. So I was surprised to find that as soon as I started the job I would not only have creative writing students, but students from engineering, law and other faculties, who would come to see me simply because they wanted to talk to a black professor. Some would see me almost as a counsellor. They would talk to me about their problems, both at university and at home. They would even talk to me about other members of staff if they felt they didn't understand their perspective. I thought it was important for them to have someone they could trust, and I realised I could be that guy.

The writer Bernardine Evaristo started at the university at the same time as me and, soon after, so did Will Self, a writer and public intellectual for whom I have great respect. Some people see us as 'celebrity professors', but we don't see ourselves like that. Students love the fact that lectures might start with a book signing or CD signing, but we take our work very seriously. I love lecturing. I love standing in front of students and seeing their faces light up when I burst into poetry. I don't enjoy the bureaucracy, though, and I can't get excited about reaching government targets, but when I'm standing in front of a group of students I come alive.

I have devised a module called 'Writing Poetry for Performance', which I've been told is the first of its kind. It isn't a module which has a performance poetry component, or the option to study performance poetry, interview performance poets or write some poetry and leave it at that. With my module you *have to perform*. Students can look at the work of other poets, they can study the history of performance poetry and the oral traditions of the world, but whatever they do, however they got there, this module comes down to them expressing themselves, using their own, original performance poetry. I encourage them to be personal; I encourage them to be political. It can get quite intense.

Over the years I have performed in universities all over the world but now, as I get older, I find myself lecturing in them. I use the term loosely because my lectures usually involve a lot of performing. I have guest-lectured in universities in South Korea, North Korea, Shanghai, Beijing, Tripoli (Libya), Mexico, Argentina, South Africa, Memphis, Ohio, India, various branches of the University of the West Indies, and I also accepted the position of Visiting Professor at De Montfort University in Leicester.

★　★　★

So there I was, in 2012, tending to my students, doing my performances and writing my novels, when I was invited to have a cameo role in a new TV drama — a drama with a difference. It would be set in 1920s Birmingham and it was to be called *Peaky Blinders*.

The Peaky Blinders were a real gang that once controlled parts of Birmingham similar to Mafia operations elsewhere. I was the first person cast for the programme, and my character is based on a real guy, called Jimmy Jesus, but for legal reasons he is called Jeremiah Jesus in the series. The real guy was a Jamaican who fought alongside Birmingham battalions in the First World War. He got on so well with the soldiers that he came back to England and stayed, He settled and became a preacher-cum-gangster.

We weren't sure how the series would be accepted when it was first launched — it could have flopped — but after the first three episodes, it was massive. We realised we were onto something. Then the second series felt like a school reunion, with a few new guys who were joining the Peaky clan. By the third series we were on a roll, and we all love the filming, although we all have very different styles. Cillian Murphy, for instance, is so understated that you sometimes cannot be sure whether or not he's acting. I'm louder and more animated, and as soon as Paul Anderson is in costume he's in character. We've become a team, and we have great fun. Cillian and I are always talking about music and the bands we're listening to, but the moment those cameras start rolling we get straight down to business.

Peaky Blinders made the production company proud, it made the writer, Steven Knight, proud, it made the cast proud — but most of all it made Birmingham proud. In the first series I was the only person in the cast actually from Birmingham, so when I walked around the city people told me how proud they were. Fans of the show started dressing like the Peaky Blinders, there was a cocktail named the Peaky Blinder, and then a pub. Personally, I really like seeing it in German, Spanish and Mandarin as I travel the world.

56

Crying in the Chapel

Due to my hectic lifestyle and constant travelling over almost four decades, I haven't been in regular contact with family members over the years other than my mum, although I have kept the lines of communication open. I have always been aware of what's been going on in the lives of my brothers and sisters, and of Pastor Burris's kids, especially Trevor, who is, in every sense except by blood, a brother.

I know my family are very proud of me, but it frustrates me sometimes that none of them have read my work more thoroughly. I don't think any of them could do a three-minute lecture on what my poetry or writing is really about — if they had, I would have employed them! I sometimes feel they're proud because I'm famous, and not because of what I stand for or have created. If I think about that, it does break my heart a little. Still, family is family and sometimes you have to take care of each other and love each other unconditionally.

In 2012 I was made aware of what was happening to Pastor, who was still in the States, and getting older and older. He had started to show signs of dementia, and he needed a carer. His situation was complicated, due to US citizenship issues, but it transpired that he was being ripped off by an unscrupulous woman who was siphoning cash from him but not doing much in the way of caring.

I started calling him regularly around this time and could hear he was fading. In October 2013 Trevor went over and couldn't believe the appalling conditions his dad was living in. This woman had completely neglected him while helping herself to his money. So Trevor said, 'We're going back to England', and put him on a plane almost immediately.

When they arrived at Heathrow there was a scene, as he was so ill. He was taken immediately to hospital. He was in there for a while, then came out, got very sick again very quickly, was readmitted and then, on 13 January 2014, he died. I visited him before he passed. All his kids saw him. But this is where it gets weird. We began making arrangements for the funeral. There was no autopsy or anything but the hospital had his body and told us, 'He's a foreign national — you'll need to pay the costs.' The family was presented with a bill for £18,000, which they couldn't afford.

The hospital wouldn't give us the body back until they got the money. I was astonished. I went to one doctor and said, 'This is crazy, you're holding the body to ransom. What are you going to do? Are you going to bury him? If so, can we come to the funeral?'

They went on about him not being a UK citizen, and how the government was clamping down on 'NHS tourism'. But he'd been in

England since he was a very young man. He was one of those guys who'd worked all his life, never gone sick. He'd worked in security, welding, all sorts of jobs. I explained how he'd become a US citizen only after he'd retired, and that he'd paid his National Insurance contributions all his working life. For a while it was like a gangsters' stand-off from *Peaky Blinders*: 'We've got your dad and we're not gonna give you the body unless you pay up.'

In typical surreal Zephaniah fashion there was a twist to the story. I was actually doing promotional work for the regional health authority, helping to publicise awareness of HIV in the black community in the West Midlands. In fact, it was a doctor from the very hospital Pastor died in who'd got me involved. I calmly pointed this out, and there was much hand-wringing and apologising, with them saying 'It's not us, it's the government.' A week later, they called to say, 'It's okay. You can have him back. No charge.'

At the funeral, Pastor had an open casket, and people were filing around to pay their last respects. Now, I'd been to many funerals in my life, and I'd never cried at one before, but when it was my turn at the casket I looked at Pastor's face and quickly hurried into a corner — where I just cried and cried. I mean *really* cried. It took me over — an emotional reaction I could do nothing about. When I composed myself, I expected people to be staring, or that some aunties would come to comfort me, but it seemed no one had noticed. A couple of acquaintances were chatting casually nearby: 'Yeah man, how you doing? Long time no see. Y'alright Benjamin, man.'

I don't remember crying when my dad died, but there was something about that last moment looking at Pastor that really touched me. He'd been like a real dad to me and, despite him chickening out on marriage and breaking Mum's heart, I'd obviously held stronger feelings for him than I was aware of.

Mum came to the funeral, although she hadn't visited him in hospital, so she never said goodbye as such. She told me after he died that she thought he was the only man who had ever really loved her. When she was in the kitchen he would come up behind her and put his arms around her or cover her eyes, saying, 'Guess who?' or give her a peck on the cheek — playful little gestures that meant a lot. She'd never had that kind of affection from my dad. And she said, 'You know, I'll never forget those things . . . black men don't do that kind of thing very often.'

57

Talking 'Bout a Revolution

I thought by this age I'd be a lot more relaxed about politics, happy to say, 'I did my bit', but whenever I have an audience in front of me, I find I'm compelled to really speak out. I feel as angry now as I did in my twenties.

If I look around the world, especially to the US, I'm in shock at the levels of racism still very much in evidence. I would never have predicted the rise of the alt-right, neo-fascists or the KKK, feeling so emboldened, so self-righteous, that they'd be taking to the streets and talking about *their* rights! And in the UK, I never imagined the EDL (English Defence League) or Britain First emerging, given that we'd seen off the NF ages ago. I knew we weren't ever going to live in a perfect world, but by the 1990s I thought we'd come too far to ever go back.

I think it's easy for people like me, who grew up in Birmingham, or for people who spend a lot of time in major cities, to think everyone is cool, but it's really not like that in the majority of the UK. I believe it's because politics is driven by fear — it keeps going on about the 'other'. And it's in areas where there are no black people that you seem to get the most fear, with people panicking, saying, 'What if they all start coming here?'

Capitalism needs wars but it also needs a fear industry. It always has to have a new enemy. I was doing an interview a couple of years ago, where the interviewer played a recording of me speaking in the 1980s. Back then I said: 'We always need an enemy; right now it's the Russians but I can imagine in a couple of decades it being something like . . . Islam.'

When I think about the political landscape in the not-too-distant future, I believe capitalism will eat itself. The idea of any economy having perpetual growth is ludicrous. It's like it relies on two big things, and they always talk about them, no matter what else is happening in the world. These are car sales and how the supermarkets are doing. Is Sainsbury's making a profit? Is Tesco making a profit? And it's like some big disaster if car sales dip by half a per cent, or Tesco's margin drops a couple of million pounds. Then you hear: 'Oh no, the economy's broke and we're doomed!' To deal with that they have recessions and bail out the banks to pump up the bubble; then the bubble floats for a few years before it bursts again. This cycle of boom and bust is unsustainable. One day there'll be a bust we cannot recover from. Then the most important currency won't be made of silver, gold or paper — it'll be made up of the relationships and trust with have with each other.

That's no excuse to be lazy or to give up, though. We've still got to play our part to improve things. People are going hungry, we need to take care of our old folk, we need to provide kids with the best education they can get, but we can't sit back and rely on capitalism to take care of it. We've still got to struggle, because it's like all the rights and gains made to better people's lives in the UK over the past sixty years are being chipped away.

I'm convinced the widening social gap started with Thatcher. People always quote her saying, 'There's no such thing as society', but the one thing I recall her saying, which I thought was shocking, was that if a man is taking the bus at the age of thirty he's a failure. That set the tone. Constant achievement became king, as if taking the bus meant a person was some kind of tramp. And this message fed into the 'loadsamoney' culture that's still with us.

Before the 1980s, I never saw the kind of greed you have now, where people want to accumulate as much wealth as possible, not caring about others and stepping on them. I was listening to a Commons debate soon before this book went to press. Theresa May was hiding behind some statistics, and Jeremy Corbyn said to her: 'Have you not seen the people sleeping in train stations? Have you not seen the soup kitchens?' And no, they haven't. The people who are really rich — or who facilitate obscene wealth — do not see, and cannot see.

One of my well-known poems is 'Money Rant'. Although financial systems are complex, at a basic level there's something very simplistic when you strip it down. In effect money is an IOU. It began in China, with people exchanging things. One day someone said, 'I'll give you a note.' Then the ruling system took it over and said, 'OK guys, we'll do that.'

The Oxford Book of Money, published in 1995, used 'Money Rant' because they said my poem explained the culture of money really well and made that explanation accessible. Money only works because we believe in it. If I'm going to do a deal with you, and I give you money, you will accept it because you know that the person you go on to give it to will also accept it. If I go to a chimpanzee and he has grapes and I have a banana, we could swap. If I went to the chimpanzee and he has grapes and I only have a £5 note, he's not going to be interested. He doesn't know the narrative — the one that says: 'I promise to pay the bearer on demand the sum of . . . ' All the humans know the narrative.

When it comes to labelling me, I would say the closest description of what I am is an anarchist. People always mock you if you say that because they think it's about going crazy, and I could respond by giving the examples of the Free Territory of Ukraine in 1918–1921, Catalonia between 1936 and 1939, and the many Asian and African communities that survive without help from a central government. But I don't have to; look at what happened after the fire at Grenfell Tower on 14 June 2017 — the immediate aftermath of that completely avoidable tragedy was an example of anarchy in action. At a time when people urgently and desperately needed their government and their local council, they weren't there for them. So the people organised themselves. People who had counselling skills volunteered; others worked out where the donations would go; some set up food centres. All that assistance was done without government help.

If we are going to have government, then can we at least have responsible government? If someone asked me what I would do with the structure we have right now, I'd say renationalise the railways and keep the NHS out of private hands. But I come from the Marcus Garvey school of political thought — doing whatever is necessary to achieve something. Some aspects of life actually work well with a capitalist approach. Personally I'm quite competitive; if I'm playing dominoes or tennis, I want to win!

If you really want to mess up the economy, get everybody to grow their own food or do favours for other people. Can you imagine how much it would upset the ruling systems if people started growing their own food? One of the things they really don't like is people saying, 'Let's be self-sufficient.' But back in Jamaica, that's how many people lived right up until recently. In fact, the simpler, more self-sufficient way of life is still thriving in parts of the Caribbean.

One time, in about 1987, in Jamaica, I gave my grandmother the equivalent of £60 in cash. And she said it was the most money she'd ever held in her hand in her life. I said to her, 'But you've got a house, you've got a farm. You must have needed money for that.' Her reply opened my mind to a different kind of economy.

'No, we didn't need money,' she said. 'Mr Baker over there, I gave him some yam, so he laid the foundations . . . to get the brickwork done I went to Mr Lawrence over there, and gave him some dasheen and sweet potato and did some childcare.' To get to her land, she had to walk through other people's plots, so it made real sense when she said the most important currency for her was the relationship she had with her neighbours.

When I asked if her garden was organic, she said, 'I plant something here, then I plant something next to it that tells the flies to go away.' Companion farming, it's called. But she didn't call it that; it was just natural. That's why it's so evil that you now have companies like Monsanto wanting to copyright rice or take seeds out of a natural crop so a person can't grow it without having to buy the copyright version.

And look at the arms trade — something that is evil by definition. As this book goes to print, Saudi Arabia is waging a despicable war in Yemen and the UK government is doing nothing about it. It just keeps selling them more arms. This is an instance when we should be saying no but, because of shareholders, and how important economically the arms trade is, we don't.

It's amazing when you see a country that's recently had a coup. You walk into a palace and think, *This was recently a government.* How were they overcome? Just a couple of props pulled out made it collapse. Say there's ten props; you only need to take out a couple. In China their revolution was initially started by a few people talking in a room. We now know that what Mao in China, and Castro in Cuba, did

352

was revolutionary even compared to other revolutions. Others might have appealed to students and intellectuals, but Mao and Castro, and Ho Chi Minh in Vietnam, went to the poor people; they went to the fields and said, 'See this land you're working on, you can take it over. Come with us.' By the time they got to the cities, they were massive.

★   ★   ★

These days, a lot of political discussion has shifted from being about class and inequality to being about personal identity. I used to have a simple formula: if you were upper or middle class, then you would inherit a house and/or money when your parents died, and if you were working class, you'd inherit debt. People were always worrying about how they'd pay for a relative's funeral. But that's all changed. If I had children they'd inherit my house, but I still wouldn't see myself as middle class. People are confused about class identity now because those kinds of social markers aren't so cut and dried. The labour force is fragmented and the concept of solidarity has been eroded by the culture of the individual.

I was speaking to this old-style socialist recently, and I realised how out of touch he sounded, talking about the rank and file, as if people still worked in factories and were going to down tools and march out on strike. Most of them are stuck behind desks and not even in a union. Exploitation is everywhere. All the factories I knew when I was growing up in Birmingham are now privately owned office spaces and workshops or loft apartments.

If you want to have a peaceful revolution, everybody needs to undergo a big mindshift and say: 'We're not paying for this. We're not doing this.' But these days it's like everyone wants to go shopping. I look at advertising now and think, *What the hell?!* Do people really believe this nonsense? Capitalism is extremely seductive. It's why I like to buy clothes that are out of fashion or see films once all the fuss has died down. I want to avoid the hype.

In China and other parts of the developing world, as capitalism takes hold, more people are getting an obsession with skinniness. Places where anorexia was unheard of thirty years ago are now subject to the same dogmas as the West. You see the obsession on social media with thinness via the craze for things like the thigh gap, or the rib cage; young people essentially oppressing themselves and each other for the fact they're not skinny enough. It starts out with advertising, but anxiety about body image spreads like wildfire via social media platforms and is so corrosive to the young psyche.

As dominant as the cult of the individual seems to be, there are also numerous rewards for mediocrity. I was watching a breakfast TV show recently featuring a vlogger who had published a bestseller by writing about domestic stuff. All she was writing about was being at home with the kids. It didn't sound like she had much of a sense of the world or what was going on politically; she was just writing about the day the washing machine broke down.

I thought back to my mum in the 1960s, washing all her clothes by hand; nappies made of terry cloth being boiled clean on a stove and seven kids to look after. These days people are being indulged with fame for mastering their kitchen utensils or baking a cake. All I know is that the world has changed a hell of lot since the days of Angela Davis.

58

Let's Get Metaphysical

I've a friend who's a doctor. He works in palliative care, he sees a lot of death, and he knows when people are dying with regrets. He says the people who are facing it calmly, regardless of how much money they have, are the ones at peace with their families, or those who have lived a full life or have tried things — marriages, ventures of some kind — even if they didn't work out. It's the 'giving it a go' that helps us feel more sanguine in the end. The ones who are screwed up are the people with regrets about not doing stuff: 'I coulda been a contender' — all that.

I don't fear death, but I don't want to be there when it happens. Women and children are definitely tougher than me when it comes to tolerating pain. I've watched people die painfully and recently someone said to me, 'Do you know how boring it is waiting to die?'

When it comes to the other side — God, the afterlife — I think there's something there but we don't understand it, so we make up stories about heaven and hell. Look at the whole of nature; apart from one or two exceptions it's the female who gives birth. When it comes to the creation story, supposedly a man does it. It

356

seems we need these simple stories for our little brains . . . and it's the same with death. We can't imagine it, so we tell a story: you go to a place, either good or bad, and you'll be judged.

Orthodox religion says we are bodies with spirits attached, which I reckon is a crazy way of thinking. You don't *have* a spirit — you *are* a spirit, with a body attached, for a time. We are so centred on the material because we're here, dragging our bodies around, along with all our stuff.

I'm fascinated by near-death experiences. It doesn't seem to matter which culture someone comes from — whether Christian, Muslim, punk, anarchist — there are so many similarities. I know someone who was on stage in Spain. It was raining; he touched the microphone, then *boom*! He was electrocuted. He technically 'died'. He left his body but when he was finally revived, he said, 'There is a god — not Jesus or whatever, but there's *something*. When I left my body, I could feel my mortgage going; all this stuff, just leaving. It was wonderful. You open like a flower, join the universe. Then you're sucked back in and you've got a backache. And stuff to worry about.' He didn't want to talk about it too much because he didn't want people committing suicide. I did a lot of research on the subject. I wanted to do a TV programme about it but no one wanted to run with it. One of the reasons I'm fascinated by near-death experiences is that I witnessed a profound incident of the unexplained when I was young.

A few of us guys were at Pastor Burris's

sister's place one day. Aunt Maud had a daughter called Kay — a teenager, about eighteen or nineteen. She was girlie, chatty, friendly. We were all sitting around the table in Aunt Maud's kitchen and Kay walked in, then walked out the back door without saying hello, which was strange, so we followed her out and couldn't see her. Not a trace. She couldn't have carried on walking; she would have had to climb a fence. We were like, 'Where's she gone? That's not like Kay. She wouldn't ignore us.' We were Jamaican guys, trying to be down-to-earth. You can imagine. 'What kinda ting Kay do, man? Why she a hide somewhere?'

Very soon afterwards, one of her nephews came rushing into the house, shouting, 'Kay's in hospital, she got run over!'

We said, 'What?!' We all looked at each other. We had all seen her, as clear as anything; not only me, all of us. As it transpired, the hospital said her heart had stopped for a short time and they'd had to revive her. We talked to her afterwards and she didn't remember anything. She was in a coma. She lives in America now. I'm convinced that when her heart stopped she 'walked' through the house.

There's a group of scientists who believe in a concept they call the Science of Eternity. They're rational thinkers but they also believe in a higher power and spirituality. The simplest way to explain their theory is to apply the analogy of frequencies, like radio waves. Say we listen to Radio 1; we know there are people broadcasting from a studio. That's real, but it comes to us through a frequency. Turn the dial a bit and it's a completely different reality — you could be hearing *Woman's Hour* on Radio 4. Human beings operate on a frequency too. We have electricity in us; our brains operate on a frequency, but there are other frequencies, where other things exist.

We can be here, but right now something else is happening on a different frequency — the past, the future, the otherworldly. The scientists who believe this are not cranks. I think it's likely that all this sort of thing will be explained through science at some point. I think people can sometimes attach to a different frequency and see something and come back. And I think that's what happened with Kay.

★   ★   ★

If you sit quietly and really get in touch with yourself, you can get in touch with the experience people think of as God. Monks will find it easier because they don't have lots of possessions. We've got all this *stuff* and all these concerns that make it hard to switch off, even for an hour or so. To get to God, we've developed this need for an intermediary — the church, priest, whatever — but I don't think it's necessary; we just need to meditate and sit with ourselves. Get in touch with yourself and you'll get in touch with God.

If I've done something bad, I sit with my conscience. I go over my day and think, *Do I need to apologise to anyone?* I can deal with my own conscience. But some people can't. They have to go to the priest and tell them they've sinned. And that's a whole other risky business — being in a closed space with a celibate man, telling him your deepest secrets. It's never going to end well, is it? (Actually, there's no passage in the Bible where it says a priest should be celibate.)

If for some odd reason you want to understand my religion, it's important to understand this — I have no religion. I have been very religious in the past, but then only found more religion, and with so much religion upon me I went on pilgrimages to the holy sites of the world. I wanted to meet as many holy people as I could, but I came back with no religion.

My name and my upbringing may link me to Christianity, Islam, Judaism and Rastafari, but I don't want these things to get in the way of seeing the spirit within. I would like to be remembered as someone who really believed in One Love. You can have the love of your friends, your wife, husband, family and your pets. But I have One Love for every living thing, and that includes the earth itself, because it too is alive.

Sitting silently is what I do. I sit so silently that the noises around me disappear and the loudest thing I can hear is my breath and the sound of my blood moving around my body. I sit some more until these sounds are replaced by the sound of my inner silence, and then I am connected. Why would I need a religion to do that?

I can understand people not going for this.

When people talk or write about these things, they can, and almost always do, sound mad, or at least like they're tripping. But talking and writing about meditation is not where it's at; it simply has to be experienced. Words don't do justice to what I experience through meditation, and I have never read an account to match my experiences in meditation. So I'm not going to attempt that here.

59

A Year of Division

By the time this book is published I'll be sixty. I can't believe it. I felt really low on my thirtieth birthday, because although I had travelled extensively, done countless great gigs and met lots of great people, I felt as if I'd hardly done anything. I spent that birthday telling everyone that zero to thirty had gone so fast, and if I did that again I would be sixty, and that's really old. So now I'm nearly really old, and I'm tempted to look back over the years, like old men do, but that's a little difficult at the moment because I'm still trying to get over 2016 — a year notable for the number of high-profile people who died. Everyone has their personal list but for me it was David Bowie, Leonard Cohen, Prince, Billy Paul, Carla Lane, Fidel Castro, Zaha Hadid, Phife Dawg, Muhammad Ali, Jo Cox and Maurice White, to name a few. Then, at the end of the year, I went to China to get away from Christmas, and while I was there George Michael and the Birmingham poet Yussef Ahmed died within days of each other. It was a terrible year in many ways.

In June 2016, the referendum on Britain's continued membership of the European Union was one of the most divisive times in British politics that I've lived through. In the past, politics around race have been divisive; fox hunting, sexual and gender debates have been divisive, but there was something unique about the EU referendum. I think it's because it was a stark yes or no referendum — two campaigns that led to an event, the vote.

For all of my political life Tony Benn had been the greatest influence on my thoughts about the EU. I had heard him talking about his distrust of the European project on television long before I met him, and by the time I got to know him his views had not changed. Of course, I thought about it for myself, but after hours of talking to Tony, and thinking it through, I had come to the conclusion that we should leave. Leading up to the vote there was so much misinformation and many — not all, but many — of the loudest voices on the leave side were those of the xenophobes and the racists.

I really didn't want them to distort my view of the debate and the debaters, so when asked to do *Question Time* for the BBC, *The Agenda* for Independent Television (ITV) and other TV programmes, I was neutral and listening intently to all sides of the debate, but in the end my views changed and I voted to remain.

I strongly believed there were some really important left-wing arguments for leaving the union, but those views were not being aired. In the end, 48 per cent of people who voted voted to remain, and 52 per cent voted to leave — the Brexiters winning for the most part on a platform of racism and scaremongering.

Lincolnshire, where I live, had the biggest leave vote in the country, and didn't I know it. People would start conversations with me by saying, 'I'm not a racist but . . . ' and anyone at the listening end of a conversation that starts this way knows the person talking will go on to express their deeply felt but cleverly disguised hatred for you.

Some people used the result of the vote to shout racist remarks at me. One drove by and shouted, 'The Europeans are leaving, and you're next, nigger.' The worst things were finding a note in my letterbox telling me to get out while I'm still alive and having a 'packet' of human excrement thrown over my gate, with a note! The extreme right rose up and racist attacks all over the country increased around this time, so it's difficult to know how far my experiences were representative of other people in Lincolnshire, but I have to say I felt very lonely and vulnerable then.

If there were another Brexit-type vote held in Britain that asked, 'Should black people be in this country or not?' I think we'd be out. I consider myself to be patriotic, because I care about England, and I care about the UK, but I don't feel the need to wave a flag. If I wasn't patriotic then I'd leave, like certain sports stars who want to live the luxury life elsewhere since they've become famous. I'll live with my people and die with my people. But it's impossible trying to explain to a racist how a black man can be a British patriot because he doesn't see you as rightfully British in the first place. There's still so much work to do out there.

Lincolnshire is one of the few places in the world where they still call black people 'coloured'; it's one of the few places in Britain that still has a shop that specialises in selling golliwogs; it's also one of the only counties in Britain where you will find many people living in the house they were born in, and where people will tell you with pride that they have never left the county.

There's a part of me that says Brexit wouldn't be so bad if the government knew what it was doing. But Theresa May is probably going to go down as the weakest and worst prime minister in British history. I want to ask the people who voted leave, 'Do you think this is going well? Is this what you expected?'

In universities a lot of students are worried. There's panic in the research community. A lot of funding for research into things like cancer comes from working across borders, pooling resources across universities. What began as a posh politician's arrogant gamble was decided by the kneejerk reaction of an electorate who had lost faith in politicians. These people were not interested in the full picture and statistics, and many hadn't thought it through. They just wanted to give Cameron a bloody nose. They made their decision on a really simplified issue — the *Daily Mail* version of being English or 'foreign'. I don't think I've met a university student who voted to leave. Anyone who is thinking about their future is seeing their options closing down.

60

Know Thy Self

When I told many of my neighbours about the racism I was receiving around the time of the Brexit vote, most seemed to be saying it was sad, but it was my problem. There was a handful of people who offered to help me by installing cameras around my house and generally being vigilant, but overall it was a very gloomy time, and I was on my own.

I've had gloomy times, I've had hard times and I've had good times, but most lives are like that. I have known people who outwardly seem to be very successful, but they've been extremely unhappy. I don't believe you can have a completely happy life all the time. We can only have lives that are full of moments, and we have to try to make sure our happy moments outnumber the unhappy ones.

I remember being in a police cell when I was sixteen and wondering what would become of me. The cell was about the size of a double bed, and the walls felt as though they were closing in. I looked around and thought I would be in and out of police cells and prisons for the rest of my life. For a time I thought that I, and people like me, were condemned to forever be in places like that, but then I also remembered that I once had

366

a dream of becoming a poet and leaving some kind of positivity in the world. Then I shook my head, I mean really shook it, as if to shake away all those negative thoughts. Yes, I did all kinds of things to survive and stay alive, but even when I did bad, even in darkest moments, I still had a deep belief that I could do better, and that I deserved better.

I've witnessed the thug life, the pimp life, the street-fighting life, because I've been right in the middle of it, but I've always been an observer. I'd always watch people and think, *He's a character. That one thinks he's the boss.* There were things I did even as a child, such as running away from approved school, where I'd think, *This is going to end up in one of my books or poems.* I jotted it all down in my memory.

I needed a chance, and when the chance came I took it. Having said that, just taking the chance is not good enough; I had to do some hard work as well. I wasn't blighted by the culture of entitlement that affects the social media generation. I don't believe the glib sentiment that if you simply 'follow your dreams' you'll make it. Maybe if your talent matches your expectations you'll make it but you might not. There might be cultural or class barriers stopping you. And if you don't make it, you'll need your own internal sense of self-worth to fall back on.

At this age people often ask me what I think is my greatest achievement, and I find it very difficult to pick one or even to rank them in any order of importance. Turning away from crime could be one of the greatest things I've ever done, but so could reaching the age of thirty without being shot.

Every time I visit South Africa I am filled with pride. My part was very small, but being involved with the anti-apartheid movement makes me think that I played a part in changing that country for the better. Actually Mandela told me it did. But my pride is also tinged with anxiety. There will never be another Mandela, but I fear that the ANC and its leadership are not focused on uniting the country and fighting corruption the way he was.

I was also very involved with raising awareness about the plight of the people of East Timor, and again I'm very proud of having played my little part in the liberation of that small nation, but I think we failed when it comes to Palestine. This is a country that for decades has suffered a brutal occupation — you can go online and see Palestinians being killed every day — but the people of Britain don't seem that aware of their suffering because very little about their oppression is covered in the mainstream media.

The shameful treatment of the people of the Chagos Islands by the British government is hardly known by the people of Britain, and the government would like it to stay that way, because they know most decent people would be outraged that a whole nation of people were moved from their homeland to make a military base for a so-called ally. Then there's West Papua. I know it will be free one day; I wanted to help free them before I was fifty; now I'm almost sixty and they're still not free. So there's another failing of mine. Yes, for me this is personal.

I really wanted to free the world, but at home, as I write this, I think one of the greatest injustices in the country of my birth is the number of people who are dying in custody. In police stations, prisons, immigration centres and psychiatric units the vulnerable are dying. Many are taking their own lives as a result of depression and other mental health problems, but many are dying as a result of the brutality they experience at the hands of the people who should be looking after them.

★ ★ ★

My mum has been the one constant and most important person throughout my life. She never helped with my writing or anything creative, and she's read very little of my work, but she has loved coming to my performances, and she really loves it if I point her out in the audience. When I started out she didn't really understand what I was doing because there were no examples of other people doing anything similiar. She understood what performance poetry was because Jamaica was full of poets, and in the part of Jamaica where she lived the oral tradition thrived but, like a lot of immigrant parents, she wanted what she believed was the best for me: a trade, or better still a profession, and 'a nice black gal fi marry'. It was only when I started to appear on TV, and people began to tell her what my poetry meant to them, that she realised I had something to say that was valid, and that my work had some merit.

A lot of people from the Caribbean say that when they die they want to be buried back in Jamaica but Mum says, 'None of that for me. I want to be buried here. This is my home.' She's Birmingham through and through. She's only been back to Jamaica once since she came here, and she was counting the days until she could return to the UK. She hasn't set foot outside of England since.

★ ★ ★

As I've been on the planet for nearly sixty years, it's inevitable that I've witnessed the passing of those relatives who immigrated to Britain in the 1950s and '60s. Around 2013 or so, the health of Mum's second husband Brother Wright began to deteriorate. First he started having problems bending and lost dexterity in his fingers. I realised things were getting bad when he told me he couldn't work on his cars anymore and asked me to sell them, along with his engines and all of his car spares. I was a fully signed-up member of the Triumph Classic Car Club, so I sold them all very quickly to someone who came and took the lot. He got a bargain.

As things got worse he began to make lots of references to death. His favourite place was the conservatory at the back of his house, where he'd set up his sound system and kept his CDs, tapes and records. As he got weaker he would spend more time there, and one day I came to see him and asked him how he was. As he rocked in his rocking chair, he said, 'I'm just sitting here waiting to die.' He would often say similar things. His arthritis was very bad and there were a couple of times when he went upstairs and couldn't get back down because of his knees.

On one of these occasions an ambulance was called and he was taken into hospital, where he spent a couple of days, but as he was about to be discharged a doctor broke the news that he had stomach cancer. As the doctor began to list all the different treatment options, Brother Wright interrupted him, saying, 'Stop. I'm not interested in you trying to keep me alive for a few extra weeks. I'm eighty-four. I've outlived all my friends and I've had a good life. So please, just manage my pain and let me go at my appointed time.'

It was tough to hear, but it made sense. On 21 June 2017 he asked to be moved to Marie Curie Hospice in Solihull, where he passed away on 28 June. He was buried at Greenhaven Woodland Burial Ground near Rugby on 5 July. It was a green burial in a woodland area with a simple, non-religious ceremony that I led.

★   ★   ★

When transferring my poems from the stage to the page, I've always tried to capture the essence of my live performance. I've always written with my voice in mind. I have to hear the words in my head before I can commit them to the written word but, try as I might, I am acutely aware that

I can't capture everything the way it sounds within me. Like a martial arts technique, my poetry works best when it goes via the quickest route to the nearest spot, which is from my brain, the source, to my mouth. Writing it down is another step removed from the source to the receiver. To fully appreciate it, to connect with its essence, you have to be in my head or in my audience.

My style is born out of the living, oral tradition of poetry — an art form that has always been part of everyday life in Jamaica. I grew up with that rhyme and rhythm coming down to me from my mum, who grew up hearing numerous parables and fables that had their origins in Africa. As the older generations pass on, younger people will get further and further away from those origins.

When it comes to the arts I think my greatest achievement was the creation of the British performance poetry scene. Of course, I didn't do it by myself. There was Linton Kwesi Johnson, John Cooper Clarke, Jean Breeze, Joolz and others, not to mention collectives like Apples and Snakes, who dedicated themselves to promoting poetry. But in the late 1970s and early '80s there was no real performance poetry scene in Britain. Michael Horovitz and others organised poetry performances in the 1960s and early 1970s from time to time, and I understand they were numinous events. Alan Ginsberg and other beat poets would come over and perform, and although the poets themselves were free-minded, progressive and all about peace and love, the

372

scene was white and a bit too hippy for we, the new generation of punks, Rastas and hip-hoppers.

This is why in 1979 I said we needed to create a culture of performance poetry and spoken word in Britain. I wanted to see a time when it was really cool for someone to take their date to a poetry reading on a Saturday night, and it happened. I wanted to see a time when the music press would write about poetry like they wrote about music, and it happened. I wanted to see a time when lots of performance poets would be able to earn a living from their craft, and that too has happened. The scene is alive and well and all over Britain. In fact, all over the world talented people are earning a living from their craft, and more importantly millions of people are enjoying it.

But I'm not sitting back and relaxing. Not in times like these when the extreme right is on the rise all over Europe, when black people are still five times more likely to be stopped and searched by the police than their white counterparts. Not when homelessness is rapidly rising, soup kitchens are opening up across the country, and women are experiencing institutionalised sexism and suffering so much due to poverty. It's difficult to relax when I live under a political system that is constantly creating refugees and then rejecting those refugees. Instead of relaxing I've released a new album, *Revolutionary Minds*, and, because I feel the political need, I'm back on the road with my band. What's really inspiring me now is that, as I look out from the stage, I see that the majority of my audience is under thirty.

Poetry has the power to heal and the power to destroy; it can be used to liberate and, after liberation, to celebrate. In the beginning was the word, and the word became poetry, and I discovered it and found that it was great. I have loved many books with all my heart, I have campaigned to get books to the bookless, and keep libraries alive, for they live too. But the greatest poetry is collected inside I.

I have had books stolen from me, I have misplaced books and left them on trains and park benches, and I still want to get the blighters who took them. The idea that any book of mine ends up in a wastepaper bin, or sits on the shelf in a lost property office vexes me. The book is one of the greatest pieces of design ever conceived. They have survived upstarts like radio, TV, the internet and various book burners, and I love them, but they are books, and as much as I love books (and my bass guitar), they are material, and the attachment to material things, whatever that may be, is the root of all suffering.

The poetry within me is not owned, yet it is a part of me, and once it is spoken it becomes a part of anyone who opens their mind and receives it. If misfortune, sickness and death will come to us all, then we should let some poetry into our lives to ease the pain.

Poetry has wrapped my heart when my heart was naked. Poetry has eased much of the pain I have experienced. I have dedicated my life to

374

poetry and 'the struggle', but ultimately I have been on a life-long quest to find inner peace. Anyone who has come to my home and seen how much time I dedicate to t'ai chi and meditation knows this. The peace of which I speak is not simply an absence of war, or something that comes about because a treaty has been negotiated; there is no way to peace, because peace *is* the way. Poetry helped me speak to the world; it helped me to represent my age and my ageing; it is a part of me, but in the end it's about knowledge of self.

★   ★   ★

Peace. I'm out of here.

Acknowledgements

Benjamin Zephaniah (that's me) is most grateful to Nicola Crossley, Kerri Sharp, Iain MacGregor and the whole team at Simon & Schuster for their creativity and their passion. Robert Kirby, Aoife Rice, Jodie Hodges, Rosemary Scoular, Kate Davie and Rebecca Haigh at United Agents for representing me so well over the years. Andrew Richardson and Margaret Murray done good too, and although they haven't worked on this book, I have to send some love out to Neil Astley for taking my poetry from the stage to the page, and to Emma Matthewson for being by my side for much of my creative journey.

Linton Kwesi Johnson told me not to take my life for granted, Roger McGough told me to stop beating myself up, and Jean 'Binta' Breeze told me that love is the answer. They all contributed to me.

We do hope that you have enjoyed reading this large print book.

Did you know that all of our titles are available for purchase?

We publish a wide range of high quality large print books including:
Romances, Mysteries, Classics
General Fiction
Non Fiction and Westerns

Special interest titles available in large print are:
The Little Oxford Dictionary
Music Book
Song Book
Hymn Book
Service Book

Also available from us courtesy of Oxford University Press:
Young Readers' Dictionary
(large print edition)
Young Readers' Thesaurus
(large print edition)

For further information or a free brochure, please contact us at:
Ulverscroft Large Print Books Ltd.,
The Green, Bradgate Road, Anstey,
Leicester, LE7 7FU, England.
Tel: (00 44) 0116 236 4325
Fax: (00 44) 0116 234 0205

PIG

Helen Browning and Tim Finney

In a frosty field on the longest night of the year, eight piglets snuffle their first breath, and jostle close to their mother to feed. Over the six months that follow, Helen Browning and her partner Tim Finney follow their adventures to show how pigs become the mischievous, competitive, intelligent and inventive characters that we know them to be. In doing so, they demonstrate why it is so crucial that the welfare of our farm animals — and equally, the way we manage our countryside — takes centre stage in the contemporary discussions around food, climate change and the loss of wildlife. Drawing on a lifetime's worth of knowledge, PIG is an exploration of our relationship with farm animals, with nature, and with life itself.

OUR GREAT CANAL JOURNEYS

Timothy West

For more than half a century, a shared love of canals and narrowboats has been inseparable from the marriage of Timothy West and Prunella Scales. The two iconic actors have spent many of the happiest days of their life together enjoying the calming pleasures of watching land and nature unfold before them at four miles an hour. In 2014, Tim and Pru took to the canals of Britain and beyond with a television crew and a brief to record their best-loved trips along the most beautiful waterways they could find. Not only does *Our Great Canal Journeys* recount their careers and travels, but it also explores the trials — and the joys — of ageing, and how Prunella's struggle with dementia has both changed, and yet failed to change, their lives together.

BOOKWORM

Lucy Mangan

When Lucy Mangan was little, she was whisked away to Narnia — and Kirrin Island — and Wonderland. She ventured down rabbit holes and Womble burrows, into midnight gardens and chocolate factories. She wandered the countryside with Milly-Molly-Mandy, and played by the tracks with the Railway Children. With *Charlotte's Web*, she discovered Death, and with Judy Blume it was Boys. No wonder she only left the house for her weekly trip to the library or to spend her pocket money on amassing her own book stash at home. In *Bookworm*, Lucy relives our best-loved books and their extraordinary creators, and looks at the thousand subtle ways they shape our lives. She also disinters a few forgotten treasures to inspire the next generation of bookworms and set them on their way.

SOMEBODY I USED TO KNOW

Wendy Mitchell and Anna Wharton

What do you lose when your memories begin to disappear? What do you value when this reframes how you've lived, and how you will live in the future? How do you conceive of love when you can no longer recognise those who are supposed to mean the most to you? When she was diagnosed with dementia at the age of fifty-eight, Wendy Mitchell was confronted with the most profound questions about life and identity. Her demanding career in the NHS; her ability to drive, cook and run — the various shades of her independence — were suddenly gone. *Somebody I Used to Know* is both a heart-rending tribute to the woman Wendy once was, and a brave affirmation of the woman dementia has seen her become.